TEACHING
AND LEARNING

READINGS IN
THE PHILOSOPHY
OF EDUCATION

GENERAL SERIES EDITOR, HARRY S. BROUDY

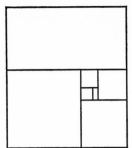

TEACHING
AND LEARNING

EDITED BY DONALD VANDENBERG

UNIVERSITY OF ILLINOIS PRESS
URBANA, CHICAGO, LONDON
1969

© 1969 by the Board of Trustees of the University of Illinois
Manufactured in the United States of America
Library of Congress Catalog Card No. 69–17365

Paper: 252 00008 0
Cloth: 252 00009 9

To My Teachers

GENERAL SERIES PREFACE

Readings in the Philosophy of Education is a series of books each of which reprints significant articles, excerpts from books, and monographs that deal philosophically with problems in education.

The distinctive feature of this series is that the selection of materials and their organization are based on the results of a three-year project supported by the U.S. Office of Education and the University of Illinois. A team of philosophers of education with consultants from both philosophy of education and general philosophy scanned thousands of items. Their final selection was presented in a report entitled *Philosophy of Education: An Organization of Topics and Selected Sources* (Urbana: University of Illinois Press, 1967).

Unfortunately, not all college libraries are equally well stocked with the items listed in the report, and even with adequate resources, getting the appropriate materials to the student is a formidable task for the instructor.

Accordingly, several members of the original team that worked on the project agreed to bring out this series. The projected books are organized in two groups. One will devote a separate volume to each of the following problems in education: the nature, aims, and policies of education; curriculum; and teaching-learning. The second group will be made up of a number of volumes each of which will bring together significant materials from one of the following philosophical disciplines: epistemology; metaphysics; value theory; aesthetics; and the philosophy of science. This volume belongs to the first group, dealing with the philosophical dimensions of teaching and learning.

The first group of books will make available to the student some important and representative statements that philosophers of education, utilizing the resources of epistemology, metaphysics, value theory, logical and linguistic analysis, social philosophy, philosophy of science, and the philosophy of religion have made about problems of education. Used as a set, these volumes are appropriate for the first course in the philosophy of education whether offered to undergraduates or on the master's level. Individually or in combination they can also be used in courses in administration, methods, principles, curriculum, and related fields.

Each of the volumes in the second group approaches the problems of education from one of the standard divisions of general philosophy, and individually or in combination they are suited to advanced and specialized courses. Some instructors may wish to use both types in their courses.

Donald Vandenberg, the author of this volume, was one of the original research assistants on the Philosophy of Education Project. His own work has explored the import of existentialism and phenomenology for the study of education.

HARRY S. BROUDY
General Series Editor

PREFACE

I have tried to avoid replicating readily available materials, to exclude whatever belongs to educational methods or to the psychology, sociology, and history of education, and to restrict inclusion to items that contain arguments and points of view that are philosophically and contemporarily tenable and defensible. Because I do not really know (nobody does) what is readily available, or when ideas become amenable to empirical research or are of "mere" historical interest, or what is currently tenable, I am sure that I have failed to apply these principles of selection adequately in spite of my best intentions. But I do believe that they are the appropriate criteria of selection for a volume of this kind however difficult their application.

The principles of classifying and ordering these materials are likewise controversial issues in philosophy of education and are accordingly explained in context in the introductory essays. These essays also attempt to indicate what to look for and to supply a minimal context and structure for the whole. Structure is necessary, but which one? Or whose? I have accordingly tried to help the reader make interrelations of his own by selecting readings that would speak for themselves, by arranging them in such a way as to minimize the need for editorial exposition, and by asking some questions indicative of the kinds of interrelations that can be made to obtain a structure for the problems different from that represented by the table of contents. I have also dared hope that the readings would illuminate the commentary as well as the reverse.

Most of the work on this volume was done at the University of Calgary. I would like to express my gratitude to the Department of Education Foundations and the library there for the use of their facilities, particularly to Miss Annette Yuar, whose complete cooperation in respect to interlibrary loans was invaluable. I would also like to thank the authors, editors, and publishers who have allowed me to reprint their materials, particularly Dr. William O. Stanley, who, as editor of *Educational Theory,* allowed me to reprint one-third of these selections. I am also happy to have had the stenographic assistance of Miss Karen Archer at Penn State.

D. V.
Pennsylvania State University

CONTENTS

PART ONE

EPISTEMOLOGICAL CONSIDERATIONS

EPISTEMOLOGY VERSUS PSYCHOLOGY OF LEARNING

The selections in this section serve to define the epistemological dimension of education; that is, their authors mention the cognitive aspects of teaching and learning that can be investigated solely through philosophical methods.

Green discusses certain features of teaching in order to distinguish instructing from indoctrinating, training, and conditioning. These features—weighing evidence, examining reasons, pursuing truth—are precisely the concerns of epistemology. What will count as evidence? What are good reasons? What is truth? When Green says that instructing is "more central" to the concept of teaching than is training or indoctrination, he in effect suggests that the epistemological consideration of teaching activities is "more central" to the understanding of teaching than are learning theories developed by psychologists. Somewhat oddly, he does not find a type of learning that is "central" to the concept of learning. Instructing, however, differs from indoctrinating, etc., in the greater amount of intelligence displayed in the actions of the learner, i.e., when the learner is concerned with weighing evidence, asking questions, and so on. If one says that this kind of learning is "central" to the concept of learning, he emphasizes the features of learning that are open to epistemological consideration.

Maccia indicates what these features are from the side of the learner when she asks about the kind of learning that is also knowing. What is knowing? By asking the question within the context of the expanding use of educational technology, allegedly justifiable by theories in psychology of learning, however, Maccia seems to be in agreement with Green. If he means that concepts of learning taken from the psychology of learning are not of the most importance to teaching or to the kind of learning that should accompany teaching, then he raises Maccia's question about the kind of human learning that should be promoted in the classroom. Be this as it may, the two selections introduce the issues of the epistemology of education in a complementary way. The next section will treat these issues in diverse ways and in greater depth.

THE CONCEPT OF TEACHING

Thomas F. Green

At the outset one must recognize, then, that the concept of teaching is molecular. That is, as an activity, teaching can best be understood not as a single activity but as a whole family of activities within which some members appear to be of more central significance than others. For example, there is an intimate relation between teaching and training. . . . One reason for this is that teaching is often conceived to involve the formation of habit, and training is a method of shaping habit. Thus, when engaged in training, we may often say with equal propriety that we are engaged in teaching. The two concepts are closely related.

Nonetheless teaching and training are not identical. Training is only a part of teaching. There are contexts in which it would be a rank distortion to substitute the one concept for the other. For example, it is more common, and perhaps more accurate, to speak of training an animal than to speak of teaching him. I do not mean there is no such thing as teaching a dog. I mean only that it is more accurate in this context to speak of training. We can, indeed, teach a dog to fetch, to heel, to point, and to pursue. There is in fact a common saying that you cannot teach an old dog new tricks. The use of the word "teaching" in each of these cases has its explanation. It has to do with the fact that the actions of a trained dog are expressive of intelligence; they involve obedience to orders. Indeed, a well trained dog is one which has passed "obedience trials."

But the intelligence displayed in such cases is limited, and it is this which renders the education of an animal more akin to training than to teaching. What should we think of a trainer of dogs attempting to explain his orders to an animal, giving reasons for them, presenting evidence of a kind that would tend to justify them? The picture is absurd. Dogs do not ask "Why?"

Reprinted from "A Topology of the Teaching Concept," *Studies in Philosophy and Education,* 3 (Winter, 1964), 286–290, 313–316. By permission of the author and the editor of *Studies in Philosophy and Education.*

They do not ask for reasons for a certain rule or order. They do not require explanation or justification. It is this limitation of intelligence which we express by speaking of training rather than teaching in such circumstances. . . .

I am concerned only to observe that training resembles teaching insofar as it is aimed at actions which display intelligence. In this respect training has a position of central importance in that congeries of activities we include in teaching. Ordinarily, however, the kind of intelligence aimed at in training is limited. What it excludes is the process of asking questions, weighing evidence and, in short, demanding and receiving a justification of rules, principles, or claims of fact. In proportion as training is aimed at a greater and greater display of intelligence, it more and more clearly resembles teaching, and one of the clues as to how closely training approaches teaching is the degree to which it involves explanations, reasons, argument, and weighing evidence. . . .

This point is strengthened when we consider what happens in proportion as training is aimed less and less at the display of intelligence. In that case, the concept fades off imperceptibly into what we would commonly call conditioning. It is natural to speak of teaching a dog to fetch, to heel, to walk in time to music. It is more of a distortion to speak of teaching a dog to salivate at the sound of a bell. It is in precisely this latter context that we speak of conditioning. Conditioning does not aim at an intelligent performance of some act.[1] Insofar as training does not aim at the display of intelligence, it resembles conditioning more and teaching less. Thus we can see that training is an activity which is conceptually of more central importance to the concept of teaching than is conditioning. We teach a dog to fetch; we condition him to salivate. And the difference is a difference in the degree of intelligence displayed.

Instruction also must be numbered among the family of activities related to teaching. Instructing, in fact, is so closely bound to teaching that the phrase "giving instruction" seems only another way of saying "teaching." There seems to be no

[1] There may be circumstances, however, in which it would be intelligent, i.e., wise, to "teach" with the aim of producing a conditioned response.

case of an activity we could describe as "giving instruction" which we could not equally and more simply describe as teaching. Nonetheless, teaching and giving instruction are not the same thing. For there are almost endless instances of teaching which do not involve instruction. For example, it is acceptable, and even correct, to speak of *teaching* a dog to heel, to sit, or to fetch. It is, however, less acceptable, more imprecise, and perhaps even incorrect to speak of *instructing* a dog in sitting and fetching.

But why, in such contexts, is it more awkward to speak of instructing than to speak of teaching? . . . When we train a dog, we give an order and then push and pull and give reward or punishment. We give the order to sit and then push on the hindquarters precisely because we cannot explain the order. We cannot elaborate its meaning. It is precisely this limitation of intelligence or communication which disposes us to speak of training a dog rather than instructing him. What we seek to express by the phrase "giving instruction" is precisely what we seek to omit by the word "training." Instruction seems, at heart, to involve a kind of conversation, the object of which is to give reasons, weigh evidence, justify, explain, conclude, and so forth. . . .

This important difference between training and instructing may be viewed in another way. To the extent that instructing necessarily involves a kind of conversation, a giving of reasons, evidence, objections, and so on, it is an activity of teaching allied more closely to the acquisition of knowledge and belief than to the promotion of habits and modes of behavior. Training, on the contrary, has to do more with forming modes of habit and behavior and less with acquiring knowledge and belief. Instructing, in short, is more closely related to the quest for understanding. We can train people to do certain things without making any effort to bring them to an understanding of what they do. It is, however, logically impossible to instruct someone without at the same time attempting to bring him to some understanding. What this means, stated in its simplest and most ancient terms, is that instructing always involves matters of truth and falsity, whereas training does not. This is another reason for observing that instructing has more to do with matters of belief and knowledge, and training more with acquiring habits or modes of behaving. It is not, therefore, a bit of archaic nonsense that teaching is essentially the pursuit of truth. It is, on the contrary, an enormously important insight. The pursuit of truth is central to the activity of teaching because giving instruction is central to it. That, indeed, is the purpose of the kind of conversation indigenous to the concept of giving instruction. If giving instruction involves giving reasons, evidence, argument, justification, then instruction is essentially related to the search for truth.

The point is not, therefore, that instructing necessarily requires communication. The point is rather that it requires a certain *kind* of communication, and that kind is the kind which includes giving reasons, evidence, argument, etc., in order to approach the truth. The importance of this fact can be seen if we consider what happens when the conversation of instruction is centered less and less upon this kind of communication. It takes no great powers of insight to see that in proportion as the conversation of instruction is less and less characterized by argument, reasons, objections, explanations, and so forth, in proportion as it is less and less directed toward an apprehension of truth, it more and more closely resembles what we call indoctrination. Indoctrination is frequently viewed as a method of instruction. Indeed, we sometimes use the word "instruction" to include what we quite openly confess is, in fact, indoctrination. Nonetheless, indoctrination is a substantially different thing from instruction, and what is central to this difference is precisely that it involves a different kind of conversation and therefore is differently related to matters of truth.

We can summarize the essential characteristics of these differences by saying that indoctrination is to conditioning as beliefs are to habits. That is to say, we may indoctrinate people to *believe* certain things, but we condition them always to *do* certain things. We do not indoctrinate persons to certain modes of behavior any more than we condition them to certain kinds of beliefs. But the important thing is to observe that *insofar as* conditioning does not aim at an expression of intelligent doing, neither does indoctrination aim at an expression of intelligent believing. Conditioning is an activity which can be used to establish certain modes of behavior quite apart from their desirability. It aims simply to establish them. If a response to a certain stimulus is trained or conditioned, or has become a fixed habit, it will be displayed in the fact that the same stimulus will produce the same response even when the person admits it would be better if he responded otherwise. This is an unintelligent way of behaving. In an analogous way, indoctrination is aimed at an unintelligent way of holding beliefs. Indoctrination aims simply at establishing certain beliefs so that they will be held quite apart from their truth, their explanation, or their foundation in evidence. As a practical matter, indoctrinating involves certain conversation, but it does not involve the kind of conversation central to the activity of giving instruction. Thus, as the teaching conversation becomes less related to the pursuit of truth, it becomes less an activity of instruction and more a matter of indoctrination. We may represent these remarks schematically:

The Teaching Continuum

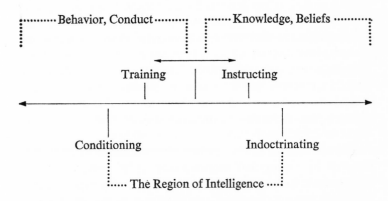

The diagram is not meant to suggest that the distinctions between conditioning, training, instructing, and indoctrinating are perfectly clear and precise. On the contrary, each of these concepts, like the teaching concept itself, is vague. Each blends imperceptibly into its neighbor. . . .

To say that indoctrination plays a legitimate role in education but is, nonetheless, peripheral to the concept of teaching is already to strike at an immensely important and powerful distinction. It is already to begin to describe the logical relations that exist between teaching and learning on the one hand, and teaching and education on the other.

Learning is commonly defined as any change of behavior. This definition, or one like it, has certain advantages for the science of psychology. It makes it possible to deal with learning as an observable phenomenon, which is important if the study of learning is to remain a scientific inquiry. Such a definition, nonetheless, is wholly inadequate to capture what we normally mean by "learning." Ordinarily we would regard a change of behavior at best as only *evidence* of learning, and we would not regard it as either necessary or sufficient evidence. A change of behavior in many contexts is not evidence that one has *learned* something new but only that he has decided *to do* something new. A bank cashier who begins to embezzle has not necessarily learned anything not learned by the cashier who does not embezzle. And this is so because it is not obvious that learning to embezzle is distinguished in any way from simply learning to keep books. In this case, as in unnumbered others like it, a change of behavior is not sufficient evidence that anything new has been learned. But for exactly the same reasons it cannot be necessary evidence either. A person may learn to do something and yet never in his life decide to do it or in any other way display his knowledge or capacities. Unless such a supposition can be shown to be absurd or meaningless, it cannot be held that a change of behavior is a necessary part of what we *mean* by learning.

The important point to observe, however, is that regardless of our definition of learning it must remain true that *every* point on the teaching continuum is *equally* a point of learning. Or, more precisely, every point on the teaching continuum, as much as any other, represents a method of bringing about learning. It is not therefore anything implicit in the concept of learning itself which distributes the teaching activities in certain logical relations along the teaching continuum. They are distributed by the logic of the concept 'teaching' and not by the logic of the concept 'learning'. People can and will learn by propaganda, indoctrination, and lies. They can be brought to adopt certain patterns of behavior by conditioning, by intimidation, by deceit, by threats of physical violence. Indeed, these different methods appear on the teaching continuum *because* they are all ways of bringing about learning and because it is true *in some sense* that teaching aims at bringing about learning. It is not true, however, that every method of bringing about learning is equally a method of teaching. Some are more central to the concept of teaching than are others.

It is because of this logical fact that the teaching concept can yield a continuum of the kind I have described. It is an immensely important fact, however, that the concept of learning cannot yield such a continuum, and that it cannot for the following reasons. The concept of teaching includes within its limits a whole assemblage of human activities. Teaching stands related to instruction, training, indoctrination, and conditioning as genus to species. But it is not the relation between genus and species which is represented on the teaching continuum. Every point within the limits of teaching is a species of a certain genus, and *in this respect,* no point is different from any other. The continuum, however, is directional; it is directional in a way that membership in a certain genus would not warrant. What is represented by the direction of the continuum is a logical relation between the *members* of the genus, indicating the extent to which they do or do not instantiate the properties of central importance in the logic of the concept. The concept of teaching is peculiar in the respect that not only does it stand related to certain activities as genus to species, but there is also *between* its species a discernible order.

If we consider learning to be a human activity, then it will also stand related to such things as drill, memorization, practice, and study as genus to species. But among the species of learning there is *no* corresponding logical order of the kind that exists among activities of teaching. That is to say, the activities of learning fall under the concept as members of a class. It makes no sense to ask whether insight is more central logically to the concept of learning than, say, drill or practice or any other learning activity. But it *does* make sense to ask whether instruction is more central to the concept of teaching than, say, indoctrination. In short, teaching is a vague concept, but learning is not.

We might discover that some activities on the teaching continuum are more efficient or effective than others in bringing about learning, or that some methods of teaching are more appropriate to certain types of materials to be learned. But these distinctions cannot be discovered in the concept of learning itself. They must be discovered by empirical study. And such studies might show that the most effective methods of bringing about learning do not fall within the province of teaching at all. If that were to happen, it would follow that teachers ought *not* to adopt the most effective or efficient means of bringing about learning. In short, teaching and learning are conceptually independent *in the sense that* we cannot discover in the concept of learning any principles sufficient to distinguish those kinds of learning aimed at in teaching from those which are not.

Now this may sound like an utterly fantastic and unwarranted claim, but it is not. Suppose it is true that by their consequences, we can identify many different kinds of learning. We can discriminate between learning habits and learning to obey certain principles, between acquiring belief sets and conditioned responses, or between learning by insight and by rote memorization. It is quite conceivable that different kinds of learning can be related to different points on the teaching continuum and, therefore, can be ordered in a certain relation to each other, and some identified as more appropriate to teaching than others. For example, there may be a certain kind of learning which would result in a non-evidential belief set, and which might therefore be related to the methods of propaganda or indoctrination. Similarly, learning certain habits or skills might be related, more or less, to training or conditioning.[10] If this is so, then different kinds of learning can be placed in an order similar to the order of the teaching continuum. But the point is that this order is imposed upon the phenomena by the logic of the concept 'teaching'. There is no such order discoverable among species of learning. We can, in short, discriminate between kinds of learn-

---

[10] I do not suppose there is in fact such a correspondence between kinds of learning and methods of enhancing learning. On the other hand, I see no logical reason why there should not be.

ing and identify which are appropriately aimed at in teaching only if we *bring to* the concept of learning some principles or presuppositions which are derived from the concept of teaching. This is, in fact, what we usually do when we "select" from studies of learning those insights and truths which we think will be of practical use in classroom instruction. The fact remains that no species of learning is more centrally related to the concept of learning than is any other, and therefore when we discover how to bring about learning, it does not follow necessarily that we have discovered how to do anything we are concerned to do in teaching.

But what is the significance of this fact? The most immediate and far-reaching conclusion is a somewhat negative one. It is not clear within what limits or on what grounds we are warranted in deriving a theory of teaching from a theory of learning. To what extent, in other words, can our knowledge of learning be made to yield, in a logically defensible way, some principles which can be normative for the conduct of teaching? Indeed, one may ask whether there is any logically well-founded principle which will suffice to mediate the inference from the management of learning to the practice of teaching.

The problem arises because the concept of learning is of greater dimensions than the concept of teaching described in our topology. But the concept represented in that topology is the one we normally employ when we think about teaching in the setting of the school. How do we know, then, that when we study certain phenomena of learning we are concerned with phenomena which fall within the more narrow limits of teaching? The fact is that apart from assumptions or presuppositions concerning the activity of teaching we do not know when our studies are relevant to the activity of teaching and when they are not. The methods of instruction and the techniques of deceit are both ways of inducing learning. On what possible grounds, then, are we more concerned to master one than the other? Can it be that at this point we manifest a presupposition that one is in some sense more relevant to the practice of teaching than the other? On what grounds can we justify such a presupposition? Apart from some theory of teaching, assumptions of this kind have no warrant, and yet without such assumptions, we have no grounds for an inference from the principles of learning to the principles of teaching. In order to profit from our studies of learning, the logically prior problem is not to develop a general theory of learning but to develop a theory of teaching. The topology of teaching described in these pages is a step in that direction. . . .

EPISTEMOLOGY AND TEACHING MACHINES

Elizabeth Steiner Maccia

The literature and discussion pertaining to teaching machines continue to grow, as do their development and use. Yet this growth is not entirely analogous to a healthful one, for we find the seeds of a cold war. The enthusiasm of one group is countered by the fear of another, with a third group in a state of confused watching. Meanwhile, the profiteers are hard at work. But we have a means that would lead to intelligent rather than emotional development and use of teaching machines which at the same time would check selfish motivation. Let us make our ideas clear and check out whether the ideas are well-founded. Let us do research.

Thought about such means has led to a twofold purpose in my adding to the already voluminous literature and discussion: (1) the presentation of distinctions as to kinds of ideas so that we do not write and talk in a careless manner which can only result in confused ideas and confusion as to the grounds upon which the ideas are founded, and (2) a consideration of epistemological ideas in relation to teaching machines so that clarification and grounding, if any, results.

Ideas about teaching machines are about whether teaching machines can provide conditions for learning. It is obvious, of course, that the context is human learning within a formal system of schooling. What is being engaged in is a technological [1] discourse, since we are dealing with the relating of means or technics (the teaching machines or their use) with ends which we have set forth as our aims (kinds of learning);

Reprinted from "Epistemological Considerations in Relation to the Use of Teaching Machines," *Educational Theory,* 12 (October, 1962), 234–237. By permission of the author and the editor of *Educational Theory.*

[1] "Technological" is used here in a broader sense than is usual, although in a sense that is beginning to find its way into the literature. See my paper, "The Separation of Philosophy from Theory of Education," *Studies in Philosophy and Education,* 2 (Spring, 1962), 158–169.

and it falls within the discipline of Education,[2] as it involves human learners within a formal system of schooling.

Immediately, one recognizes that ideas falling within related discourses are involved. The question as to teaching machines providing the conditions for learning depends upon answers to other questions: What is learning and what conditions are related to learning so defined? What kind of learning should we bring about in our classrooms? The second question arises because "learning," whether it be defined in terms of behavior changes or mental states, is taken to be valuationally neutral and because there are other sites of learning, such as the home. That is to say, learning encompasses both good and bad learning. Surely, we do not consider all learning good. To learn to cheat or to learn to be prejudicial is questionable in regard to goodness. Consequently, we must face the issue of what the good man is or what kinds of learning should be aimed at. But more, we must face the issues of what role the school should play in bringing about goodness in men. Thus, we shall answer our question as to what kinds of learning should be brought about in our classrooms. Yet a third question arises, provided we accept knowing as the kind of learning that we ought to bring about in our classrooms: When does learning constitute knowing?

The first question marks off a related discourse that falls largely within psychology.[3] Theorizing about learning and consideration of data supportive thereto are attempts to present ideas and their grounds in answer to the query as to the conditions related to learning. This query, then, is a scientific one, for it seeks what is or what will be the case, and as such, clarity of ideas depends upon defining them in a scientific context and their grounding depends upon their meeting the canons of scientific adequacy.[4] The nature and importance of this query has to

[2] I capitalize "education" to indicate the discipline and not the process. What I have in mind is a distinction between the study of how we educate and the being educated.

[3] Sociologists are becoming concerned with learning. I would tend to support such interest on the basis that a learning theory which does not include conditions relating to the individual in a group context could only be incomplete.

[4] See my papers, "The Nature of Research" and "Empirical Theory

some extent been lost sight of and so Kendler writes: "There is always a tendency to lump together ideas that have a common origin. Although the recent development of the teaching machine is obviously an outgrowth of Skinner's operant conditioning programs, it would be useful to isolate . . . the teaching machine from Skinner's atheoretical, ultrapositivistic orientation. It is my belief that if we come to grips with problems that properly belong to theories of learning . . . we may increase the effectiveness of the teaching machine." [5]

The second question marks off a related discourse that falls largely within philosophy and more particularly within ethics and social philosophy. Theorizing about what constitutes a good person and a good school in a good society, and so what constitutes good behavior or good mental states and the related proper role of the school, and consideration of supporting grounds for such theorizing are attempts to answer the query as to what kind of learning we ought to bring about in our classrooms. Clearly this inquiry differs from both the scientific and the technological. We cannot approach this query as we would the scientific one. The concern is with what ought to be and not with what is or what will be. We are concerned with right effort or right conduct or moral goodness. Furthermore, no answer is to be found in technological discourse as to whether teaching machines are the means for learning. The answer must be given prior to our technological discourse. As Broudy puts it: "The advent of the teaching machine . . . only serves to make us ask anew: Just what is teaching and what are teachers for?" [6] Once this question or philosophical questions similar to it are answered, technological discourse can proceed fruitfully. How can we check out whether the machine can do something if we are not clear about the something in terms of which it is being checked? The point of priority should be emphasized. Otherwise we shall end up doing in our classrooms what the teaching

---

Construction," Bureau of Educational Research and Service, Ohio State University, 1961.

[5] Howard H. Kendler, "Teaching Machines and Psychological Theory," in *Automatic Teaching,* ed. Eugene Gallanter (New York: John Wiley and Sons, 1959), p. 179.

[6] Harry S. Broudy, "Teaching Machines," in *Paradox and Promise* (Englewood Cliffs, N. J.: Prentice-Hall, 1961), p. 154.

machine can do, rather than seeing whether it will do what ought to be done and discarding it if it cannot accomplish our aims. Gilbert in his discussion of programming also suggests that this is the behavior to be expected if our starting point is wrong-headed: "If you begin with a device of any kind, you will try to develop the teaching program to fit that device." [7]

The third question marks off the related discourse of epistemology or theory of knowledge. When we ask the question, "When does learning constitute knowing?" we are seeking "oughts" for believing behavior which would make it knowing behavior. We are seeking criteria that would set off right reasoning from reasoning that is wrong, such as reasoning that is prejudicial. Stated another way, we are attempting to state how true believing differs from other believing.[8] Consequently, epistemology is a normative [9] inquiry, just as ethics and social philosophy, and so falls within philosophy rather than science or technology. It differs from ethics and social philosophy in that the search is for logical goodness, not for moral goodness. Whether logical goodness is one species of, the only species of, or no species of moral goodness is another question. That is why we stated that the epistemological question arises provided we assume the moral question is decided in favor of logical goodness, i.e., logical goodness is either one or the only species of moral goodness.

In reviewing the above main queries, it must be striking that one has been omitted: Regardless whether teaching machines can provide the conditions for learning and for the kind of learning that ought to occur in our schools, how does their

[7] Thomas F. Gilbert, "On the Relevance of Laboratory Investigation of Learning to Self-Instructional Programming," in *Teaching Machines and Programmed Learning,* ed. A. A. Lumsdaine and Robert Glaser (Washington: Department of Audio-Visual Instruction, National Education Association of the United States, 1960), p. 478.

[8] "Believing" in this context is used to mean a habit for action. See C. S. Peirce, "The Fixation of Belief," in *Values in a Universe of Chance,* ed. Philip Wiener (New York: Doubleday Anchor Books, 1958), pp. 98–99.

[9] Normative in this context is not a statistical concept. We do not mean "norm" in the sense of a population tendency, but in the sense of an ought. The tendency of a given population may well not be what it ought to be. Consider a population whose habits for action tend to be superstitions.

development and use relate to the present emerging situation? This is the practical question. For example, even though we may find that teaching machines cannot produce conditions for learning where the learning is an insight into values (and Broudy seems to think this is what we would find: "Particularly when the learning is an insight into values, does the machine have a hard time of it.") [10] while teachers could, and insight into values is taken to be an aim of education, nevertheless we might have to resort to teaching machines due to a present and continuing severe shortage of adequate teachers. The often-quoted article of Ramo [11] is another illustration of practical discourse. In this article he sets forth the broad outlines of educational technique, including the use of teaching machines, which he holds to be in keeping with the world ahead. He does not claim acceptability, only feasibility.

But is not feasibility all that matters? Why bother with any discourse other than practical? Why not make all research, action research? Surely, no one would deny that if we are to do something, we can only do it by taking into account what our situation permits. However, if we let the situation limit our inquiry, then neither shall we have a basis for attempts to change our situation to permit us to do something else (is there no way of changing the situation so that the severe shortage of teachers can be eliminated?), nor shall we be prepared to do something else should our situation change in ways that are not now seen. Technological, scientific, philosophical, and practical research are all needed and we must be clear about what we are up to, if intellectual peace is to reign and Education is to go forward. . . .

Further reading

Broudy, H. S., "Educational Psychology as a Rationale of Method," in *Building a Philosophy of Education* (Englewood Cliffs, N.J.: Prentice-Hall, 1962), pp. 337–339.

Guzie, T. W., "The Philosophical Approach to Learning Theory," in *The Analogy of Learning* (New York: Sheed and Ward, 1960), ch. 1.

[10] Broudy, *op. cit.,* p. 152.
[11] Simon Ramo, "A New Technique of Education," *Engineering and Science Monthly,* 21 (October, 1957).

Henle, R. J., "Philosophy of Knowledge and Theory of Learning,"
   Educational Theory, 8 (October, 1958), 193–199.

Komisar, B. P., "The Non-science of Learning," *School Review*,
   74 (Autumn, 1966), 249–264.

Smith, B. O., "Logic, Thinking, and Teaching," *Educational Theory*,
   7 (October, 1957), 225–233.

DEVELOPING THE MIND

When it is stipulated that the pupil's learning should also be knowing, i.e., when teaching and learning activities are intended to develop the pupil's mind and it is deemed desirable to give him criteria so that he can attest to the truth of what he learns, then the educational problems involved become the philosophical problems of epistemology—How does the mind know anything? What procedures enable one to validate his knowings? What is good evidence? What is the nature of data? What is truth?

The pupil can learn many things that are not true—nonsense syllables, that Eskimos live at the equator, that the creation of the world took six days, that Pluto was god of the underworld, or that "might makes right." He cannot know these things, however, because of epistemological considerations: good evidence does not support them. To insure to the pupil that his learnings are also knowings, procedures have to be provided to enable him to validate his learnings. These give him some warrant for believing what he learns and for believing that what he learns is what he is entitled to know. In utilizing these procedures the pupil develops his mind.

Each of the following selections suggests such a procedure. Each recommendation depends upon answers to the epistemological questions accepted by the author. Different answers to the latter questions involve different educational recommendations. The presence of differing *legitimate* answers to the basic questions supplies one of the minor joys of philosophy, for the coexistence of differing viewpoints makes each point of view somewhat less than adequate, which only intensifies the original questioning for the stout-hearted: how does the mind know anything? The issues involved are so complicated that there is room for disagreement about the importance of epistemology to educational problems, e.g., McMurray. This, and other problems, stem from the intimate relation of epistemology to metaphysics, particularly to the metaphysical problem concerning the nature of the mind. The connection is obvious: How can the mind know anything? What is the nature of the mind? Should mind be called *mind, intelligence, reason, intellect, understanding, consciousness, spirit,* or what? Wondering how the mind can know anything is inevitably bound up with wondering what the mind is.

In other words, the selections that follow are "solutions" to the educational problem based upon provisional solutions to the epistemological problem of how the mind can know anything. These in turn are intimately related to provisional solutions of the metaphysical problem of the nature of the mind. These selections emphasize the epistemological dimension of teaching and learning, whereas selections included in Part Two emphasize the metaphysical dimension. They overlap because of the inseparability of epistemology and metaphysics. For example, John Dewey accepts biological evolution to the extent that he denies the existence of the mind in an ordinary or classical sense of the word, i.e., as an entity of some sort. Mind is simply a function of the total biological organism interacting with the environment; it is the purposeful element in human activity. It was appropriate for him to use the word *intelligence* for this metaphysical conception of the nature of mind.[1] The epistemological dimension of teaching and learning for Dewey has to do with the development of the pupil's intelligence by providing an environment that would encourage purposeful activity, for this enables his learning to become knowing through utilization of the procedures of problem-solving as they are explained in the selection. Other selections also focus upon the epistemological consideration of the development of the pupil's mind because the authors advocate procedures to insure that what the pupil learns constitutes knowing, but underneath their recommendations lurk conceptions of the nature of mind, and these are metaphysical considerations.

The arrangement of the selections requires some explanation. The ordering principle comes from Dewey's predominant influ-

----

[1] If someone were to suggest that Dewey utilizes a biological view of mind in order to avoid the controversies of metaphysics, we reply that he thereby reduces his metaphysics to biology but does not escape making claims that are essentially metaphysical.

ence in philosophy of education in this century. It is tempting to amend Emerson's and Whitehead's comments about Plato to fit Dewey: "Dewey is philosophy of education and philosophy of education is Dewey." "All of philosophy of education is a footnote to Dewey." These overstatements to make the point are less misleading if one recalls that footnotes are sometimes more interesting and more illuminating than the text. At any rate, the sheer number of philosophers of education who were and who still are experimentalists of one kind or another is great enough to demand inclusion of Dewey. It used to be said that in order to understand Dewey, one had to understand what he opposed. It may now be truer to say that in order to understand those who oppose Dewey, it is first necessary to understand Dewey. For this reason the major sections of this volume begin with rather substantial selections by Dewey. The view most like Dewey's appears immediately after his, and then there is a gradual progression to the view most unlike his.

Dewey, therefore, provides a touchstone, for the most significant question that an educational philosopher might ask of a piece of writing in education might very well be, "How does it stand with respect to Dewey?" This kind of question may appear to be merely academic to teachers, but for students the ordering principle has pedagogic value. It is too easy to mix ideas that belong to contrasting views, or to confuse contrasting views, because the "same words" are used to say very different things. The views can be differentiated by contrasting them with Dewey's view, especially with regard to (a) the procedures recommended to enable the pupil to insure that his learnings constitute knowings, (b) the nature of good evidence, (c) the pupil's pursuit of truth, (d) the development of the pupil's mind, and (e) the nature of mind. After doing this, comparing the authors with each other should be relatively simple.

The order of the selections is not meant to be prejudicial to any view either in this or in subsequent sections. They can still be read in any order; e.g., if one thinks it is necessary to understand what Dewey opposed in order to understand Dewey, he can read the selections in reverse order. What he opposed was more or less reiterated by those philosophers of education who opposed him.

LEARNING AS PROBLEM SOLVING

John Dewey

. . . Thinking *is* the method of intelligent learning, of learning that employs and rewards mind. We speak, legitimately enough, about the method of thinking, but the important thing to bear in mind about method is that thinking is method, the method of intelligent experience in the course which it takes.

I. The initial stage of that developing experience which is called thinking is *experience*. This remark may sound like a silly truism. It ought to be one, but unfortunately it is not. On the contrary, thinking is often regarded both in philosophic theory and in educational practice as something cut off from experience and capable of being cultivated in isolation. In fact, the inherent limitations of experience are often urged as the sufficient ground for attention to thinking. Experience is then thought to be confined to the senses and appetites, to a mere material world, while thinking proceeds from a higher faculty (of reason) and is occupied with spiritual or at least literary things. So, oftentimes, a sharp distinction is made between pure mathematics as a peculiarly fit subject matter of thought (since it has nothing to do with physical existences) and applied mathematics, which has utilitarian but not mental value.

Speaking generally, the fundamental fallacy in methods of instruction lies in supposing that experience on the part of pupils may be assumed. What is here insisted upon is the necessity of an actual empirical situation as the initiating phase of thought. Experience is here taken as previously defined: trying to do something and having the thing perceptibly do something to one in return. The fallacy consists in supposing that we can begin with ready-made subject matter of arithmetic, or geography, or whatever, irrespective of some direct personal experience of a situation. . . . But the first stage of contact with any new material, at whatever age of maturity, must inevitably

Reprinted from *Democracy and Education,* by permission of Macmillan Company. Copyright 1916 by Macmillan Company, renewed 1944 by John Dewey. Pp. 180–190.

be of the trial and error sort. An individual must actually try, in play or work, to do something with material in carrying out his own impulsive activity, and then note the interaction of his energy and that of the material employed. This is what happens when a child at first begins to build with blocks, and it is equally what happens when a scientific man in his laboratory begins to experiment with unfamiliar objects.

Hence the first approach to any subject in school, if thought is to be aroused and not words acquired, should be as unscholastic as possible. To realize what an experience, or empirical situation, means, we have to call to mind the sort of situation that presents itself outside of school, the sort of occupations that interest and engage activity in ordinary life. And careful inspection of methods which are permanently successful in formal education, whether in arithmetic or learning to read, or studying geography, or learning physics or a foreign language, will reveal that they depend for their efficiency upon the fact that they go back to the type of the situation which causes reflection out of school in ordinary life. They give the pupils something to do, not something to learn; and the doing is of such a nature as to demand thinking, or the intentional noting of connections; learning naturally results.

That the situation should be of such a nature as to arouse thinking means of course that it should suggest something to do which is not either routine or capricious—something, in other words, presenting what is new (and hence uncertain or problematic) and yet sufficiently connected with existing habits to call out an effective response. An effective response means one which accomplishes a perceptible result, in distinction from a purely haphazard activity, where the consequences cannot be mentally connected with what is done. The most significant question which can be asked, accordingly, about any situation or experience proposed to induce learning is what quality of problem it involves.

At first thought, it might seem as if usual school methods measured well up to the standard here set. The giving of problems, the putting of questions, the assigning of tasks, the magnifying of difficulties, is a large part of schoolwork. But it is indispensable to discriminate between genuine and simulated or mock problems. The following questions may aid in making such discrimination. (*a*) Is there anything *but* a problem? Does the question naturally suggest itself within some situation of personal experience? Or is it an aloof thing, a problem only for the purposes of conveying instruction in some school topic? Is it the sort of trying that would arouse observation and engage experimentation outside of school? (*b*) Is it the pupil's own problem, or is it the teacher's or textbook's problem, made a problem for the pupil only because he cannot get the required mark or be promoted or win the teacher's approval, unless he deals with it? Obviously, these two questions overlap. They are two ways of getting at the same point: Is the experience a personal thing of such a nature as inherently to stimulate and direct observation of the connections involved, and to lead to inference and its testing? Or is it imposed from without, and is the pupil's problem simply to meet the external requirement?

Such questions may give us pause in deciding upon the extent to which current practices are adapted to develop reflective habits. The physical equipment and arrangements of the average schoolroom are hostile to the existence of real situations of experience. What is there similar to the conditions of everyday life which will generate difficulties? . . . No amount of improvement in the personal technique of the instructor will wholly remedy this state of things. There must be more actual material, more *stuff,* more appliances, and more opportunities for doing things, before the gap can be overcome. And where children are engaged in doing things and in discussing what arises in the course of their doing, it is found, even with comparatively indifferent modes of instruction, that children's inquiries are spontaneous and numerous, and the proposals of solution advanced, varied, and ingenious.

As a consequence of the absence of the materials and occupations which generate real problems, the pupil's problems are not his; or, rather, they are his *only as* a pupil, not as a human being. Hence the lamentable waste in carrying over such expertness as is achieved in dealing with them to the affairs of life beyond the schoolroom. A pupil has a problem, but it is the problem of meeting the peculiar requirements set by the teacher. His problem becomes that of finding out what the teacher wants, what will satisfy the teacher in recitation and examination and outward deportment. Relationship to subject matter is no longer direct. The occasions and material of thought are not found in the arithmetic or the history or geography itself, but in skillfully adapting that material to the teacher's requirements. The pupil studies, but unconsciously to himself the objects of his study are the conventions and standards of the school system and school authority, not the nominal "studies." The thinking thus evoked is artificially one-sided at the best. At its worst, the problem of the pupil is not how to meet the requirements of school life, but how to *seem* to meet them—or how to come near enough to meeting them to slide along without an undue amount of friction. The type of judgment formed by these devices is not a desirable addition to character. If these statements give too highly colored a picture of usual school methods, the exaggeration may at least serve to illustrate the point: the need of active pursuits, involving the use of material to accomplish purposes, if there are to be situations which normally generate problems occasioning thoughtful inquiry.

II. There must be *data* at command to supply the considerations required in dealing with the specific difficulty which has presented itself. Teachers following a "developing" method sometimes tell children to think things out for themselves as if they could spin them out of their own heads. The material of thinking is not thoughts, but actions, facts, events, and the relations of things. In other words, to think effectively one must have had, or now have, experiences which will furnish him resources for coping with the difficulty at hand. A difficulty is an indispensable stimulus to thinking, but not all difficulties call out thinking. Sometimes they overwhelm and submerge and discourage. The perplexing situation must be sufficiently like situations which have already been dealt with so that pupils will have some control of the means of handling it. A large part of the art of instruction lies in making the difficulty of new problems large enough to challenge thought, and small enough so that, in addition to the confusion naturally attending the novel elements, there shall be luminous familiar spots from which helpful suggestions may spring.

In one sense, it is a matter of indifference by what psychological means the subject matter for reflection is provided. Memory, observation, reading, communication, are all avenues for supplying data. The relative proportion to be obtained from each is a matter of the specific features of the particular problem in hand. . . . The same principle applies to the use to be made of observation on one hand and of reading and "telling" on the other. Direct observation is naturally more vivid and vital. But it has its limitations, and in any case it is a necessary part of education that one should acquire the ability to supplement the narrowness of his immediately personal experiences by utilizing the experiences of others. Excessive reliance upon others for data (whether got from reading or listening) is to be depreciated. Most objectionable of all is the probability that others, the book or the teacher, will supply solutions ready-made, instead of giving material that the student has to adapt and apply to the question in hand for himself.

There is no inconsistency in saying that in schools there is usually both too much and too little information supplied by others. The accumulation and acquisition of information for purposes of reproduction in recitation and examination is made too much of. "Knowledge," in the sense of information, means the working capital, the indispensable resources, of further inquiry, of finding out, or learning, more things. Frequently it is treated as an end itself, and then the goal becomes to heap it up and display it when called for. . . . Pupils who have stored their "minds" with all kinds of material which they have never put to intellectual uses are sure to be hampered when they try to think. They have no practice in selecting what is appropriate, and no criterion to go by; everything is on the same dead static level. On the other hand, it is quite open to question whether, if information actually functioned in experience through use in application to the student's own purposes, there would not be need of more varied resources in books, pictures, and talks than are usually at command.

III. The correlate in thinking of facts, data, knowledge already acquired, is suggestions, inferences, conjectured meanings, suppositions, tentative explanations—*ideas,* in short. Careful observation and recollection determine what is given, what is already there, and hence assured. They cannot furnish what is lacking. They define, clarify, and locate the question; they cannot supply its answer. Projection, invention, ingenuity, devising come in for that purpose. The data *arouse* suggestions, and only by reference to the specific data can we pass upon the appropriateness of the suggestions. But the suggestions run beyond what is, as yet, actually *given* in experience. They forecast possible results, things *to* do, not facts (things already done). Inference is always an invasion of the unknown, a leap from the known.

In this sense, a thought (what a thing suggests but is not as it is presented) is creative—an incursion into the novel. It involves some inventiveness. What is suggested must, indeed, be familiar in *some* context; the novelty, the inventive devising, clings to the new light in which it is seen, the different use to which it is put. . . . The educational conclusion which follows is that *all* thinking is original in a projection of considerations which have not been previously apprehended. The child of three who discovers what can be done with blocks, or of six who finds out what he can make by putting five cents and five cents together, is really a discoverer, even though everybody else in the world knows it. There is a genuine increment of experience, not another item mechanically added on, but enrichment by a new quality. The charm which the spontaneity of little children has for sympathetic observers is due to perception of this intellectual originality. The joy which children themselves experience is the joy of intellectual constructiveness—of creativeness, if the word may be used without misunderstanding.

The educational moral I am chiefly concerned to draw is . . . that no thought, no idea, can possibly be conveyed as an idea from one person to another. When it is told, it is, to the one to whom it is told, another given fact, not an idea. The communication may stimulate the other person to realize the question for himself and to think out a like idea, or it may smother his intellectual interest and suppress his dawning effort at thought. But what he *directly* gets cannot be an idea. Only by wrestling with the conditions of the problem at first hand, seeking and finding his own way out, does he think. When the parent or teacher has provided the conditions which stimulate thinking and has taken a sympathetic attitude toward the activities of the learner by entering into a common or conjoint experience, all has been done which a second party can do to instigate learning. The rest lies with the one directly concerned. If he cannot devise his own solution (not of course in isolation, but in correspondence with the teacher and other pupils) and find his own way out he will not learn, not even if he can recite some correct answer with one hundred per cent accuracy. We can and do supply ready-made 'ideas' by the thousand; we do not usually take much pains to see that the one learning engages in significant situations where his own activities generate, support, and clinch ideas—that is, perceived meanings or connections. This does not mean that the teacher is to stand off and look on; the alternative to furnishing ready-made subject matter and listening to the accuracy with which it is reproduced is not quiescence, but participation, sharing, in an activity. In such shared activity, the teacher is a learner, and the learner is, without knowing it, a teacher—and upon the whole, the less consciousness there is, on either side, of either giving or receiving instruction, the better.

IV. Ideas, as we have seen, whether they be humble guesses or dignified theories, are anticipations of possible solutions. They are anticipations of some continuity or connection of an activity and a consequence which has not as yet shown itself. They are therefore tested by the operation of acting upon them. They are to guide and organize further observations, recollections, and experiments. They are intermediate in learning, not final. . . . But it is not easy to secure conditions which will make the getting of an idea identical with having an experience which widens and makes more precise our contact with the environment. . . . As we have already seen, thoughts just as thoughts are incomplete. At best they are tentative; they are suggestions, indications. They are standpoints and methods for dealing with situations of experience. Till they are applied in these situations they lack full point and reality. Only application tests them, and only testing confers full meaning and a sense of their reality. Short of use made of them, they tend to segregate into a peculiar world of their own. . . .

It can hardly be said that many students consciously think of the subject matter as unreal, but it assuredly does not possess for them the kind of reality which the subject matter of their vital experiences possesses. They learn not to expect that sort of reality of it; they become habituated to treating it has having reality for the purposes of recitations, lessons, and examinations. That it should remain inert for the experiences of daily life is more or less a matter of course. The bad effects are twofold. Ordinary experience does not receive the enrichment which it should; it is not fertilized by school learning. And the attitudes which spring from getting used to and accepting half-understood and ill-digested material weaken vigor and efficiency of thought.

If we have dwelt especially on the negative side, it is for the sake of suggesting positive measures adapted to the effectual development of thought. Where schools are equipped with laboratories, shops, and gardens, where dramatizations, plays, and games are freely used, opportunities exist for reproducing situations of life, and for acquiring and applying information and ideas in the carrying forward of progressive experiences. Ideas are not segregated; they do not form an isolated island. They animate and enrich the ordinary course of life. Information is vitalized by its function, by the place it occupies in direction of action. . . .

LEARNING AS ENQUIRING

Joseph J. Schwab

The introduction of a substantial component of doubt in the teaching of science is, however, only a first necessary change. Its virtue is limited and its effect one-sided. It conveys the point that hesitancy, failure, and error occur in science but not how they occur nor that they are rarely literal errors. Hence, the use of a doubt component by itself will almost certainly have a dangerous side effect. It will exhibit the ordinary hazards of enquiry as misinformations which are identified and rectified only by accident.

What is wanted, therefore, is a mode of discourse which will exhibit the hesitancies of enquiry for what they are: signs of the complexity of the problems which science dares solve, and objects of systematic re-search and rectification.

If we are to exhibit error and incompleteness as objects of re-search and rectification, we can do nothing less than renounce our dependence on a rhetoric of conclusions. For the systematic rectification of error and incompleteness can be exhibited only if conclusions are made visible from the first as the outcomes of enquiry and not as apparitions of truth revealed by the author of the textbook.

With conclusions seen as outcomes of enquiry, the discovery of error and incompleteness and their progressive rectification can also be shown as outcomes of the continuing enquiry: the consequences of expanded study of the subject, leading to recognition of over-simplicity of first formulations, leading, in turn, to the search for new conceptions to embrace new data and thus render the whole interpretation more nearly co-extensive with the complexity of the subject.

This is to say, quite obviously, that the constitutive components of scientific knowledge—principles, data, interpretations

Reprinted from Joseph J. Schwab and Paul F. Brandwein, *The Teaching of Science* (Cambridge, Mass.: Harvard University Press), by permission of the publishers. Copyright, 1962, by the President and Fellows of Harvard College. Pp. 64–71, 100–102.

—as well as the constituted conclusions, must become the materials regularly taught and learned in science courses.

The phrase "the teaching of science as enquiry" is ambiguous. It means, first, a process of teaching and learning which is, itself, an enquiry, *"teaching* as enquiry." It means, second, instruction in which science is seen as a process of enquiry, *"science* as enquiry." The ambiguity is deliberate. Both of these meanings are parts of the idea in its complete form. The complete enquiring classroom would have two aspects. On the one hand, its materials would exhibit science as enquiry. On the other hand, the student would be led to enquire into these materials. He would learn to identify their component parts, detect the relations among these parts, note the role played by each part, detect some of the strengths and weaknesses of the enquiry under study. In short, the classroom would engage in an *enquiry into enquiry*.

Such a completely enquiring classroom requires teaching and learning skills which are not the common habits of our schools. Its aim is not only the clarification and inculcation of a body of knowledge but the encouragement and guidance of a process of discovery on the part of the student.

For the student, this means relinquishment of habits of passivity, docile learning, and dependence on teacher and textbook, in favor of an active learning in which lecture and textbook are challenged. The lecture and textbook cease to be authoritative sources of information to be learned and become materials to be dissected, analyzed. For, in one form or another, the materials of such a classroom are not statements of truth but reports of enquiry. Hence, the student's attention is not on something said but on something done. The oral and written material presented him still, inevitably, are sayings. But the student's attention is not upon the statements as statements—words and assertions to be learned—but on what the words and assertions are about: the thoughts and the actions of a scientist which have gone into the making of a piece of scientific research.

In penetrating the statements to the actions and thoughts they report, the aim of the student's reading, listening, and learning is active in a still further degree. He is not merely to discover what the scientist did and thought but what each thought and action contributed to the enquiry and how effectively it contributed. It is in this sense that his work is an analysis and a challenge of the text.

For the teacher, the transformation of the conventional classroom into a completely enquiring one also demands new skills and habits. A student does not learn to "learn for himself" merely by being told to do so. Still less can he discover for himself what sorts of parts exist in a scientific enquiry, what their roles and connections are, and so on. He cannot be expected, in short, to know automatically what to look for in a report of scientific enquiry, what questions to ask of the material he is reading. On the contrary, this is the first and major responsibility of the teacher.

In the dogmatic classroom, the role of the teacher was to explain what the book left unclear and to test the student's grasp of what he was told. Now, his role is to teach the student how to learn. His responsibility is to impart to the student an art, a skill, by means of which the student can teach himself. This art consists in knowing what questions to ask of a report of enquiry, when to ask them, and where to find the answers. This kind of skill is learned by doing, by exercise, and is taught by guiding the doing.

Hence, the enquiring classroom is one in which the questions asked are not designed primarily to discover whether the student knows the answer but to exemplify to the student the sorts of questions he must ask of the materials he studies and how to find the answers. The student and the teacher both have before them, let us assume, a report of an enquiry. The teacher's first question might well be, "What was this research about?" Now, nowhere in the report is there a statement of the form, "This research is about. . . ." Hence, the question is not in the dogmatic mode, designed to find out whether the student has read and literally remembered what he has read. Rather, it is intended to convey to the student, by example, that this is one of the questions (and one of the first questions) which must be put to a report of enquiry.

There may be no statement in the report of the form, "This research is about. . . ." But there is a title to the research report, and almost every statement in it has as its subject some part or aspect of what the research is about. Hence, when the first, major question finds no ready answer, the teacher asks subordinate questions: "What is the title of the report? What did the experimenter do to the animal? Why did he do it?" The student may be able to answer some of these questions immediately. If he cannot, he is invited quite matter-of-factly to inspect the report which is before him, to find out from it what the experimenter did to the animal, and so on. For, again, the aim of the questioning is not to convey the meta-lesson that the student is expected to have memorized the report but to convey three other matters.

First, it is intended to convey the point that these subordinate questions are the pathways by which one can discover the answer to the major question—what the research was about. Second, the question and the search of the report teach, as a second meta-lesson, that the student can himself find the answers to them. Third, when the answers to the subordinate questions have been found, the teacher asks, again, the original major question. And this time, the student discovers that he now knows what the research was about. Hence, his third meta-learning is that questions can be answered and problems solved, not by looking for *a statement* of the answer or solution but by looking for materials which can serve as data—raw materials—from which an answer can be formed.

When the first major question has been answered and the first meta-learnings have made a contribution to shaping the skill of enquiry, the teacher moves to second and third major queries, following each by the subordinate queries which teach the student how and where to find the answers to the major queries. (What some of these further major queries are, we will note later.) In successive discussions of successive reports of enquiries, this skill is further shaped and refined. The student will have learned to ask and answer the first and easiest of the major questions for himself; these questions, when put by the teacher, now find ready answers and the teacher moves on to ask other major questions and show by appropriate subordinate queries how answers to them can be found.

He also will begin to evoke *alternative* answers to questions from different students. He will set the alternatives in juxtaposition to one another and ask the kinds of questions which send the answering students to the report in search of evidence for the soundness of their respective answers. He will then so guide the students by exemplary queries about implications and consequences that students will discover which of the alternative answers is soundest and why.

By these means, the following meta-lessons are taught: that there is room for alternative interpretations of data; that many questions have no "right" answer but only most probable answers or more and less defensible answers; that the aim of criticism and defense of alternative answers is not to "win the argument" but to find the most defensible solution to the problem.

All this is part of the art of conducting discussion. It is through discussion that the skill of enquiry into enquiry can be conveyed, and it is through discussion, too, that the art, once learned, can be carried on in a group. For discussion is the form of human communication in which the essence of communication is maximized. The conveying of information is followed by behavior which is itself information—information on what meanings were conveyed and what behaviors were evoked by the first conveying. This second relay of information then modifies the communication-behavior of the first speaker—the teacher. He can adjust his second communication so as to correct or change the effect of his first communication. In the same way, communications by the student evoke feedback from the teacher which informs the student of the consequences of his first communication and thus teaches him how to modify his further behavior and later communications. Thus the teacher and the students become cooperative and communicating pursuers of a common problem.

Such educative discussion, be it noted, is a far cry from some of the popular notions of "discussion." It is not a debate carried out to impress an audience, to obtain domination, or to defeat an opponent. It is not a random and undisciplined expression of personal opinions. Rather, it is the means for cooperative learning and conjoint work on a challenging and intellectual problem. . . .

It is important to recall, now, that we are discussing only one version of the enquiring curriculum—the most complete one, one which combines to the highest degree both aspects of the matter: *science* as enquiry and *learning-teaching* as enquiry. This complete version of the enquiring curriculum is by no means the only version nor necessarily the most desirable version in all schools for all students. Of the two components—science as enquiry and the activity of enquiring—it is the former which should be given first priority as the objective of science teaching in the secondary school. . . .

The importance of *difference* must be the subject of a closing note. I have in mind differences between modes of enquiry within the natural sciences; differences between scientific enquiry and enquiries which aim to decision and action; further differences between these and the activities appropriate to humane objects. Respect for these differences will mark a responsible treatment of science as enquiry, whether by way of narrative or through other devices.

The all too likely alternative is escape from distinction and discrimination in the interest of a simplicity which will provide slogans and a uniform procedure for the school curriculum in general. If this occurs it will end by conveying, not science as enquiry, but a doctrine about knowledge and enquiry which is more questionable and less useful than our present dogmatic teaching of science.

American education has twice in recent times committed this sin of vulgarization on a considerable scale. Once, it was a wave of uncritical commitment to the notion that a rote method could replace intelligence because all subject matters and problems were of one kind. This thoughtless commitment gave us the spate of courses in "scientific method" in the case of the sciences, and in "straight and crooked thinking" in other parts of the school curriculum. The other and larger was the corruption of John Dewey's complex and distinguished conception of learning and the learned.

There are again signs of such tendencies—two of them. On the one hand, there is a growing tendency to escape the diversities of enquiry by conceiving it as primarily a matter of simple "controlled experiment," of technical proficiency. Under the sway of this false simplicity, many science classrooms are being converted into research microcosms in which every high school student, regardless of interest and competence, is supposed to act, on a small scale, like a scientist. He is required to master techniques and to collect data. But the intellectual problem of interpreting these data is avoided and the problem under enquiry is treated as something given. Meanwhile, the textbook continues to be a rhetoric of conclusions and the end result is little nearer the mark of the teaching of science as enquiry than our former habits.

The second tendency is to reduce the diversity of enquiry to a matter of teaching "method," of giving some time to "process" as well as to "content"; in short, to divorce "content" and "method" and treat both of them as orthodoxies by a rhetoric of conclusions. The result of this procedure will be to surround science with an even greater aura of religious certainty than that which has created our present educational problem.

Let me emphasize once again what is involved in the notion of difference. First, the treatment of science as enquiry is not achieved by talk about science or scientific method apart from the content of science. On the contrary, treatment of science as enquiry consists of a treatment of scientific knowledge in terms of its origins in the united activities of the human mind and hand which produce it; it is a means for clarifying and illuminating scientific knowledge.

LEARNING AS APPROPRIATING

Foster McMurray

A large part of that kind of learning which is stimulated and directed in the formal school is appropriative, an activity of borrowing from the culture certain of its resources. Where learning by appropriation is deliberate and thoughtful, the objective content of learning is most often cognitive, a matter of knowledge or of that which is amenable to intellectual control. I do not deny that pupils, both in and out of the formal school, are constantly learning a great deal more than the purely intellectual and cognitive resources of their culture. They are learning habits and attitudes, values and habits of evaluating, securities and fears, emotional responses and stable dispositions, of infinite variety. But that which they appropriate deliberately, under guidance, and by intelligence is mainly to be classed as some form or another of knowledge. The reason is that thoughtful learning employs languages and language systems, and that part of learning which seeks for its content the clearly formulated resources of a culture must turn in the main to propositions which purport to represent states of affairs in the world of common experience.

This initial attempt to describe what happens in a formal school might be regarded as questionable or controversial. In a society as fearfully concerned as ours with questions of value and with healthful personality development, the intellectual and cognitive is apt to be "put in its place" as something considerably less than the entire content of good learning. In a community of educators who have been stressing the factor of creativity in learning, there might be a tendency to take offense at a set of meanings which revolves around the idea of appropriation—or "mere" appropriation, as a progressive might say—of public knowledge. The traditional school is often characterized as that

Reprinted from "The Problem of Verification in Formal School Learning," in *Essays for John Dewey's 90th Birthday* (Urbana, Ill.: Bureau of Educational Research, 1950), pp. 47–49, 56–58. By permission of the author.

kind of institution which hands on, or down, the accumulated knowledge of older generations, whereas the modern school, apparently, is in some way quite different in that regard. But the suggestion that there is or ought to be a difference at *that* precise point, is quite misleading. For a progressive educator will insist that in his kind of school, contrasted with traditional kinds, pupils learn more rather than less of the knowledge which mankind has accumulated. And it seems to me that this is a claim which he ought to make and might even have a right to make.

Therefore, I take it as roughly true, and as probably agreeable to all thoughtful educators, that a major part of learning in the formal school is to be classed as appropriations of publicly accumulated knowledge. But I should like to go one step further than this, into the truly questionable, and say that pupils ought to learn as large a part of that public domain as they may be encouraged to learn, and that the more of public knowledge we are able to communicate, the better equipped our pupils will be for successful living. In just a moment I shall explain why this is a controversial position. First, however, let me explain why the position seems desirable or theoretically necessary.

Successful living is the outcome of actions within and upon the environment which convert the energies and materials of the universe into agencies for the satisfaction of needs. To use intelligence in this process is to discover regularities in the ways of the universe which may be counted upon, the kinds of interference we might introduce into causal processes, and other possible recurrences which might be subjected to manipulation or rearrangement in our behalf; in other words, the use of intelligence is the attempt to predict what will or might or could happen, and to act in such a way as to avoid or prevent or encourage or rearrange processes and changes in a way favorable to us.

Although all parts of a cultural heritage are significant, in the sense that they are potentially not neutral with respect to our efforts toward successful living, nevertheless it may be said that those parts of the culture which inform us concerning the probable character of the universe, and concerning what kinds of actions within a foreseeable range of events will produce what kinds of results, are to be called cognitive, or are to be designated as knowledge. From this definition it becomes obvious that knowledge is that part of our cultural heritage which is most directly useful to us in making such predictions as will enable us to gain control over our relationships with environment and thereby increase the likelihood of success in living. If we will admit that the most carefully tested kinds of cognitive resources are those which we designate as the sciences, then it seems to follow that the more knowledge we are able to acquire, and the better tested or verified our knowledge is in the public form from which we make our appropriations, then the more likely we are to be living in an environment both predictable and controllable for satisfaction of needs. For these reasons, I urge that the educator bend his efforts toward encouraging the appropriation of knowledge in the greatest possible amounts.

If what I have just said seems as plausible to you as it does to me, then you might wonder whether my position is in any real sense controversial. Who, in contemporary society, could attempt to controvert this description of knowledge and its importance? This question leads me directly into the problem for discussion.

As I interpret the experimentalist theory of education, its supporters would say that we cannot attach educative value to mere sizeableness in amounts of appropriated knowledge. They would offer two reasons. First, they would say that it is better for a pupil to learn a few things well than a great many bits of information poorly or incompletely. Second, they would say that the amount of knowledge acquired or appropriated by a learner is a function of his problem-solving activities, and that, therefore, questions of amount are as indeterminate as the number of problems that might arise in the biography of the learner.

These two arguments are related and perhaps not really different in any important regard. If an experimentalist is asked why he would prefer that the learner appropriate only a small portion of our total cognitive resources, and come to know this relatively small amount well, his reply would reveal a basic doctrine of the experimentalist school of thought, and this basic doctrine also underlies his argument that the amount of knowledge appropriated is a function of the learner's success in problem-solving. This doctrine is the theory that as a learner attempts to appropriate knowledge from the public stores, his initial understanding of that which he is borrowing has the status of mere information; this information, no matter how well verified or warranted by the scientific public, cannot achieve the status of knowledge until the learner has tried it out as a resource in problem-solving, and by testing in action, verified for himself its instrumental value.

This theory reflects deep philosophic insights, of the kind for which we honor Mr. Dewey. . . .

The suggestion I have to make is that when a learner is contemplating executive action, the prediction which guides his overt behavior is a prediction about the environment with which he has long been familiar, and therefore, that what he verifies, and increases in its cognitive status, is a hypothesis about what will happen in his empirically presented environment.

At first glance, my suggestion must seem rather dull and insignificant, but I should like to claim for it a power to clarify that which experimentalism has obscured, and also to suggest that this proposed language system is more adequate as a foundation for educational theory.

I might begin an attempt to clarify by explaining why the term "environment" has been used as it was just a moment ago. It is said that the predictions which are verified in executive action are predictions about the environment. The environment of the learner is that part of the common world which has appeared directly in the learner's empirical experience. It is that part of the world to which the learner might attend or respond, which has been discriminated in perception, and toward which more or less stable ways of behavior have been developed. It is, in other words, the world of common sense, the world of familiar things, processes, and persons. It is that part of the world which is made known to us through the avenues of sense and by direct handling, or through physical and social involvement. The anticipations of what will happen, which are verified or refuted in executive action, are meaningful to the learner only in terms of this familiar and empirically presented environment.

There is a reason for this emphasis upon environment, which

is that the propositions which embody our cultural cognitive resources are *not* expressed in the language of common sense by which we name, describe, and think about our empirical environments. The language of science describes relations and recurrent states of affairs within a public world or universe, a world which is mostly unknown, in a direct empirical sense, by any one person. It is a language which uses many constructs which go far beyond the range of experiences possible for any individual person. A large or at least a significant part of this public universe is a construction by inference through elaborate logical connections, which touches the known environment only in a few strangely abstracted places and suggests a connection of events, only a few separated points of which can appear to our actual observation.

This public world of construction by inference is that which the learner, and the ordinary citizen who is not participating in scientific research, does not or cannot build into his own knowledge structure by any process of testing and verifying. That a learner may appropriate the available knowledge about a public universe, and convert it into individual knowledge, has not been doubted. Nor has it been doubted that this conversion of appropriated resources requires a testing of *some* kind. What then is the connection between testing in action and the appropriation of knowledge from the public domain?

The process of appropriating knowledge begins in an act of communication. The learner hears or reads a statement having empirical content, and in some way descriptive of recurrent states of affairs in the common universe. If the reading involves communication, then the learner is able to make sense of what he reads, or to understand it. But this initial comprehension of meaning is not yet knowledge. It is something like an imaginative picture of a possible existence, and perhaps involves a diagram or a scheme of operations which will make this possible existence demonstrate its actuality. If the learner accepts the authority of the scientific public, he assumes that this imaginative construction or picturization is true, but he does not yet know what the quality of experience would be like if he were living in an environment which revealed the characters and powers claimed for it by science. For it must be remembered that the learner's environment, which is that part of the public world which enters directly into the learner's experience, and to which he may respond, does not share those powers which science is claiming for the universe.

The second phase of appropriation is the confrontation of a problematic situation which arises within the experienced environment. This problematic situation becomes an opportunity for advance (in cognition by appropriation) only if the learner plans an action within and upon the environment which is different, by virtue of his initial comprehension of communicated materials, than it would have been had he not become familiar with these materials.

The injection of this difference depends upon the learner's ability to interpret his environment as signs of that kind of world which he constructs after the manner of the scientist. That is, he interprets the observable and familiar environment as the scene or setting for other elements and processes which are not directly observable within the environment, but which will yield indirect evidence for their practical existence, provided that certain operations are performed. This evidence will also be directly observable within the familiar environment.

In conclusion, let me repeat what has been observed earlier. The learner, in his appropriations from our cognitive resources, uses scientific materials to construct a picture of a world which extends beyond the narrow limits of his directly observable environment. In his acts within environment, from which, so to speak, he can never escape, he assumes that the broader world is as he pictures it, and that his own environment is continuous with this unexplored and public world. He assumes, that is, that some phase or process of an imaginatively constructed and logically inferred public world is the unseen background for a forefront which is his own environment. If his action succeeds, he has not thereby verified, either partially or totally, the truth of what he has appropriated. But he has in fact verified something else, and added to the sum of his knowledge. What he verifies is the prediction that certain operations upon the environment will produce foreseen results within that environment, and, therefore, what he comes to know, in the act of appropriation, is that subsequent experiences, or interactions between the self and the environment, are subject to control in certain ways. But whether or not scientific knowledge is true remains a question for the scientific public to determine. For that which the learner verifies in action is his correctness in appropriation rather than the empirical truth of that which is appropriated. Therefore the common universe, which is the referent or object of our public knowledge, remains for the learner a logical construction, the empirical truth of which he assumes rather than knows.

LEARNING AS SYMBOLIZING

Frank C. Wegener

Now unlike many of his followers and interpreters, Dewey has said that functional processes of learning should terminate in an approximation of expert subject matter. Even back in 1910 when he wrote "How We Think," he urged that in "process and product" we do our actual thinking in resolving a problem and then achieve logical order in the product of [this] reconstruction of the experience. At least he did emphasize the logical product. But his emphasis was on the functional process. He said: "Method means that arrangement of subject matter which makes it most effective in use. Never is method something outside of the material." [1] Of course here his point is the inseparability of method and content. Still it does emphasize the functional order of things. Again he said: "The subject matter of education consists primarily of the meanings which supply content to existing social life. . . . There is need of special selection, formulation, and organization in order that they may be adequately transmitted to the new generation. But this very process tends to set up subject matter as something of value just by itself, apart from its function in promoting the realization of the meanings implied in the present experience of the immature." [2] Subject matter is therefore studied, for Dewey, within a means-ends context, and not in the older logical context, the logic of the relations of the subject itself as it exists in itself. In fact Dewey would not accept such a statement [or conception of logic] at all. It would appear that Dewey does believe in the approximation of the subject organization of the expert. But we may ask, "What is the organization of the content by the expert?" Although I do not find that Dewey has

Reprinted from "The Logic of Subject Matter," *School and Society*, 77 (May 16, 1953), 306–308. By permission of the editor of *School and Society*.

[1] John Dewey, *Democracy and Education* (New York: Macmillan Co., 1916), p. 194.

[2] *Ibid.*, pp. 226–227.

explicitly stated this fact, it would seem to imply that the expert, too, has organized his thought functionally and instrumentally. That the content should have a logic in itself would hardly be claimed by Dewey. Hence we should be a little wary of believing that Dewey's logic of subject matter is the same as the logic of a given content in itself.

I do not want to extend this discussion on Dewey's point at this time. Suffice it to say that Dewey's instrumentalism and nominalism never quite allowed a genuine recognition of anything we might call an intelligible order in itself, be it reality or subject matter. Dewey never seemed to get outside of the circle of experience with its subjective emphasis.

My critique, however, is directed more toward those educational theorists who center their thinking in "education as adjustment" and the meeting of "child needs."

It seems to me that members of this group have taken an unnecessarily belligerent and contemptuous view of subject matter during the past few decades. There was a time when they loudly proclaimed that "we know no-subject-matter-set-out-in-advance!" The criticisms of the more moderate progressives and the conservative counterrevolutionaries in education did much to restrain the excesses of these theorists. Yet their voices are still heard today in some quarters. By and large, however, there has been a fresh awakening to the need for organized subject matter. Of course, the reaction has gone too far in some places and there has been a return to prosaic teaching of subject matter in many schools. This reaction, too, is unfortunate.

Thus far, then, we find the following "either-or" choice: (1) teaching subject matter directly in an old-fashioned manner; or (2) trying to follow Dewey's instrumentalism with the incidental teaching of subject matter in means-ends relations.

Intelligibility in itself. If we adhere to principles of the "Organic Philosophy of Education," we shall modify, reconstruct, and utilize both of the above as complementary relations. In place of the old approach to formal subject matter as content to be memorized, if this be true, we shall seek the intelligibility of the content in itself. With respect to Dewey's methodology we shall make at least two modifications: (1) include dialectical method as valid as well as his preferred scientific method; and

(2) relate shared means-ends relationships toward the understanding of the intelligibility of subject matter in itself.

Scientific method is accepted as one mode of procedure, but not as the only legitimate one. I take it that "scientific method" includes the whole notion of the instrumentality of mind, problem-solving of emergent problems, and empirical verification after the mode of science. It is evident that such a method is applicable to a large area of life activities. It is not necessarily an appropriate method for nonscientific studies in the arts, humanities, or philosophy.

Dialectical method should be utilized in areas transcending empirical verification. Where thought cannot be reduced to observing, sensing, and verifying in an empirical or experimental manner, our teachers should not hesitate to use dialectic in encouraging the use of reason.

The pedagogical values of the means-ends participation is too well established to challenge its desirability. It should be used. Even here, however, we must insist on some reconstruction of the full significance and use of this principle. Participation by the immature raises the problem of intrinsic and extrinsic controls. Dewey placed his emphasis largely upon the intrinsic concept, almost too idealistically. Our philosophy of complementary principles demands a prudent ratio of the intrinsic-extrinsic relationship on a sliding scale.

The defense of intelligibility *in se* can be argued and delineated on two different levels, the philosophical and the educational. The complexities of the former would involve us more than need be at this juncture with problems of metaphysics and epistemology. Let us examine the claim of intelligibility *in se* on the relatively simple level of elementary subject matters. At least we may see the point of the whole discussion.

Traditional elementary-school subjects, such as arithmetic, grammar, history, geography, reading, writing, and music, furnish us with ample examples. What is the logic *in se* of arithmetic or grammar? Does it have an intelligibility in itself which is independent of the intelligibility of practical or functional usage?

Functionalists stressing incidental learning seem to believe that meaning is derived solely from seeing the functional relationships of such matters to their uses. Number is learned incidentally and functionally as related to games or work. Grammar is learned functionally as difficulties are encountered. Geographical facts are learned incidentally as social or historical problems are met. It is thus assumed that most of the traditional content will be learned in functionally needed situations.

But this is only one half of the intelligible process. The error lies in "psychologism" to the extent that only the psychological principle is stressed to the exclusion of the logical intelligibility of the content in itself. Some teachers when asked why they did not teach the relations of a given subject matter replied that they were not interested in the content itself. Or they may have replied that such content would be known functionally in the long run. More specifically arguments have centered about the "times tables" in elementary arithmetic or the "parts of speech" in grammar. Conservatives have defended the "memorization" of the parts of speech and also the "times tables" for future use. Progressives have frequently defended the omission of such "essentials."

Where do we stand on this argument? The answer seems to be that there are two kinds of defensible intelligibilities: *the functional and the intelligible relations of the subject itself.* We have said enough about the functional intelligibility. But let us see the intelligibility *in se,* which does not mean sheer "memorization" in the recommended context. The "times tables" themselves have a logical intelligibility in themselves. Systematic learning of the "times tables" does not require only memorization; *real learning requires insight into the real relationships of these numbers in their logical sequence.* The progression of the "ones" and "twos" and "threes" provides a discernible and discoverable sequence which is intelligible in itself. "Dialectically" considered there is a problem, or a series of problems, within the field itself. The problems are comparable to what might be called "pure mathematics" as opposed to "applied mathematics" on a higher level. I say "dialectically" for one can well imagine how a Socratic teacher might proceed to lead youngsters through the "times tables" by asking questions. "Now that we have learned our 'threes'," he might say, "How are we to discover our 'fours'?" "If three times one is three, and three times two is six, and three times three is nine, what then is four times one, and four times two?" The child is not at the moment interested in *functional application.* He is interested in logically intelligible relationships when he is being taught in this manner. He has shifted his thinking from the level of *practical thought* to that of *intelligible thought.* Or in terms of problems, he has ascended from a practical or particular problem to the level of problems in the intelligibility of a given field. He may descend to the level of practical problems again with new insight for his application. When he begins with a practical problem he is proceeding inductively; when he descends from the level of intelligibility to the level of practice he is proceeding deductively. Both are necessary.

The same is true with grammar. A child may make a mistake in the course of some activity in his speech. A correction may be made on the practical level. However, if the youngster is to understand his error and correction, it will be necessary for the teacher to lead his thinking into the whole-part relationships of grammar itself, which possesses intelligibility in itself. Elevated to this level of study the youngster should be led into the problems of the field of grammar itself. What are the parts of speech? Why do we have them? How did they originate? What is the difference between a noun and a verb? An adjective and an adverb? Diagramming of sentences was at one time an honorable technique for seeing the intelligible relationships of grammar. But why has this fallen into discard? Because "functional" or "incidental" learning theories have supplanted the traditional conception of "formalized subject matter."

Thus we see clearly two doctrines of educational theory in contrast. The modern instrumental doctrine stresses "learning through experience" which is usually interpreted in terms of "life problems" and "life adjustment." Perhaps I should say "frequently." School curricula should then revolve about "life activities." But we have illustrated and delineated a doctrine of *intelligibility in se,* within logically organized subject-matter fields, which provides another basis of curricular organization. Beyond the level of practical or prudential curricula is that level of curricula which has *intelligibility in itself* along subject-matter lines. One level requires the other in a total educational process.

One level is that of understanding in logical relations, and the other level is that of practical application.

. . . They are complementary in their relationship. The intelligible level must be understood objectively, but the process of assimilation into the active personality of the learner requires particular application.

. . . The relationship between the psychological and the logical intelligibilities is that of organic polarity. Traditional or formal education made the error of reducing education to the one-pole-ism of the logical curriculum and logical procedure. Modern or functional education made the error of reducing education to the one-pole-ism of the psychological curriculum and psychological procedure. These two errors can be corrected by the organic principle of polarity which recognizes the dependence, independence, and interdependence of the two necessary poles of such realities. In this case we have the necessary poles of psychological and logical intelligibility, curricula and educational procedures; both must exist organically within our educational theory and practice.

Thus this means in effect that we must see that our pupils understand the logic of subject matter, whether in mathematics, science, or grammar, and that at the same time they must learn the functional intelligibility of these subject matters. Or in other words, they must achieve theoretical and practical understandings organically.

LEARNING AS ACQUIRING

Harry S. Broudy

. . . Methods of teaching and learning are also related to a theory of knowing, for clearly one outcome of learning is cognition. Thus for Dewey methods of teaching, methods of learning, and methods of thinking all follow the same design. The analysis of knowledge in Chapter 5 stressed its beginnings in the perceiving of actual individual things and its development through abstraction into concepts (ideas) and propositions that asserted truly or otherwise that concepts were related to each other in a certain way.

So while an Experimentalist or Instrumentalist theory of knowing accents the learner's efforts to predict what will extricate him from some predicament, a Realist account of the matter will stress the attainment of accurate concepts and precise relationships among them. Clearly, the strategy of teaching, just as the organization of the curriculum, will differ depending on what is stressed.

Similarly, the role of mind in learning will differ in the two types of theory mentioned above. For Pragmatism and Experimentalism, mind is intelligent, purposeful action; it is a quality of behavior, not something inside the head. Just being aware of the nature of something, of its properties and relations, is not to be dignified by the name of "knowing." [5] We are not arguing, however, that awareness of a pattern of relations carries its own guarantee of truth. But to deny that such awareness is cognitive runs counter to common sense and, what is more important, would make cognition a combination of noncognitive elements.

A Realistic theory of knowing, on the other hand, takes awareness and consciousness as a basic aspect of mind. In

Reprinted from *Building a Philosophy of Education*, 2nd ed. (Englewood Cliffs, N.J.: Prentice-Hall, 1961), pp. 339–348. By permission of the publisher.

[5] See, e.g., C. I. Lewis, *Knowledge and Evaluation* (LaSalle, Ill.: Open Court Publishing Co., 1946), pp. 9 ff., and John Dewey, *Logic: The Theory of Inquiry* (New York: Holt, Rinehart and Winston, 1938), pp. 143–144.

awareness the perceived situation is grasped in both its concrete richness of sound, color, shapes, sizes, and smells and as objects in their relations. Mind is the "form of forms." Realism, therefore, tends to think of the mind as a processor of data—sorting, classifying, and connecting them—all sortings are equally good, so to speak. To persuade the learner to perceive, classify, and relate as does the expert in a given domain of knowledge is the unabashed objective of Realistic teaching method.

Once these "intervening processes" have been shaped, the student is expected to use this cognitive equipment for solving problems, and part of the curriculum is designed to provide practice in doing so.

In summary, Realistic methodology can be expected to be interested in perceptual reorganization, concept attainment, abstraction, and insight as basic to the learning process. Other theories of knowledge can be expected to stress other aspects.

We shall distinguish in the teaching-learning process the following phases: I. Motivation, II. Presentation, III. Trial Response, IV. Insight or achievement of the model response, V. Incorporation into habit or mastery, and VI. Testing.

I. Motivation. It is a truism that the more the learner apprehends a situation as relevant to his concerns, the greater his attention, effort, and learning. An important part of method, therefore, is to know what the concerns (interests) of pupils really are. Educational psychology has helped us map these interests for various age levels.[6] Yet interests are symptoms of deeper and more pervasive urges to self-determination, self-realization, and self-integration. Insofar as knowledge is apprehended as relevant to these motives, the pupil will not be indifferent to it. But so poorly are these three drives defined in the young child that it is difficult for him to comprehend the relevance to them of much that he is asked to learn in school.

[6] For example, H. C. Lehman and P. A. Witty, *The Psychology of Play Activities* (New York: A. S. Barnes, 1927). Dale B. Harris found that adolescents ranked manners and courtesy 4th in 1935 and 10th in 1957, getting along with other people 7th in 1935, but 3rd in 1957, sex adjustment 13th in 1935 and 7th in 1957. The daily schedule and civic responsibilities, however, continued to occupy 15th and 14th (the last two) places respectively. See his "Life Problems and Interests of Adolescents in 1935 and 1957," *School Review,* 23 (Autumn, 1959), 33–50.

Self-determination, self-realization, and self-integration manifest themselves differently at the ages of 5, 10, and 15 years. The key to the pupil's interest is, therefore, how he translates the meaning of success. The energies of the learner, one can be sure, will be channeled accordingly, and much of it does not require school learning.

Nevertheless, the desire to know, to understand, and to perceive clearly are no less natural and ubiquitous than to be strong, agile, and popular. Indeed, the intellectual curiosity of young children is as well known for its strength as for its lack of discrimination. That children prior to adolescence are revolted by aggregates of unrelated "facts" such as the population of Tanganyika, the number of telegraph poles to the mile, and the size of steamships is contrary to the experience of every parent who has listened to an interminable series of "Do you know what?" and the answers to them.

Motivation is often distinguished as being intrinsic or extrinsic. A task is intrinsically motivated when it is done for the sake of performing the task, extrinsically when the reward for performing the task lies beyond the task itself. Now there is a sense in which intrinsic motivation cannot be contrived or engineered. For if a pupil is already interested in a task, no extrinsic motivation is needed; if he is not interested, resort must be had to some goal other than the task itself, in which case the motivation is extrinsic. For this reason, activity programs have no problems of motivation, for either the child is already involved in the learning task or the task is changed to one in which he is involved. An interesting point is raised if it is asked whether an activity program really does rely on intrinsic motivation. When, for example, children absorbed in play *learn about* the dances of Indian children, are they interested primarily in playing or the Indians?

With a more conventional program, however, the pupil who is not interested in learning at a level on which he cannot operate successfully may become interested if the level of the task is brought within his capabilities. For example, a pupil who loses interest in a chemistry problem he cannot solve may become interested in one he can. The motivation thus remains intrinsic. If, however, this gambit does not succeed, the subject-matter teacher cannot abandon or change the task. He has to resort to extrinsic motivation, either in the form of a more remote goal, e.g., the learner is expected to stick with the chemistry problem because he wants to become an engineer some day, or in the form of loyalty to a moral principle, such as "One ought to persevere in worthwhile tasks even when one gets no pleasure from doing so" or "One ought to carry out one's commitments to the teacher, school, etc." There is also the cruder motive of avoiding punishment.

This moral appeal is out of place if the teacher has the duty of making the task interesting or the pupil interested. The appeal to self-discipline is also out of place under these circumstances because this kind of control is called upon only when one's commitment to a task breaks down. To be loyal to the demands of a task despite boredom and distraction is really loyalty to a concept of self rather than to the task. It is hard to see on what grounds the pupil should be expected to develop such self-discipline or how one is to develop it if it is insisted that all learning activities be intrinsically motivated.

II. Presentation. The strategy of motivation decided upon, the teacher presents the learning task. Pupils are directed or invited to discuss, read, recite, perform an experiment, watch a demonstration, or solve a problem. The teacher may talk, demonstrate, ask questions, give orders, invite questions, etc. . . . The manner of presentation depends on the sort of outcome expected, and where different types of outcomes are stressed . . . the teacher is expected to be skillful in instituting problem solving, concept attainment, improving a skill, and appreciation.

Presentations are more or less abstract. The more verbal, the more technical, the more theoretical they are, the greater their demand on the abstractive potential of the pupil. Visual aids, examples, diagrams, and demonstrations concretize presentation. Invoking the familiar is another way of lowering the cognitive stress or the abstractive demand on the learner. . . .

Whatever the devices or procedures, the primary objective of the presentation is to make the pupil *ready* to carry out the instructions. That is why every act of presentation is completed by ascertaining whether the learner is clear as to *what* he is being asked to do, and what a satisfactory response would be like. Of course, if a pupil is *completely* clear in these matters, the learning is over. However, this is rarely the case, so the teacher continues with the presentation until there is reason to believe the pupil has understood the requirements of the task.

It is at this point that analysis of task-types helps the teacher to adjust the mode of presentation both to the type of task and to the learning-readiness of the pupil—or, if possible, of the class as a whole.

III. Trial Response. Another ingredient in the learning process is a trial of some kind. It can be a motor act, such as writing or riding a bicycle; it can be a verbal one, like reciting; it can be memorizing something, recalling something, rearranging symbols in the form of inference, or building something—the list is practically endless. The important matter is that the learner has to make some kind of trial symbolically, with his muscles, or both.

We should not construe this activity too narrowly. We cannot learn to ride a bicycle without trying to ride it, but neither can we learn to read without reading, or to think without thinking. Even in just noting something the mind is active—reaching out to its object.

Unfortunately some educators have restricted "doing" to the use of the large muscles. Much of what is sound in the activity program is now in danger because, rightly or wrongly, the public is under the impression that in such programs there is no place for the cultivation of the mind. In their fear of merely verbal learning some schools have turned their classrooms into workshops or little communities where children learn to live together. But if these schools are true to Dewey, they will remember that behavior becomes intelligent as we *note the connections* between what we try and undergo. In other words, symbolic trials are the crux of the matter even on an Experimentalist philosophy.

As far as method is concerned, the trial phase cannot be regarded as automatic. The pupil may hesitate to make the trial for any one of a thousand reasons, or he may not make enough trials, or he may make the wrong trials, or in the wrong way. It is at this stage that the teacher is almost indispensable to the pupil.[7]

The trial response may be no more than an imitation of the instructor's presentation or the uttering of words found in a textbook, or it may be an attempt to use what has been presented in an unpracticed situation, or with very few clues, it may be an attempt to solve a problem of some sort.

The teacher at this point, if necessary, corrects the trial performance or he confirms its correctness. Trials and needed corrections ensue until the pupil has within himself a model of the correct response. He not only knows that it is right, but he has the *feeling* of rightness as well, or what may be called insight.[8]

IV. Insight—The Model Response. The next step in learning is a judgment by the learner as to whether the response has been adequate. . . .

This is a really crucial step in learning. When the learner can evaluate the trial in terms of the task, we have one kind of situation, e.g., when a boy examines his answer to a problem in arithmetic and judges it to be right or wrong, or when falling from a bicycle, he is aware that what he is doing is somehow not right.

When the learner cannot make this judgment, then we have the slow staggering progress characteristic of trial-and-error learning. It takes many trials before chance or the mysterious unconscious workings of reward and punishment give the nervous system the sense to distinguish the right from the wrong response.

In trial-and-error learning, the learner may not *see the connection* between the stimulus and the response that actually

[7] For some experimental light on the effectiveness of such guidance, see Robert C. Craig, *The Transfer Value of Guided Learning* (New York: Teachers College, Columbia University, 1953), p. 65 *passim*.

[8] It may be that psychologically the value of the trial lies in the stimuli that the learner creates when he makes the response. These stimuli can presumably become cues to the subsequent responses or attitudes toward the task. See O. Hobart Mowrer, *Learning Theory and Behavior* (New York: John Wiley and Sons, 1960), ch. 7. The trial also builds up what E. C. Tolman has called "sign-gestalt expectations." See his "Theories of Learning" in *Comparative Psychology*, ed. F. A. Moss (Englewood Cliffs, N.J.: Prentice-Hall, 1934), pp. 367–408.

brought the success. For example, when Thorndike's cat could not get out of the cage except after a long trial-and-error experience, the gestalt psychologists pointed out that the situation was too complex for the cat to apprehend as a pattern. . . .

Seeing, feeling, or apprehending a new *pattern* of experience is the moment of learning. The gestaltists call it insight or that sudden awareness of completeness, fitness, or suitability with which we are all familiar. . . . Whether the task is to organize muscle sequences, as in swimming, golfing, and penmanship; or whether it is to connect a new stimulus to an old response; or whether it is to recognize that A is the sign of B; or whether a new pattern of meanings is to be carved out of a welter of meanings organized in other ways—regardless of what is to be learned, the *learning moment* is the one in which the organism achieves the organization. . . .

It is the business of instruction to help the learner become aware of the pattern that constitutes the right response. Not all tasks are as automatically self-evaluating as swimming. One can give the wrong answer to a problem in arithmetic without immediately suffocating. In the place of immediately felt pains or pleasures resulting from success or failure, the teacher supplies clues; often her pleasure or displeasure or her verbal report is the chief clue.

The same sort of correction is needed for the perfection of details after the main pattern is apprehended. Thus the boy who learns to stay afloat and to move forward a bit in the water has learned the main pattern of swimming, but he is not yet aware of the subpatterns in the learning sequence.

We can now see the proper place of repetition in the learning situation. Traditionally, it was called drill or practice, e.g., repeating the lines of a poem to be learned by heart, repeating the multiplication tables, trying repeatedly to play the right notes on a piano, or trying to hit the right letters on a typewriter. Educational psychology has taught us that repetition *as such* does not improve performance. Properly varied repetition is the opportunity to form patterns when previous attempts have failed.

If the moment of conscious learning is an insight into a new pattern or the attainment of a model response, then is learning an all-or-none affair? If the answer is in the affirmative, what meaning shall we attach to the improvement of learning?

Our answer would seem to be that at any given moment we either do have an insight or we do not. The differences among learnings consist in the patterns apprehended. Some are more extensive than others. For example, I may have the insight that $(a + b)^2$ is an instance to which the binomial theorem applies. Yet I may not have the insight that it applies to $[(x + y) + b]^2$. I may have mastered the pattern of typing words but not phrases.

Similarly, how well we know a subject is measured by the extent of the network of patterns we can comprehend. It follows, therefore, that a learning task that is well structured, which can be patterned, is more easily learned than one which is an agglomerate of unrelated items. It follows also that part of what we mean by teaching is the disclosure of complex and hidden patterns that are not easily accessible to the pupil.

A learning may be improved, therefore, in several ways: we may try to get an insight into subpatterns within a larger pattern already apprehended, e.g., perfecting computational patterns after the theory of the equation has been apprehended, or we may seek a larger pattern that will include smaller patterns that have been apprehended separately, e.g., seeing the general causes of war after having studied the causes of a number of different wars. Finally, one can try to improve the efficiency of a learned response, that is, achieve mastery.

V. Incorporation into Habit. The tendency to seek patterns, more inclusive patterns, and more subtle patterns is the habit of acquiring knowledge. Part of the habit will be formed by the satisfaction the learner gets from knowing; part of it comes from the tendency of an incompleted pattern to prod its owner to complete it.[12] These factors establish the dynamic tendency of a

[12] B. Zeignarik, "Das Behalten erledigter und unerledigter Handlungen," *Psychologische Forschung,* 9:1–85, translated and condensed in W. D. Ellis, ed., *A Source Book of Gestalt Psychology* (New York: Harcourt, Brace, and World, 1938).

piece of learning to find opportunities for further use, and this further use establishes the habits.[13]

Mastery comes with the incorporation of learnings into habit. The moment of learning is the moment of insight into a pattern: when the learner has within himself the model response and judges that it is correct. But this is still not mastery; one would hardly care to be operated on by a medical student who has just had his first insight into a surgical procedure.

Mastery makes the successful performance efficient and reliable. In brief, it becomes habitual and semi-automatic, leaving the master free to *think* about the variables in the situations that call for judgment. Mastery without insight and practice is virtually impossible, but insight without mastery is not infrequent. Because not everything in the curriculum need be mastered, efforts to teach for mastery are sometimes misguided and frustrating.[14]

VI. Testing. The teaching act is completed by a test in which the pupil is asked to perform the "learned" task without the total complement of clues and aids furnished him during the learning.

It has been observed that this "pay-off" trial is far more potent in shaping the pupil's learning than anything else, because one of the things only the unusually dull student fails to grasp is what pays off in rewards. It is by their tests and not by their printed syllabi that the true aims of the schools are known.

Many school tasks are really exercises of the operations of the mind with little direct relation to life outcomes. Naturally one hopes that school outcomes will produce life outcomes; one hopes that reading Shakespeare in school will result in going to Shakespearean plays in life, but this we cannot test.

It would make everyone involved in the educational enterprise happier if schools promised only those outcomes they have a chance to observe and test at least once in school. It is risky to promise that even observed learnings will operate in life; it is

---

[13] Some men will maneuver a whole evening for a chance to tell a joke or story they particularly fancy.

[14] Cf. Harry S. Broudy, "Mastery," in B. Othanel Smith and R. H. Ennis, eds., *Language and Concepts in Education* (Chicago: Rand McNally, 1961).

sheer recklessness to promise this about learnings that have not been observed at all.

Insight, the moment of learning, and mastery, the perfecting of habit, are therefore the objectives of teaching method. The means for achieving insight can be characterized as matching the learning readiness of the pupil with the cognitive or noetic demand of the task. Roughly this demand corresponds to the level of abstraction at which the learner is asked to operate. The closer a task is to perceptual experience the more concrete it is; the more a task is couched in concepts, theory, and symbols that do not resemble what they represent, the more abstract it is.

When the pupil fails to learn, one can suspect that discrepancy between the abstraction levels of the task and the learner is responsible. To restore congruity of abstractive levels is the strategy of teaching method, and the strategy is applicable to motivation, presentation, trial, insight, and testing, that is, to all phases of teaching method.

LEARNING AS ACTUALIZING

Etienne Gilson

To teach, any sensible man would say, is to give lessons at school or elsewhere, in or on any subject. It is to cause a person to do something—for instance, to read and write—by instruction and training. But if you had desired to hear a sensible man, you would not have invited a philosopher. The true philosopher's business is precisely to ask questions which common sense considers settled, and, let us add, rightly so. Should it be resolved that all teaching will be suspended in schools until a world convention of teachers agrees about what it is to teach, pupils could joyfully envisage an exceedingly long vacation. The words of a philosopher can bring about no such visible effects; they are the words of a soul quietly talking to itself, but they can be heard by other souls, and invisible effects may attend the silent realization of their meaning.

Let us therefore start from common sense in order to go beyond it. To teach, the dictionary says, is by instruction to enable or to cause a person to do something. And indeed, all teachers know that they are causes. I would even suggest that the simpler their teaching is, the better they know this. At the end of the year a professor of metaphysics may well wonder what he has caused his pupils to do that they could not already do on the very first day they entered his classroom. But there is no place for such doubt in the mind of the primary-school teacher. At the beginning of the school year he has been given a batch of boys and girls, none of whom could read a line, and, marvel of marvels, at the end of the same year they all can read. By both instruction and training, the teacher has caused them to read, and his reward is not in his salary, for quite a few other jobs would enable him to keep soul and body together, which is about all he does; his true reward is the joy he has taken,

Reprinted from Etienne Gilson, *A Gilson Reader,* ed. Anton Pegis (New York: Doubleday and Co., 1957), pp. 300–309. By permission of the publisher.

despite his hours of discouragement, in seeing his efforts progressively rewarded first by his best pupils, then by all the others. There was something they could not do, and now they all can do it, and he is the cause that they can. Here we are at once stumbling upon a truly metaphysical question. So long as we quietly enjoy teaching, no problem arises; but as soon as we begin to wonder why we enjoy it, we must ask the next question: Why is there pleasure in exercising this kind of causality?

Were we left to ourselves, we might have to wait a long time before finding an answer. We might even despair of ever finding one and quit bothering about the question. Such failures to find an answer can always be blamed on the question; we simply conclude: It does not make sense. But, precisely, this one does, and we can apply for an answer to those who asked it before us. If we believe in teaching, we should also feel willing to be taught.

The first remark to make on this point is that, properly speaking, to learn by being taught is not to invent. Improperly speaking, to invent is to teach oneself. Grown-up people are doing it constantly, and children begin to do so much earlier than we think. As soon as a human being knows something, he begins to enlarge the amount of his knowledge by a personal effort. But unless we use words in a loose way, we cannot say that this process of personal reflection, however fruitful it may be, constitutes a real teaching. When we are learning from a book, the problem becomes different; the book and its author are our teachers. There is teaching here because there is a teacher who is another than the pupil. This personal relation between two distinct human beings is essential to teaching; no man is to himself his own teacher in any department of human life, and we all know this even from common language. When a man says, "I am my own master," he merely means that he has no master. So also in the order of teaching: to be oneself one's own teacher does not mean not to learn, but it certainly means to have no teacher at all.

Now what is this precise relation which we find between teacher and pupil? I have just been using the word "master," and although there is some tendency to shun it in our day, or at least not to use it with the fullness of its implications, it still retains some of them. Besides, it is not used only in the language of schools. The master of the house or the master of a merchantman is supposed to have control over the house or the ship. In medieval universities a master was the holder of a degree giving authority to teach. Today, as in the thirteenth century, a master's control extends not only to his pupils but often to their masters. In all such cases, the notion of master implies that of authority. By its very nature it is not a democratic notion. Assuredly, we are doing our very best to make teaching as democratic as possible. . . . Yet, when all is said and done, the very act of teaching implies the admission of a certain inequality, not indeed in nature, nor even in intellectual ability, but at least in knowledge. A man knows something, others do not know it; there is no way for the teachers to cause it to become known without putting it, willy-nilly, in the heads of his pupils. There can be no equality between a cause and its effect. To cause is to act upon; to be caused is to be acted upon, and no pedagogy will ever do anything about this.

In the case of teaching, however, this is not the whole story. When we light a wood fire, all that the wood has to do is to be burned. Wood is completely passive with respect to burning, but children are not so with respect to learning. When they enter a school, however young they may be, they have already exercised, practically at every waking moment of their lives, the extraordinary operation called cognition. Mysterious as it is, knowledge is a natural function of man. Children walk because they have legs, they breathe because they have lungs, they see because they have eyes, and they know because they have an intellect. Not only do they know, but they love knowing, just as they love breathing and walking. Let us rather say that they cannot help doing these things because no organ can help performing its natural operations.

Yet we all know that it takes them an effort to learn what they are taught in schools. The reason is that teaching in school confronts the child with a kind of knowing operation he is not yet used to performing. However simple we may try to make it, what we teach in schools always remains a typically adult learning. Left to himself, provided only he is out of early infancy, a child performs marvelous intellectual operations. The first time he says "dog," he has already seen things, perceived analogies between them, formed the abstract concept of a class, and attached a name to it. Any normal child achieves this feat without even being aware of it, and he repeats it endlessly without effort. On the contrary, as soon as we teach him to read, to write, or to count, we ask him to perform operations that are not natural to his intellect, because they are about symbols and no longer about things. The recognition of this fact accounts for the multiplication of images and pictures in modern school-books, and we all know their danger as well as their usefulness. By putting pictures under the eyes of the child, we are inviting him to exercise natural cognition, which he loves to do, but, by the same token, we are postponing the time when he will have to make the very effort we must cause him to make if he is to be trained to think in an adult way. There is no natural relation between the letters of the alphabet and the sounds they are supposed to represent, nor between the words and the things they point out, nor yet between numbers and the possible concrete objects whose substitutes they are. Now these are precisely what we consider the simplest things to teach: reading, writing, and arithmetic; but they are indeed the least natural things to learn. This is the reason why learning them requires from the child such an effort, the very same kind of effort he will be asked to furnish throughout the whole course of his studies. If we think of it, most of what we are teaching consists of techniques, either scientific or linguistic, whose practical useful-ness, supposing it exists, the young student cannot see. Since he cannot see it, the effort required for the mastering of such techniques is made doubly hard because, in his mind, it has no justification.

This is precisely the point at which the teacher not only has a part to perform but becomes a necessity. We should not imagine that school children know nothing more than what they are taught in schools. In fact, what we teach them is but an infini-tesimal part of their knowledge, but it is precisely made up of what, without us, they would never learn. No wonder, then, that in the good old days teachers were so commonly called masters. Where an effort is required, to obtain it by persuasion is by far the best thing to do, when it can be done; otherwise, there is no other recourse than to authority, unless, of course, we renounce obtaining it.

Now, to obtain from the pupil this effort upon himself, which he can see no reason to give, except the words we say, is the highest and noblest part in the work of the teacher. It also is by far the most difficult one, so much so that we are all trying to ease the difficulty. The present tendency to make everything as easy to learn as possible is perfectly justified so long as it is a question of teaching those elementary techniques which are part and parcel of the mental equipment of a civilized man. The three R's need not be made more difficult than they naturally are, but beyond the level of elementary education, while there is still no reason to make things harder than they actually are, we should not wish to rid our pupils of the effort necessary to learn them. First of all, the thing cannot be done; where the pupil has no personal effort to make, he needs no help and consequently no teacher. Next, if the difficulties are inherent in the teaching matter at stake, they usually can be simplified up to a point, but we cannot eliminate them without eliminating the matter itself. Hence the sometimes bitter disappointment of so many grown men and women when they remember their school years. How is it, they sometimes say, that I have had three or four years of this and that, and yet I don't know it? The reason often is that, when a subject is made easy to the point of ceasing to be what it is, it is simply not being taught.

This first way of avoiding the difficulty is a question of programs, schoolbooks, and teaching methods. If mistakes are made there, the teachers are in no way responsible for them. But there is a mistake for which some teachers are responsible, and I myself have made it so often that I feel entitled to say something about it. I beg to symbolize it by the well-known aside which escapes us after a strenuous effort to explain a difficult point: "I hope I am making myself clear." Now of course we must try to make ourselves clear; this certainly is one of the most important results to achieve for any master interested in his work, but we should not consider it *the* most important one. There is no use in displaying evidence before eyes that make no effort to see it; when they do see it, the reason is not that we made it so clear that we understood it for

our pupils; sooner or later they have to understand it by themselves, and their own effort to understand it is for them the only
way there is to learn it. The most scientifically pedagogical
methods are bound to fail if they go against the facts of nature.
In this case, the fundamental fact of nature is that no man can
understand anything for another one. No master can take his
own knowledge out of his own mind and put it in the heads of
his pupils. The only thing he can do is to help them to put it
themselves into their own minds. To the extent that he has
achieved this result, a teacher can justly feel conscious of having
attained the proper end of his professional activity.

Abstract as it may sound, this general conclusion can help to
clear up certain pedagogical controversies. For instance, if what
precedes is true, there is no fundamental difference between the
classical method, which proceeds by professorial expositions
and lectures, and the so-called Socratic method, which proceeds
by questions and answers, that is, by mode of dialogue. However you may choose to teach them, your pupils have the same
kind of intellect that you have, they use the same principles of
natural reason that you yourself are using; the only difference is
that, in your own mind, a certain number of consequences are
related to these principles and follow from them according to a
certain order which you know but which your pupils do not
know. What you achieve in teaching is precisely the communication of this order. Whether you do this by continuous exposition or by questions and answers does not make any difference.
If you are lecturing, you know the order beforehand; if you are
asking questions, these must needs be leading questions and
their order is precisely your own lead. The teacher is equally
active in both cases and he is so in the same way; and the
learner is equally passive in both cases, in the sense that his
mind has to follow the order already present in the mind of the
teacher. But there again the learner's passivity comes to an end,
for indeed, for him to reproduce this order is to produce it.
Having to answer the objection of those who precisely denied
that a master could put into the heads of pupils something that
was not already there, Thomas [Aquinas] observed that "if
questions be put in orderly fashion, they proceed from universal
self-evident principles to what is particular. Now by such a

process knowledge is produced in the soul of the learner." So the master really causes knowledge to be in the mind of the pupil; but, Thomas goes on to say, when the learner answers the truth, "this is not because he had knowledge previously, but because *he then acquires knowledge for the first time.*" And indeed, there is no other choice. The proper effect of the act of teaching is to cause a personal discovery in the mind of the pupil.

Thomas Aquinas has several times considered this remarkable problem, and apart from minor variations in the expression of his thought, he has always answered it in the same way. One of the favorite examples he uses in such cases is a comparison between the art of teaching and the art of healing. In both cases, a certain acquired learning is at the origin of the process. The physician knows what he has to do in order to heal the patient, just as the teacher knows what he has to say in order to instruct the pupil, but the physician can no more give to the patient his own health than the teacher can give his own learning to the pupil; last, not the least, the physician can do little more than to cause nature to recover health in the body of the patient, just as the teacher does nothing more than to cause the intellect to acquire knowledge in the soul of the pupil. Only . . . the relation of master to pupil is a still more intimate one than that of physician to patient, because it does not obtain between a mind and a body, but between two minds. What is the term of the teacher's action, Thomas has just told us, is that the pupil acquires knowledge for the first time; and this is true, but it has its counterpart on the side of the teacher. In order to cause his pupil to invent learning, he himself must invent again what he is teaching, or, rather, he must go again, before his pupils, through the whole process, now familiar to him, of the invention of each and every truth. The teacher, Thomas says, begins to teach in the same way as the inventor begins to invent. In other words, unless he is actually thinking aloud and engaging his own intellectual activity in his lecture, the teacher does not really teach. Incidentally, this is one reason why it is doubtful that any mechanical device will ever replace the actual presence of the real teacher. Only a living intellect, patiently preceding us on the way to truth, can effectively teach us how to think.

Although I am mostly using modern words, what I am now telling you is a very old truth, or, rather, a standing one. It can easily be found in one of the disputed questions of Thomas Aquinas *On Truth:* "When they say that a teacher transfuses his learning to his pupil, this does not mean that the learning that is in the master is to be found afterward, numerically the same, in the pupil; it means that a learning similar to that of the master is caused in the pupil by the fact of his being taught." In other words, there is no transfusion of learning in the sense that there are transfusions of blood. We can give our own blood to others; we cannot give them our own learning.

And yet, see what an extraordinary thing teaching is! St. Thomas Aquinas died in 1274—that is, nearly seven hundred years ago—and on the very moment he died, his own learning died together with him. . . . We read his words, however, and suddenly what was alive in his mind seven centuries ago begins a new life in our own understanding. How is this possible? Simply because, while reading the dead signs symbolizing his thought, our own minds have themselves formed the same notions that were in the mind of Thomas Aquinas at the time when he wrote those lines. In saying the same notions, I naturally mean to say not the very same notions which once lived in his mind but, rather, similar ones. His learning has become the cause of our learning, and still this learning is truly our own, not his. In short, Thomas Aquinas has been our teacher, and we have been his pupils, because he has caused us to produce in our own minds a learning similar to his own learning.

Here is precisely the point where the eminent dignity of teaching appears in full. Without attempting a philosophical definition of man, this at least can be said, that he is the only known species of speaking animal, and the reason why he has an articulate speech is that he has an articulate thought. The thinking power of man, which we call his intellect, is what makes him different from all the other kinds of living beings. If to teach is what we said it is, it implies the meeting of two human intellects—that is, of two human beings taken precisely in that which makes them to be men, namely, their understandings. Every other kind of job has its usefulness; consequently, it has its own dignity; but this particular one does not consist in producing material goods, in exchanging them, or in selling professional advice, or in taking care of the bodies of our fellow men. In point of fact, it is like nothing else. The relationship that obtains between the master and his pupils is that of an intellect which has already actualized its own potentialities, with another intellect whose potentialities are still to be actualized by the teaching of the master.

From this point of view, the reason for this ancient appellation should become clear. Whether or not we give him the title, the teacher is indeed a master because, owing to his intellectual maturity and his own learning, he alone is the prime cause of the whole teaching process. But the nobility of his work arises as much from its ends as from its cause. What his intellect is acting upon is another human intellect, endowed with the same natural light as his own, just as noble and irreducibly personal as his own intellect is, and which, if his pedagogy is sound, he can cause to think, but for which he cannot think. It is true that in comparison with the understanding of the master, that of the pupil is in a state of receptivity or, to use the technical term familiar to philosophers, of potentiality. But, if I may be permitted to borrow once more from Thomas Aquinas one of his more felicitous expressions, I shall say that the understanding of the pupil is in a state of "active potentiality." Without this active receptivity, Thomas Aquinas goes on to say, man could never learn anything by himself, which he certainly can do. In short, man does not have two distinct intellectual powers, the one by which to learn by himself, the other by which to learn from his teacher. The intellect by which the pupil can learn from his teacher is the very same intellect by which he can learn by himself. For indeed he has no other one. This is the true reason why the ultimate end of our pedagogy should be to teach children to learn by themselves, because, in fact, there is nothing else we can teach.

How impractical all this probably sounds! And yet how practical it is! However heavily we load our programs, and however widely we may diversify them in order to answer the future needs of all our pupils, many of them will feel later on that they have been taught many things they did not need to know, whereas what they did need to know has never been taught to them in school. There is a safe way for us to protect ourselves against this otherwise inevitable reproach, and it is to teach our pupils to learn by themselves instead of trying to impart to them an always larger amount of learning.

Should we consider it possible to do this still more than we are already doing it, no pupil would ever regret having spent so many years in school and no master would ever wonder if he has not been wrong in his choice of a career. For we now know the answer to one of the first questions we asked at the beginning of this lecture: Why do good teachers love to teach? Why do they take pleasure in exercising this particular type of causality? The answer is that since to be is to act, all beings like to exercise causality for the same reason that they like to be. Now causality is the very act by which a being gives something of itself to another being, and this is the reason why effects naturally resemble their causes. The good teacher then loves to teach because he loves to impart to his pupils the very best thing there is in him, namely, intellectual life, knowledge, truth. The generosity inherent in the very act of being finds here its highest manifestation, and the purest kind of pleasure should naturally attend its exercise. The highest reward of teaching is the joy of making other minds similar, not indeed to ourselves, but to the truth which is in us.

Further reading

Barton, G. E., "John Dewey: Too Soon a Period Piece?" *School Review*, 67 (Summer, 1959), 128–138.

Bayles, E. E., "Reflective Teaching," in *Democratic Educational Theory* (New York: Harper, 1960), pp. 188–202.

Dewey, J., "Method in Science Teaching," *The Science Teacher*, 22 (April, 1955), 119–122.

Gotesky, R., "The Lecture and Critical Thinking," *Educational Forum*, 30 (January, 1966), 179–187.

Guzie, T., "The Analogy of Learning in the Classroom," in *The Analogy of Learning* (New York: Sheed and Ward, 1960), pp. 192–203.

Hullfish, H. G., and P. G. Smith, "The Classroom as Reflective Continuity," in *Reflective Thinking* (New York: Dodd, 1961), pp. 195–211.

Lahti, A. M., "Scientific Methodology—The Education for a

Changing World," *Science Education,* 47 (March, 1963), 157–162.

Plochman, G. K., "On the Organic Logic of Teaching and Learning," *Journal of General Education,* 12 (April, 1959), 119–224.

Schwab, J. J., "The 'Impossible' Role of the Teacher in Progressive Education," *School Review,* 67 (Summer, 1959), 139–159.

Wegener, F. C., "Perception and Conception in Education," *School and Society,* 70 (July 16, 1949), 37–39.

Weir, E. C., "The Meaning of Learning and the Learning of Meaning," *Phi Delta Kappan,* 46 (February, 1965), 280–284.

CONCOMITANT LEARNINGS

Concomitant learnings are usually said to be those occurring in the teaching and learning situation in addition to cognitive learnings. They are usually taken to include any emotional, attitudinal, valuational, personality, and social learnings accruing while the pupil is busily engaged in cognitive learning.

This view was brought to the attention of the educational world by William Heard Kilpatrick, who identified concomitant learnings with the noncognitive.[1] However, the way Kilpatrick called attention to the noncognitive dimensions of teaching and learning clearly indicated that he held these dimensions to be more important than cognitive learnings, but then he should have said that cognitive learnings were the concomitant learnings; he should have said that cognitive learnings accrue concomitantly with the pupil's whole-hearted pursuit of projects. But he identified the concomitant with the noncognitive, and his sense of what concomitant learnings are has been the accepted sense ever since he popularized the term. In this sense of the word, almost all of the remaining readings in this volume are concerned with concomitant learnings.

Identifying concomitant learnings with the noncognitive dimensions of teaching and learning, however, simply will not do. If a teacher or parent is engaged in direct moral instruction, for example, and the object is to have the pupil learn to do the right thing, then any cognitive learnings necessary to promote right conduct are learned concomitantly. The amount of cognitive learnings will vary with the theory employed and with the conceptions of learning, conduct, and human nature that are involved, but the required cognitive learnings are necessarily learned concomitantly as the pupil learns to act rightly. To deny this would result in two things: (a) the transformation of direct

---

[1] For a convenient source, see his "Modern Education: Its Proper Work," Professional Reprints in Education No. 8220 (Columbus, Ohio: Merrill Books), pp. 1–26.

moral instruction into indirect moral instruction, i.e., into cognitive learning about morals, and probable failure to teach the pupil how to do the right thing; and (b) the denial of the possibility and right of anyone anywhere to be able to engage in direct moral instruction at any time.

If concomitant learnings are identified with noncognitive learnings, furthermore, the kind of "meta-lessons" of inquiry advocated by Schwab as the very procedures necessary to turn the pupil's learning into knowing would become concomitant learnings. Schwab, however, would object to lowering the importance of the meta-lessons to secondary status because that interpretation would miss the point. The meta-lessons are not to be learned concomitantly; for Schwab they are the very means of learning science as science. They are the object of the teacher's attention and intention. Analogously, Dewey would object to the suggestion that acquiring the "method of intelligence" was a matter of concomitant learning, for he turns "common sense" upside down when he says that informational knowledge should be learned incidentally (concomitantly) in the pupil's problem-solving experiences.

The fairest way to consider concomitant learnings, in other words, is to regard them as being those things that are learned but *not* as the conscious object of the teacher's or pupil's intention. They are whatever happens when the teacher is consciously trying to effect, or the pupil is consciously trying to achieve, some other learnings, probably some other kinds of learnings. This definition transcends the cognitive-noncognitive distinction embodied in Kilpatrick's view. This definition also avoids a premature answer to the problem of distinguishing the cognitive from the noncognitive in metaphysics: of distinguishing the epistemological from the metaphysical and the moral. Making this distinction is easier with respect to classifying writings (as for the three parts of this volume) than it is in fact. At any rate, the third section of each part of this volume includes a small sampling of writings that are primarily concerned with what is learned incidentally without the conscious intent of the teacher or pupil—as the second section in each part contains writings that are primarily concerned with what the teacher or pupil ought to be consciously attempting to achieve. It should be emphasized that it is the *writings* that are thus classified. They disagree with each other on the matter of what should be learned directly and what should be learned indirectly. This is as it should be, for it may be the whole problem of philosophy of education, of education, of life.

The smallness of the sampling in the third (and fourth) sections in each part is in proportion to the importance of the topic thus defined. Whenever concomitant learning or creativity becomes important to a particular view, they become what the teacher or learner ought to be directly concerned with, as in the meta-lessons in Schwab's view, as in the inventing of original and creative solutions in Dewey's view. Then, however, they permeate everything and lose their identity as separate concepts. Seen this way, the topics of concomitant learning and creativity remain relatively unimportant of logical necessity, and this is reflected in the size of the sampling.

In the Kilpatrick tradition, Epperson and Schmuck attack programmed instruction and its apparent philosophical basis, warning us of the dangers that threaten when concomitant learnings are ignored. That a philosophical realist can also become concerned about programmed and machined instruction for fear of omitting what it ignores is clear in the article by Broudy quoted by Maccia and in his "Socrates and the Teaching Machine." [2] In the second selection, Wirth calls attention to possible effects of some educational practices in a way that echoes Kilpatrick. Epperson and Schmuck identify their view in the Dewey-Kilpatrick tradition, however, and there are no such obvious signs respecting education in Wirth's article. Which of the views of the preceding section, if any, would be most conducive to promoting the values that Wirth calls attention to? Does Wirth oppose the same concomitant learnings that Epperson and Schmuck do? What agreements and disagreements are there on what these two selections oppose and on what they recommend?

[2] In *Phi Delta Kappan*. 44 (March, 1963), 243–246.

A CRITIQUE OF PROGRAMMED INSTRUCTION

D. C. Epperson and R. A. Schmuck

A critical look at the assumptions concerning the nature of knowledge made by the proponents of programmed instruction raises some additional issues. These issues arise when one attempts to answer the question of what should be "fed" into the teaching machine. Programmers making such decisions are, in essence, authorities who make ultimate decisions concerning the nature of reality and truth. This epistemology clashes with the Experimentalist position which declares knowledge to be a dynamic reality, continuously being modified as learners transact with ever-changing environments. For the programmer there can be no creative participation of teacher and learner in the process of knowing, except, of course, for those few fortunate learners acting as subjects for the development of a program. It is the teacher, or some other authority, who knows the truth and whose job it is to "stamp in" this knowledge.

This procedure for establishing truth has certain socio-political implications. The belief in an elite which makes decisions about the nature of reality, implicit in the programmed learning approach, precludes the opportunity for learners to challenge the status quo. For Realists the creative participation of learner with teacher in the process of knowing does not appear to be a goal in and of itself, and thus does not play an integral part in education for a democracy as envisioned by the Experimentalists. The democratic bias of the Experimentalists leads them to conceive of pupil participation in the learning process not only as a goal in itself, but as training both in learning how to learn and in learning how to participate fully in a democracy. The Experimentalist must conclude that the nature of programmed instruction can support simultaneously a belief in the right of educational authorities to establish "truth" and the status quo in educational methodology. This technology, therefore, can be

Reprinted from "An Experimentalist Critique of Programmed Instruction," *Educational Theory*, 12 (October, 1962), 249, 251–254. By permission of the authors and the editor of *Educational Theory*.

conceived as a further extension of our tradition of teacher-centered instruction which might serve to impede the adoption of educational reforms designed to teach more effective participation in a democracy.

Still another highly related issue brought to mind by present trends toward the adoption of programmed instruction concerns the source of educational goals. One assumption implicit in the Realist doctrine is that basic truths exist "out there" as a part of a static reality. The argument follows that as these truths are discovered they should serve as the basis for educational goals. This view contrasts markedly with the transitory nature of educational goals as conceived by the Experimentalist. Within an educational setting emphasizing programmed instruction, active participation by the student in setting learning goals is limited, if not precluded, by the prearranged sequence of subject matter on the program.

So far we have attempted to demonstrate that the methodological improvement promised by programmed instruction may, very well, result in a further entrenchment of present practices involving exercise, review, and rote. This conclusion is supported by the philosophical assumptions upon which programmed instruction is based. . . .

In relation to the learning process, programmed instruction has numerous other limitations which should be kept in mind while evaluating it as a candidate for improving the educational process. One of the most important goals of educational institutions is to equip students with skills for mastering new and different learning tasks. Pupils should learn how to learn new things. It is doubtful that an important skill which demands so much flexibility can be successfully programmed. The everyday learning tasks of executives, doctors, laborers, etc., do not lend themselves to programmed instruction. Medical practitioners could hardly afford to stand by while an educator goes through the tedium of trial and error programming of an innovation in diagnosis or treatment. The physician, like other skilled craftsmen and men in all walks of life, needs to possess skills of knowing how to learn, and it is questionable that this can be accomplished effectively through a program.

At this time, programmed instruction cannot claim under its

province any of the following: 1) learning how to seek and use varied resources in solving problems, 2) learning how to apply concepts learned in the abstract, 3) learning how to put parts together in forming a creative product (only the most elaborate machine could be expected to provide complex evaluative feedback for this purpose), and 4) learning how to relate to other people while accomplishing a task. It becomes apparent that anyone committed to the Experimentalist position, and hence to democratic values, will emphasize these four areas which by their very nature do not lend themselves to programming. In order to teach children how to question beliefs based on authority effectively, opportunities must be offered which allow them to challenge sources of information. These democratic skills can hardly be promoted until programs are built to *receive* as well as to give feedback. With the current unbalanced power relation between the program and the child, the learner is not a creative participant in the process of evaluating and modifying the "truths" presented by educational authorities. . . .

In this period of advanced technology with emphasis on efficient production, the Experimentalist will not be able to turn his back on this programmed instruction movement. The real question that the movement raises is: Is it possible to participate in a reconstruction of educational procedures by adapting to these currents of change without being seduced by the apparent advantages for teaching efficiency offered by programmed instruction?

It appears unrealistic to conceive of significantly modifying the social forces at work leading educators to a general acceptance of programmed learning. We deem it important, therefore, to comment constructively on the ways in which programmed instruction might be used creatively as part of an Experimentalist educational reform. One might ask first: *How can programmed instruction serve the goals of educational reconstruction?* There seem to be ways in which programmed learning could be integrated into classrooms with a problem solving focus. First, if the curriculum were developed so that boundaries of subject matter, as we currently know them, were blurred and a problem solving, "real life" orientation prevailed, it would be possible to use programs and machines just as teachers, peers, books, supplies, movies, and television would be used, as other resources with unique contributions to the learning process. Programmed materials could be used when more detailed information concerning a particular class of phenomena is required for more mature problem solving. Or secondly, the student could compare a program with other sources of knowledge on the same topic and critically evaluate the usefulness of these various sources of knowledge for solving the problems he faces. Here the program represents an object of criticism. Thirdly, in the process of building programmed curricula, decisions concerning the content of a program might provide the stimulus for a re-assessment of traditional subject areas in the school curriculum. This re-evaluation could lead to attempts to help the student creatively integrate across traditional subject matter areas through the presentation of general problems on programs. This means that a more careful selection of concepts to be programmed would add to an educational process focused on establishing conditions for individual inquiry, problem solving, and creativity. For instance, there might be an attempt to delete obsolete fragments of information which do not lead to an effective solution to contemporary problems.

We also want to ask: *How can programmed instruction overcome criticisms aimed at a philosophical Realism?* A variety of modifications could be made in program construction and classroom practice in alleviating some of these objections. First, shorter programs could serve as bridges in getting the student over certain "blind spots" in the educational process. They would never be used as the primary mode of instruction in the solution of any one class of problems, such as problems of economic exchange or international understanding. Secondly, more consideration must be given by programmers to the variety of cognitive styles which are present in individual pupils. For instance, it seems quite appropriate from findings in social psychological research to use different life examples for pupils from different social backgrounds. Presumably it is the case also that children with various intellectual resources differ in their cognitive orientations to the task of learning. Conceptually adept students are able to handle more abstract levels of knowledge, while other students operate more effectively when presented with concrete illustrative materials. Along these lines it is quite appropriate, for instance, for less conceptually adept students to learn from a programmed system which utilizes two, three, or even four sense modalities. Psychological research concerning learning to read has led to similar conclusions.[8] Thirdly, programs should be constructed so that they are subject to continual collaborative modification by teachers and pupils.

Negative criticisms leveled at the derivatives of a philosophical Realism can be somewhat diminished if instructional techniques incorporate procedures for dealing directly with pupil expectations also. Modifications in the procedures of classroom management should be made so that pupils are alerted and rewarded for being critical of the content, sequence, and illustrative materials represented in the program. This critical, evaluative process can be realized in two ways: First, opportunities should be set up so that pupils can give feedback to the program as they are engaged in machine learning. Secondly, pupils should be taught to question and debate the conclusions drawn by the programmer with their peers and teachers. Procedures like these must be institutionalized and supported by teachers or we run the risk of developing passive, dependent accepters of realities as they exist for the programmers. Stamping in the "truth" should be avoided if we are to create a society in which critical inquiry and creative discussion are prominent.

Still another question arising from our analysis is: *How can programmed instruction overcome the criticisms aimed at its apparent neglect of the learning context?* For programmed learning to hold significance for the learner, certain contextual conditions should prevail in the classroom. First, group standards in support of individual differences must be developed and clarified. A clarification of the group standards centering around the individual's relations to the program and his relationships with other pupils is an essential objective for the teacher. Individual differences should be accepted and encouraged by the peer group. Different styles and paces of learning would best be seen as natural outgrowths of the variety of human resources

[8] Grace Fernald, *Remedial Techniques in Basic School Subjects* (New York: McGraw-Hill, 1943).

that exist in the peer group. This variety should be valued by students, with each being thought of as making his own unique contribution to classroom life. In addition, immediate application situations should be provided for pupils so that materials received from the program gain a meaning outside of their program context. This should facilitate retention and render new concepts more useful.

Finally we ask: *How can educators resist the pressures from the entrepreneurial world to adopt programmed products?* New programs should be studied thoroughly, giving special attention to their rigidity or flexibility for modification, their applicability to a problem solving centered classroom, and their appropriateness for the variety of individual cognitive styles that exist in most instructional groups. We must not run the risk of adopting another educational tool which discriminates against the lower class child who operates from a different cognitive frame of reference than the middle class child.[9] We should endeavor to make all educational decision makers, teachers, administrators, and others, as sensitive as possible to the limitations of machine teaching and of educational technology in general. And finally, we should constantly pursue alternative modes for improving educational efficiency and effectiveness. We cannot afford the luxury of complacency with any one technique of instruction in a world so in need of individuals who possess the flexibility to deal effectively with the complexities of modern living.

Our purposes in this article are to call to the attention of educational reformers the basic philosophical and psychological assumptions upon which programmed instruction is based, to suggest some consequences of the adoption of such an instructional technique, and specifically to indicate that the programming movement is potentially conservative. . . .

[9] D. R. Miller and G. E. Swanson, *Inner Conflict and Defense* (New York: Henry Holt and Co., 1960).

THE EMPEROR'S NEW CLOTHES

Arthur G. Wirth

The following observations were prompted by the author's reading of literature in the existentialist vein and a re-reading of his daughter's copy of Hans Christian Andersen's "The Emperor's New Clothes." There are less rewarding things that educators can read today.

Attention will be focused on a theme, common to both of the sources, which is worthy of careful consideration. . . . Simply stated, the theme deals with a warning of the dangers of man's manipulation of man and of accompanying self-alienation and delusion. There is the urging that straightforward, radical truth-telling is the indispensable instrument for redemption. . . . It shall be maintained, further, that the disease of human manipulation and self-alienation is a society-wide phenomenon which has left unmistakable marks on educational policies and practices, and that, if the threat is as ominous as maintained here, serious re-examination of many educational practices is in order. . . .

It is maintained, first, that the influence of technology and [the] rationalization of work, with all of its admitted material benefits, has tended to make man a cog in the machine, interchangeable as a machine part. Secondly, man's manipulation, subtle or unsubtle, in the world of work has been accompanied by a disintegration of a common world-view in western culture which helped hold it together. The breakdown, due to the challenge of the older faiths and traditions by devastating criticism arising from new levels of awareness and knowledge about man and his world, has not been accompanied by a new synthesis to replace it. A result . . . has been a wide-spread feeling of anxiety—a condition of *anomie,* which in its acute manifestation, has been accompanied by the feeling that "God is dead."

In flinching from the void and shrinking from the onerous

Reprinted from "Existentialism, The Emperor's New Clothes and Education," *Educational Theory,* 5 (July, 1955), 152–157. By permission of the author and the editor of *Educational Theory.*

responsibility of facing up to the facts of his existence and moving on from there painfully but with veracity, modern man, consciously or unconsciously, has resorted to modes of life which have required the surrender of his person. Three of these are mentioned here for purpose of illustration.

First is the willingness to dull one's awareness of self by becoming an unthinking molecule in the mass. "Human existence becomes mass existence. The individual loses himself in types that grow compellingly from propaganda and movies and from the leveling every-day of everyone. Lost, he pursues a collective self-consciousness by participating in vast collective power." [3]

A second tendency, similar to the first, is submission to monolithic political mass movements and the all-powerful, all-wise State. "Technology has become a principal factor of the political situation. In a world in which God was deemed dead and nihilism triumphed, it was precisely by their actual nihilism that unscrupulous men could rise to leadership. These 'Neanderthal Men' with technology have done limitless violence to untold others whose mysterious submission urge accommodated the demands of force." [4]

The rootless, the driven, the fearful, the products of a destructive world are "like a symbol of the human world's bottomless pit." [5] "They are at the mercy of a political machinery that looks something like this: Active are only the functionaries of a merciless bureaucracy; man is the piece of paper which (as identification, as credentials, as conviction, as classification) gives him a chance, restrains him, or erases him; obstacles pile up to the point of absurdity and sometimes vanish suddenly; incalculable interventions govern people's existence, work and way of life. If you want to know who gave the orders, no authority can be located. No one seems to bear the responsibility." [6]

The quotation reflects the particular European experience of the last two decades, but there are qualitative similarities or

[3] Karl Jaspers, *Existentialism and Humanism* (New York: Russell F. Moore, 1952), p. 66.
[4] *Ibid.,* p. 76.
[5] *Ibid.,* p. 77.
[6] *Ibid.*

tendencies in many of the corporate entities in which our own lives are enmeshed.[7]

Finally, there is the surrender to orthodoxy. Ultimately this is done at the expense of silencing personal questions and doubts at crucial points and accepting that which is humanly unbelievable, perhaps *because* it is unbelievable. "I don't believe it but it must be believed," in the spirit of Tertullian, is the price paid for nestling in the secure arms of orthodoxy—even when the essential fact is camouflaged by scholarly rationalization. The price is steep.

This does not mean that there are no valid insights to be gained from a careful appraisal of the tradition. This, in fact, will be imperative for the coming synthesis, but the tradition must be re-valued and re-interpreted always in terms that ring true for us. It must constantly be made our own. We cannot tolerate its being used as incantation or accept it at the price of dishonesty with ourselves. The unbending integrity of Albert Schweitzer in his approach to a validation of his ethics is instructive in this respect. "Only if it offers itself to us as something arising from thought can it become spiritually our own." [8]

The existentialists have shared in seeing and sensing the nature of the manipulative tendencies of our era and the unprecedented threats to human freedom, and they stated their misgivings with an unmistakable note of urgency. "Civilizations have perished before. What is new today is that all of mankind is threatened, that the menace is both more acute and more conscious, and that it does not only affect our lives and property, but our very humanity. . . . We regard it as possible that man may be doomed, or that he may turn into a different animal disconnected from all that we are, seek, love, and have made." [9]

Similar warnings from other sources have not been lacking in recent years. There has been the wide circulation of George Orwell's *1984* and Aldous Huxley's *Brave New World* with

[7] C. Wright Mills, *White Collar* (New York: Oxford University Press, 1951), and Fred C. Blum, *Toward a Democratic Work Process* (New York: Harper and Bros., 1953).

[8] Albert Schweitzer, *Out of My Life and Thought* (New York: New American Library of World Literature, Mentor Books, 1953), p. 123.

[9] Jaspers, *op. cit.*, p. 83.

their dramatic projections of the future world of manipulated man. The danger is that we shall interpret these as having applicability only to those beyond our shores. David Riesman [10] in his characterization of the other-directed character has made clear the danger of contamination among ourselves. The news media furnish us with more direct evidence: brain-washing and forced "confessions" beyond our borders; within, the constant din of the big lie in big advertising, the cloak of pseudo piety in high places, the effort to drug the body politic by the sleazy, bludgeoning techniques of supersalesmanship in national political campaigns, the use of the half-truth (by the Right and the Left) in the form of slogan, catch-word, and innuendo to create fear aimed at stifling the voice that would question or protest.

If this social analysis is essentially sound and the issue for society is as critical as has been maintained, those who are concerned with the preservation of human individuality have a compelling obligation to examine their institutions to see if these are supportive of responsible freedom or of counter tendencies. The obligation for applying the test in the field of education could not be ignored. Before turning to this task, several other existentialist themes should be noted as invaluable tools for such an inquiry. The first consists of a warning about a not uncommon disposition to use devices of self-deception and rationalization to hide basic life facts from ourselves. Here the works of Dostoevsky,[11] Sartre, and Nietzsche may be revealing. They are, in their way, as instructive on this score as the works of the Freudians. We are reminded that valid judgments are possible only if accompanied by a thoroughgoing exposure of evasions and illusions that deceive us. Finally, there is the insistence that each of us bears personal responsibility, in whatever capacity he finds himself, for throwing his weight on the side of actions consistent with the values of human freedom and individuality. Forces and practices which threaten these for one threaten them for all. We create the future by our actions. Granting the power of manipulative tendencies, each of us personally makes the

[10] David Riesman, *The Lonely Crowd: A Study of the Changing American Character* (New Haven: Yale University Press, 1950).
[11] See particularly Fyodor Dostoevsky, *Notes From Underground* in *The Short Novels of Dostoevsky* (New York: Dial Press, 1945).

choice to bow before them or to oppose them guided by the truth as he sees it. "Veracity" and "personal responsibility" are thus key concepts in the argument. In a world of dissonance, "truth and truthfulness are everything today, the only sure possibilities." [12]

What, then, are some of the consequences of this position if applied to the field of education. . . ? The question to be put is: Are there practices conducive to manipulation and self-alienation?

Such an investigation would not fail to reveal items to reassure us, but there would be much, too, to cause us to take pause. We suggest here a few illustrative items of the second type.

There is, for example, the much-condemned but time-honored practice of encouraging or forcing students to accept and repeat words which they have never made their own. Few would subscribe to it as methodology, but rationalizations for the practice are easily produced. "The quality of the students is declining and there *is* the ground to be covered." Besides, students learn to know and love the game. How much time of the American student is still spent on culling from books or notes elaborate descriptions of the Emperor's Clothes. Examinations are taken and passed where descriptions of cloth, buttons, and trimmings are dutifully made. Somehow, in spite of our not ignoble statements of purposes, many of our students seem to have had little practice or encouragement in making use of their own eyes and experience. We still label as a rarity the student who says that *he* sees nothing on the man but a pair of long, red woolen drawers. Our students' behavior must bear some evidence of their experiences with their teachers. As we become aware of the real societal danger, such practices will become anathema. We can have no truck with devices which cause students to veil or deny their own perception of their lives and their world. Our emphasis will have to be concentrated on a search for methods which cause our students to become self-involved in honest inquiry with those of us who "teach." Rewards and penalties will have to be modified accordingly. We cannot

---

[12] Jaspers, *op. cit.*, p. 44.

relax our vigilance against infiltration of the manipulative even as newer methods such as those involving "group-process" are involved. There are fruitful hypotheses here, but we shall have to watch particularly the concept of consensus that it does not get distorted into coercion.

Since one of the features *par excellence* of the manipulated society is the use of the half-truth as slogan to dull and bludgeon men into dupes, this item might well be on the check-list for examining the health of our institutions. Sad to say, the technique is far from absent on the fields of academic jousting. . . . Instead of seeking honestly to understand the position of a critic, the emphasis is placed on setting him up as straw man to be destroyed by loaded "evidence" and catchy cliches. . . . The question concerning self-alienation when applied to the American system of examining and marking students could not fail to give us uncomfortable moments. The spectacle of students nervously gorging reams of ill-digested stuff . . . and then . . . being herded into huge halls to be confronted with hundreds of "objective" questions, which will be machine-scored (for speed and avoidance of human error) and sorted out "scientifically" to conform to the "curve," is hardly an inspiring sight when measured against objectives like self-development and honest inquiry. How strong, too, are the pressures on students to pursue the mark for the sake of the mark? It cannot be maintained that there is no need to obtain evidence of competency, but is the price we pay for the present paraphernalia really worth it in terms of the results achieved? The difficulties of attempting reforms in this area are onerous, for re-examination of marking practices inevitably forces a re-examination of major educational premises. That, perhaps, is exactly what is needed. . . .

Very simply put, these questions together with policies they suggest are as follows: What are present practices which (to use an existentialist phrase) make for "authentic living"? Encourage and foster these. What are practices which put pressures on students and staff to live according to other men's purposes, to ignore or deny their experience, to be untrue to themselves? Expose these, eliminate them where possible, and seek alternative courses of action. In the meantime don't become morbid or defeatist. There is much candor and courage among us. We must live in the faith that men will rise to meet the unprecedented challenges confronting them. Each of us can concentrate on his own actions where he is. It is important not to set perfection, in our own setting or in the world setting, as our goal. This dooms us to defeat and despair before we start. Man and his world are incomplete and far from predictable. The goal should be to create the conditions which make possible the continuation of unshackled inquiry and fulfillment of the person.

In the struggle to preserve the integrity of the person, the principal enemies are the forces of deception and manipulation in all their forms. In choosing to expose and oppose them we can hopefully take to heart the final words of Hans Christian Andersen's little story: The emperor who had been tricked by the villainous tailors was parading down the avenue in unadmitted exposure. The people, too ashamed to admit that they were able to see nothing, were "oohing" and "ahing" at the splendor of the emperor's new robes.

Suddenly a little girl's clear voice rang out above the murmurs of the crowd. "But he has nothing on!" she cried.

And soon her words spread through all the gathering, and others whispered, then shouted, "BUT HE HAS NOTHING ON!"

Then the foolish emperor felt very silly indeed, for he knew that they were right. The people, too, realized that they had been tricked, and only the unashamed words of a little girl had made them speak the truth.[13]

[13] *Hans Christian Andersen's Fairy Tales Retold For Little Children* (New York: Wonder Books, 1952).

CREATIVITY

What remains in the consideration of a dimension of teaching and learning after it is defined and after direct and indirect learning are examined is the role of the pupil's independent contribution. The teacher tries to do things, some of which are achieved. Other things happen collaterally as an "accidental" result. Finally, some things happen on the initiative of the pupil. In general the pupil's contribution can be designated *creativity*.

The degree to which creativeness ought to be emphasized depends upon the point of view. It ranges from almost complete reliance upon the pupil's resourcefulness in inventing his own solutions for problems arranged by the teacher, as in Dewey, to almost complete lack of recognition of any creative capacity in the pupil, as in Gilson. The selections in the second section in each part of this volume, in fact, can be considered as being arranged in order of decreasing emphasis upon the pupil's independent contribution to the educative process. Curiously, it would be as irrelevent to speak of creativeness to someone of Dewey's persuasion, where the pupil's creative activities constitute the educative process, as it would be to mention it to someone of Gilson's persuasion, where the teacher's creative activities constitute the educative process. Only for the views in between is there scope for creative action by the pupil as herein defined.

If this classifying definition captures the essence of what the scope of creativity ought to be within teaching and learning activities, then it is very difficult to see what could be done to promote creative contributions to the educative process without turning creativity into something else, e.g., into education. Be this as it may, one way to foster creativity is for the teacher to be creative, i.e., for the teacher to have a great variety of methods available in his working repertoire. Just as each of the writings in the second section offers a method to try out in appropriate circumstances, so too does the following selection on Zen teaching offer another alternative. Although it shows the wide variety of things that can be done with pedagogic intent, its primary focus is upon developing the creativeness of the pupil.

In what respects would the devices of the Zen master offer suggestions for school teachers? Would the *sine qua non* of worthwhile creativeness by pupils be the return from "discriminating intellect" to direct experiencing as promoted by the Zen master? Could schools wherein most of the teaching and learning was similar to that discussed by Broudy and Gilson move toward Dewey by introducing Zen-like techniques? Or does formulating the difficulty of promoting creativity as Kobayashi does seem to suggest that perhaps the schools ought not to want to promote it? Is Zen teaching, or any creativeness by the pupil, anti-intellectual and anti-cognitive? Or is *satori* a method of knowing? Is it a procedure by which the pupil can insure to himself that his learning constitutes knowing?

THE QUEST FOR EXPERIENCE

Victor N. Kobayashi

It must first be emphasized that Zen *per se* is not conceived by its practitioners as a philosophy in the Western sense. In fact, the Zennist avoids an analytic approach to his Zen practice, for this interferes with the practice itself. Zen is a way of living; however, any set of practices may be described in terms of a philosophical structure; such an interpretation is presented here.[1] The reader should remember that "Zen" is outlined here as a philosophy—and should not be identified with the mental set of the practicing Zen Buddhist.

Satori: The Goal of Zen. Satori is an experience crucial for the Zennist, for it is *the* experience which he ultimately seeks. All of the techniques in Zen are geared to the attainment of this experience. *Satori* is a dramatic flash of insight; it is "enlightenment" and one experiences the moment in a total sense; the basic problem is to get at experience directly and not through the medium of formalized, structured conceptualization. Thus, as such, the experience of *satori* cannot be accurately described. The experience has been depicted by some as an experience in which the individual becomes "one with Nature," or becomes aware of Nature "in its suchness."

The Western positivist may find such a description of *satori* unacceptable, but he may become sympathetic when he considers the inherent difficulty in communicating even a relatively simple experience, such as diving into a pool: the temperature, salinity, physiological data via complex instruments may be given, but these do not exhaust the content of the experience in terms of how the diver felt. Zen accepts the ultimate impossibility of the verbalization of experience; in D. T. Suzuki's words:

Reprinted from "The Quest for Experience: Zen, Dewey, and Education," *Comparative Education Review*, 5 (February, 1962), 217–222. By permission of the author and the editor of *Comparative Education Review*.
[1] The sketch of Zen presented is necessarily brief and crude; the reader interested in further exposition should turn to the many volumes on the subject now available in Western languages.

"Satori may be defined as an intuitive looking into the nature of things in contradistinction to the analytical or logical understanding of it. Practically, it means the unfolding of a new world hitherto unperceived in the confusion of a dualistically-trained mind. Or we may say that with satori our entire surroundings are viewed from quite an unexpected angle of perception." [2]

. . . Furthermore, for some interpreters, once *satori* is gained, that is not all there is to it: "*Satori* is [not] a single, sudden lead from the common consciousness to 'complete unexcelled awakening' . . . there may be many occasions of *satori* in the course of [Zen] training, great *satori* and *little* satori. . . ." [3]

One should not let the fact that Zen is a sect of Buddhism interfere with his understanding of Zen. Zen is Buddhism in that it sees the historic Buddha as one who experienced *satori* and who saw that other men could also experience it. Zen is not a "religion" in the ordinary sense of the term; there are no deities or holy scriptures.

The Zen master may be regarded as an educator. He helps change those who are willing to be changed. His pupils are those who earnestly seek *satori*. As a person who has experienced *satori,* how does the master help the pupil in his quest for *satori?*

First of all, the Zen master is a model for the pupil. The pupil observes the Zen master in action and, in so doing, hopes to understand the attitude toward the world of one who has attained *satori*. The view of the teacher as a model for the pupil is of course not unique to Zen. There are many who believe that the teacher should be an example to his pupils in some way or another. Many Americans are frequently ambivalent about this view of the teacher, however. . . . This ambivalence may also be noted in the attitude of the teacher to himself. The situation does not hold for the Zen master; the master does not think of himself *as* a model, for in so doing he is not being Zen-like: conceiving one's self as being a model is incompatible with

[2] D. T. Suzuki, *Essays in Zen Buddhism,* 1st ser. (London: Luzac and Co., 1927), p. 216.

[3] Alan W. Watts, *The Way of Zen* (New York: New American Library, 1957), p. 158.

being a model from the Zen point of view; the Zen master cannot be conceptually self-conscious. A consideration of another aspect of teaching may help illuminate this particular point.

The Koan. The *koan* is an exercise, a problem, in which the Zen master (of certain Zen sects) reveals his orientation to the pupil. *Koans* are frequently in the form of *mondos* which are questions and answers between famous masters and their pupils. Two examples may give an idea of what a *mondo* is like:

A monk [the pupil] asked Tung-shan, "Who is the Buddha?" "Three *chin* of flax," said Tung-shan.

A monk asked Chao-chou: "What is the meaning of the First Patriarch's visit to China?" "The cypress tree in the front courtyard," said Chao-chou.[4]

As can be seen in the examples, there is no logical connection between the question asked by the pupil and the response given by the master. Why the enigmatic answer?

The worst enemy of Zen experience, at least in the beginning, is the intellect which consists and insists in discriminating subject from object. The discriminating intellect, therefore, must be cut short if Zen consciousness is to unfold itself, and the *Koan* is constructed eminently to serve this end.

On examination we at once notice that there is no room in the koan to insert an intellectual interpretation. The knife is not sharp enough to cut the koan open and see what are its contents. For a koan is not a logical proposition but the expression of a certain mental state resulting from the Zen discipline.[5]

A hypothetical "lesson plan" for the Zen master may clarify further:

1. The pupil must realize that *satori* cannot in the final analysis be grasped through cerebration. In fact, the tendency to intellectualize acts as a barrier to *satori*.

2. The pupil must realize that because verbal concepts, logic, segregate aspects of a world which is essentially continuous and unverbalizable, they are extremely limiting and even deceptive.

3. In order to realize the above, the pupil must be forced to use his intellect to the ultimate in order to see the essential limitation of the intellect. He must strongly search and strive to the point

---

[4] Suzuki, *Essays,* 2nd ser. (London: Luzac and Co., 1933), pp. 68, 69.
[5] *Ibid.,* p. 69.

where searching and striving are themselves obstacles to the attainment of *satori:* "A psychological *impasse* is the necessary antecedent of *satori.*" [6]

As Fromm so aptly put it, the Zen master removes each crutch of rationalization from his pupil, one after another, until the pupil can no longer escape unless he stops thinking and starts experiencing; tremendous anxiety is produced in the process, but the Zen master is there to reassure the pupil.[7]

There are other techniques of the same vintage as the *mondo.* In the first stages of the pupil's Zen education, he is bursting with philosophical questions. In order to remove the "crutch" on which these questions are based, the master might respond by merely grunting, by giving an answer like that depicted in the *mondo,* by slapping the pupil, or by asking another question. All of these sound like something from *Alice in Wonderland,* and indeed, it too has been used by a modern-day Zennist working in the United States.[8]

Zazen. Another device (in fact, a most important one) used in Zen is that of *zazen,* in which the pupil sits quietly, without any thoughts, yet not asleep, for some length of time. It is a practice which is difficult to master. *Zazen* is sometimes termed "meditation," but it is not "meditation" in the ordinary sense of the word: No intellection is involved.

In *zazen,* the master can be of very little help, except to encourage or to demand this procedure. He may be able to show the pupil the techniques of sitting—such as the positions found to be most stable, or the method of breathing most conducive to achieving *satori,* but the technique itself is not the important thing. The pupil, in trying to sit "for the sake of sitting," may find that the striving itself interferes with the sitting and in this way, finally may surrender himself to an "unverbalizable mode" and lead himself to *satori.* Here again, as in the *koan,* the device of *zazen* is one which helps the pupil to "get out" of the realm of intellection. The use of *zazen* also underscores another "teaching principle" of the Zen master:

---

[6] *Ibid.,* p. 71.

[7] Erich Fromm *et al., Zen Buddhism and Psychoanalysis* (New York: Harper and Bros., 1960), p. 126.

[8] Watts, *op. cit.,* p. 163.

The master can only point, guide, indicate; the pupil himself, in the end, must take the final step in achieving *satori*.

Sitting need not necessarily be the only form of this type of meditation—one can practice the "state of mind" involved in *zazen* in other activities, such as walking, working, painting, fencing, drinking tea, playing a musical instrument, and so on. Here lies the relationship of Zen to art, for it is believed that the Zen state is an important aspect in the cultivation of "controlled spontaneity" and effortlessness which is a trait of creative individuals. "A temporary leap out of cerebration" may possibly help an individual see old things in a fresh way: Chinese and Japanese Zen masters have historically been extraordinary artists and craftsmen.

All the techniques used by the Zen teacher have the aim of helping his pupil attain *satori*. It seems to be a formidable task, for it involves directing the pupil to something inherently unverbalizable and impossible to communicate directly. This particular task is one common to most educators: An educator frequently, if not primarily, wishes to communicate ideas, experiences, or insights which cannot be reduced to the form of a textbook, a lecture, or an educational film. Modern man has painfully realized that a pupil may be able to memorize a text, identify a Rembrandt or a Bach, or may even perform excellently in an examination, and yet, somehow, miss the entire point of the lesson. In spite of this fact, many educators assume in some way that the pupil can learn something other than mere skills, facts, or a verbalized body of ethical rules. The transmission of these matters is considered important, but in themselves, they seem insufficient: Teachers frequently want the pupil to become "responsible," "critical," "imaginative."

The Zen master has a similar problem. He realizes the futility of giving intellectual explanations of *satori* or of reducing Zen to a set of philosophical or procedural rules and then merely writing these on the *tabula rasa* of the pupil's mind. He realizes that the final step to *satori* must be made by the pupil, and that at all steps, the master can only guide. All the techniques he uses are ways of leading one to a certain state. Is not education an economical way of leading one to a certain state, an economical way of organizing experiences which will be meaningful to the child?

If we assume that the problems of the Zen master and the Western educator are similar in the respect discussed above, we may turn to a consideration of Zen with respect to a given philosophy of education: Dewey's philosophy. The selection is made not only because Dewey has been an important figure in educational philosphy, but also because there are certain striking parallels between Zen and Dewey.[9] The approach here will be in terms of some comparisons between Zen and Dewey.

1. Both Dewey and Zen view traditional or conventional ways of thinking as often dealing with empty or misleading verbalizations. Dewey was extremely suspicious of the dichotomies (mind-body, man-nature, means-ends, and so on) found so frequently in traditional philosophy. These distinctions, for Dewey, tended to create "problems" which have no bearing on the existential situation. "Dichotomies for Dewey, are, at best, unrealistic and *a priori* intellectualistic constructions which operate only as obstructions to sound analysis and barriers to fresh experience." [10] Dewey sought to construct a philosophy which was closer to the problems of human experience. Zen, too, is suspicious of verbal categories and concepts. But Zen seems to go further in that *any* kind of symbolic activity is basically unacceptable as a method of solution of our deep inner problems, for these "problems" really stem from cerebration. However, it should be kept in mind that *"What Zen objects to is not intellection or conceptual knowledge as such, but clinging to intellection, or to conceptualization within the clinging pattern."* [11]

---

[9] For other discussions on the similarities between Zen and Dewey, see Van Meter Ames's "America, Existentialism, and Zen," in *Anthology of Zen,* ed. W. Briggs (New York: Grove Press, 1961); Suzuki responds to this article in *Zen Buddhism,* ed. W. Barrett (Garden City, N.Y.: Doubleday and Co., 1956), ch. 9; Harold E. McCarthy's "Dewey, Suzuki, and the Elimination of Dichotomies," *Philosophy East and West,* VI (April, 1956), 35–48. There is a remote possibility that Dewey may have been influenced by Zen through his contact with Japanese philosophers in 1919. Letters to his children mention visits to a Zen monk and how Dewey was impressed by Zen in action while visiting a judo class. See his *Letters from China and Japan,* ed. Evelyn Dewey (New York: E. P. Dutton, 1920).

[10] McCarthy, *op. cit.,* p. 39.

[11] Chen-Chi Chang, *The Practice of Zen* (New York: Harper and Bros., 1959), p. 117 (italics in the original).

2. The Deweyan idea of an "esthetic experience," especially as described in *Art as Experience,* resembles the Zen *satori.* The following quotation, for example, concretely suggests the similarity. (Dewey here is speaking of the experience in terms of confronting an object of great art.)

A work of art elicits and accentuates this quality of being a whole and of belonging to the larger, all-inclusive, whole which is the universe in which we live. This fact, I think, is the explanation of that feeling of exquisite intelligibility and clarity we have in the presence of an object that is experienced with esthetic intensity. It explains also the religious feeling that accompanies intense esthetic perception. We are, as it were, introduced into a world beyond this world which is nevertheless the deeper reality of the world in which we live in our ordinary experiences. We are carried beyond ourselves to find ourselves.[12]

Dewey differs in that, unlike Zen, symbolic activity too, when properly carried out, may culminate in esthetic experiences. Theorizing, creating a unifying scientific or mathematical system, could culminate in an experience which "weds man and nature," and "renders men aware of their union with one another in origin and destiny." [13]

3. In Zen, the pupil *must* be willing to achieve *satori.* Dewey realized that in order to learn in a meaningful way, the child must be motivated, be interested, be willing to learn. Zen does not seem to offer help here except to point out that motivation is essential. Zen pupils seek out the masters. . . .

4. Concepts are instruments to action. For Zen, words are used in a somewhat unconventional way (e.g., *the koan*), a way, though, which may somehow be adaptable to the Western classroom. Dewey, too, was interested in having pupils realize the limitation of concepts and that although concepts are instruments for intelligent action, they are not tools applicable in all situations. The negative aspects of conceptual and logical thinking seem not to be emphasized by Dewey's educational spokesmen of today and perhaps there is need for such an emphasis.

5. Dewey believed that a crisis, an "indeterminate situation," is a precondition of a unifying (esthetic) experience. Any in-

[12] John Dewey, *Art as Experience* (New York: Capricorn Books, 1934), p. 195.
[13] *Ibid.,* p. 271.

quiry is based on such a precondition. A crisis is seen too, in Zen, as a necessary prerequisite for *satori*. Zen offers a method here which Dewey did not seem to have considered (although he himself apparently used it): that of "pushing" a problematic situation in its conceptual form to a point where cerebration does not resolve the situation, and that in so doing, one may achieve a unifying experience or solution. How to go about leading one to such a point may thus be a relevant problem for the educationist. As mentioned previously in reference to Fromm, the teacher here is extremely important, for in "pushing" a problem to its "dead end," there may be extreme anxiety on the part of the pupil, and the presence of a sympathetic teacher is psychologically important, if not necessary. (Teaching machines, though useful, probably cannot play the role demanded here—herein seems to lie one tenable argument against teaching machines.)

We finally come to what may be considered the most important message of Zen to Western education. It is a point which has interested the psychoanalysts.

Our educational methods seem to be almost exclusively oriented to the realm of intellection. Even in approaching the arts and the area of physical education, teaching is in terms of intellection. Modern man seems to be so exclusively involved in thinking in terms of words that he finds himself unable to free himself from a symbolic world. He is so concerned and involved in a "quest for certainty" that he sometimes fails to wonder whether symbolic thinking itself may be the source of difficulty. He fails to consider the possibility that symbolic thinking, philosophizing, cerebration, may at times be inadequate "defense mechanisms" against the realities of his problems of existence and that a "breakthrough" may be achieved via nonrational lines. Such a breakthrough may paradoxically be the key to the creative formation of new ideas or new ways of conceptual thinking.

A study of Zen suggests that a process of education wholly in a symbolically oriented realm, a realm in which systems are constructed over systems, boxes over boxes—in never-ending progression—may be a limited, and perhaps even too rigid and therefore dangerous, approach to education and life.

The cry of those who say we live in a world of excessive anxiety may perhaps be an indication of this danger.

Further reading

Ehrenzweig, A., "Conscious Planning and Unconscious Scanning," in *Education of Vision,* ed. G. Kepes (New York: Braziller, 1965), pp. 26–49.

Lanvin, E. J., "Creative Learning," *Jesuit Education Quarterly,* 21 (March, 1960), 205–219.

Maccia, G. S., "Hypothetical Thinking in Education," *Educational Theory,* 10 (July, 1960), 182–186.

Rugg, H., "Imperatives for Education," in *Imagination* (New York: Harper and Bros., 1963), pp. 310–314.

Scheffler, I., "The Possession of Adequate Evidence," in *Conditions of Knowledge* (Glenview, Ill.: Scott, Foresman, 1965), pp. 66–74.

METAPHYSICAL CONSIDERATIONS

METAPHYSICS VERSUS EXPERIMENTAL PSYCHOLOGY

These selections raise metaphysical problems because the authors question the assumptions made in the application of the "findings" of experimental psychology to the teaching and learning situation of the classroom. The reasons given to substantiate their opposition to this application serve to define in a preliminary way the dimension of teaching and learning that is open to metaphysical consideration.

Aschner rejects the applicability of Skinner's learning and personality theory to the classroom in the name of the teacher and the pupil as responsible agents. She differs with Skinner about the nature of human action. This is related to a difference about the nature of human nature, a metaphysical consideration. It is not Skinner's theory as a scientific theory *about* human nature that she rejects, but its application as if it were a true and representative picture of human nature, as if it were a metaphysical account of human nature. She buttresses her argument with the unself-conscious metaphysics of the ordinary language system allegedly supported by teachers, parents, and pupils. Soderquist, on the other hand, argues in terms of a fully self-conscious metaphysics. What Aschner says in respect to one theory, Soderquist repeats in respect to all such theories, in respect to the much broader issue of the application of scientific research to teaching, and he does so by speaking directly to the metaphysical issues involved. The introduction to the next section will explicate the issues involved in the problems raised by these selections.

VERBAL BEHAVIOR OR HUMAN ACTION?

Mary Jane Aschner

The assumptions about the nature of human action which appear to underlie Skinner's definition of verbal behavior and the one proposed here for a study of teaching differ mainly with respect to where we locate the agency and control of human action. The manipulation and control of behavior sought in the laboratories of experimental psychology have—at least in this writer's opinion—no place in the classroom.

According to Skinner's research model of verbal behavior, the individual is apparently assumed to be somewhat less the responsible agent of his own actions than a conditioned reactor to environmental stimuli. This would seem to add up to a kind of "push button" theory of conditioned behavior, typical of the stimulus-response-reinforcement model of learning theory that has so long prevailed in experimental psychology. Theoretically, that is, one can presumably produce (i.e., control the emission of) a given verbal response on the part of an individual. Once it is known why a person says this word or that remark under such and such conditions, this particular response can be elicited or inhibited in that person by manipulation and control of these conditions. His "emission" of a given verbal response, according to Skinner, is a function of many variables. An important one of these is that of reinforcement with respect to the response in question—the history of its reinforcement in the individual, and of its career in "the reinforcement practices of the verbal community" wherein he "emits" this response.[1] To the degree, then, that one achieves control over the variables typically operative in given occurrences of this response in the individual, one can assign a probability factor to it. Then, ideally, one can predict reliably, and finally control future instances of, that person's

Reprinted from B. Othanel Smith and R. H. Ennis, eds., *Language and Concepts in Education* (Chicago: Rand McNally, 1961), pp. 121–125. By permission of the publisher.

[1] B. F. Skinner, *Verbal Behavior* (New York: Appleton-Century-Crofts, 1957), p. 36.

emission of the same verbal response. On such a theory, one person can presumably manipulate and gain control over another person's verbal behavior simply by knowing how to push the right buttons on his psychological switchboard.

In contrast to the stimulus-response model for the agency and control of human action, our theory of linguistic behavior as action assumes the individual to be the responsible agent of his own verbal acts. When we observe a person speaking, we do not view him as a conditioned reactor to a set of stimuli, but as an agent taking action. He does not emit a statement; he makes one. It is something of his own doing.

The ultimate locus of control, in our view of human action, lies at the point of agency. Hence, if we accord to an individual the status of a rational social being, we are fairly obliged to acknowledge him as ultimately in control of his own utterances. This would hold whether or not his control is efficient, and whether or not he has the choice to speak or remain silent in a given situation. What someone says, in the last analysis, is up to him. At least it seems more plausibly a matter of his own doing than of someone else's.

In this view, then, our model of an act of verbal behavior is understood to be an action taken by an agent and addressed to some responding agency (whether real or imaginary, one or many). For example, a speaker engaged in discussion may be asked a question. By the conventions of discourse, he is obliged to reply to the question or be judged discourteous or out of order. In this sense, the choice to speak or be silent is not in the hands of the person to whom the question was addressed. But though the "ground rules" of the situation may thus demand response, the speaker's response is of his own making. As a reply, it is an action taken by him and addressed to his questioner. It is responding action, not a conditioned response emitted in reaction to the stimulus of being asked a certain question.

Whether Skinner is actually right in locating the agency and control of verbal behavior in the operation of environmental variables, or whether we are right in ascribing the control to a self-directing agent is not an important question to settle at this point. What is important is the fact that, in our society at all levels, the individual is typically regarded as being the responsible agent of his own actions. And certainly this outlook can be said to prevail in the classroom.

In the minimum sense, responsibility for an action is usually viewed as nothing more than agency. But when we think of responsibility in the sense that one is held accountable for his actions, we generally assign it according to some scale of degree. Our legal, moral, and social codes commonly assign agency (responsibility) to him who acts, although the degree to which he is held accountable may be limited or even cancelled, depending on the particular case. Thus a small child who shoots his brother is considered the agent of the shooting, but his father may be held legally and even morally responsible (accountable) for the child's act. This assumption of individual agency and responsibility is so built into our language system that our verbal activities are shaped by our customary ways of considering and dealing with one another.

The commonly held assumption that each person is responsible and accountable for his acts is clearly reflected in the behaviors of teachers and students in the classroom. Despite all their college courses in psychology, teachers seem not to see themselves as manipulators of student behavior by push-button techniques. Nor does anyone appear to view the student as "emitting" verbal responses conditioned to follow upon given environmental stimuli. If a student makes a mistaken or an impertinent reply to a teacher's question, he is normally corrected or called to account. Now, if this student's reply were looked upon as mere conditioned response, it would be plainly absurd to hold him accountable for it. After all, Pavlov's dog cannot be blamed for slavering when the bell rings. Rather, in such a view, the teacher would be obliged simply to conclude that he had pushed the wrong buttons. But, of course, this just is not the way people see themselves or others, in or out of school. The definition of verbal behavior proposed in this essay is frankly acknowledged to reflect the accustomed ways in which people deal with each other in group-discussion stituations. A description of verbal interaction, based on a definition assuming a view of human action consonant with that upon which the subjects of observation themselves proceed, should be useful to those who hope ultimately to bring about desirable changes in teaching.

Because language, as we have described it, is so much a part of teaching, research in the classroom is but partly served by the ideas of prediction and control used in statistical and laboratory research. These ideas concern the identification of relevant variables and of significant relationships among them regarding the antecedent conditions necessary for the predictable occurrence of given events. Of course, educational researchers hope, as we have said, to achieve this kind of prediction and control with respect to given teaching operations and desired educational results. Such research can be done by analysis of data on classroom verbal activity described in the terms of action we have suggested. For to locate the ultimate control of action at the point of agency is not to say its performance under given conditions cannot, at least in a general way, be predicted. After all, we assume the ability of one person to influence another even though at the same time we assume the individual's capacity deliberately to resist or evade as well as to accept that influence. And, clearly, the notion of teaching rests upon this dual assumption—that people influence each other, and that the individual is (or should be) ultimately in responsible control of his own actions. Nor do these assumptions bias the notion of teaching in favor of any particular educational or psychological doctrine.

It is for this reason that the educator's concern with prediction and control goes a step beyond that of the laboratory psychologist. For he must eventually put control and prediction in the hands of the teacher. The language of teaching is the language of responsible action taken to influence the behaviors of those under instruction. The teacher's two-fold dealings with language in the classroom cast him in the role of strategist and tactician in the campaign for learning. First, he acts with language, using it in the performance of almost all those actions describable as teaching. Secondly, the teacher studies and interprets verbal action; he observes what his pupils say and do under instruction. He does so in order to predict—to diagnose and adapt his teaching to the pupils' present state of comprehension and progress in learning, to appraise the quality of their reasoning, and to assess their emotional reactions to the situation of the moment. The teacher's control over his dealings with language thus determines in large measure his success (or failure) to induce the educational results for which we send our children to school. Moreover, it is the teacher's task and purpose *not* to condition the responses or the learnings of his pupils, but to develop in them their own capacities to think and act responsibly. The rational and self-directing individual is, in most views, the ultimate aim of education.

PERSONALISM AND EDUCATION

Harold Soderquist

We have come far enough along in the scientific movement in education to evaluate with some adequacy of perspective the mechanistic naturalism from which that movement has drawn rational sustenance. While indeed, educational questions which have been convincingly answered by experimental procedures are not large in number, we have made sufficient progress to be able to see ahead at least the general outlines of a new type of problem which the expansion of the scientific enterprise has itself created. The new problem is of the species which has been raised by the enormous progress of the physical sciences—the moral. For just as intergroup and international morals have not advanced far enough to make us feel safe with the destructive weapons placed in our hands through physical science, so our understanding of the conditions demanded for healthy morality on the interpersonal level is not yet at a stage to make us feel safe as users of the new knowledge and techniques placed at our disposal by the psychological sciences. . . .

Early in the present century the new prophets of the scientific movement in education announced their jubilant creed that everything which exists exists in some amount and can, therefore, be measured. Human character and aptitude, it was averred, can be analysed into existent and persistent traits. These can be quantified and measured, and the resulting knowledge will make possible prediction of behavior and success in the tasks of the school and the vocations of life.

Central in this outlook was the mechanistic principle of cause and effect, adopted whole-cloth from the physical sciences. This conception served admirably to spark research into the elements and control of human behavior and became the rationalizing principle of the psychological and social sciences in general. Thus, before the first third of the century had passed, educa-

Reprinted from "Personalistic Naturalism and Educational Method," *Educational Theory*, 3 (October, 1953), 369–370, 372–373. By permission of the author and the editor of *Educational Theory*.

tional scientists had come to view man as a machine, a biological and very complex one indeed, but a machine nevertheless, amenable to scientific analysis as to structure and scientific control as to behavior. From this point of view a concern with consciousness as a phenomenon was considered a hindrance to a confident and all-out experimental attack on behavioral problems. The individual's subjective sense of self and freedom was of no scientific significance.

The mechanistic philosophy became, then, the rationale of the psychology which has until recent years made up the methodological core of the teacher-education curriculum. Nor can there be any doubt of its benefits. The deterministic view of the child as a product of his history—his inherited constitution, his temperament, and most of all, his experiences—has certainly made for greater objectivity of teachers in their attitudes toward children, and has dissipated much of the oldtime penal atmosphere of the schoolroom. Just as the scientific outlook has led to the softening of teacher-child relations, so it has mellowed society's dealings with human delinquency in general, at least in the democratic parts of the world. It has outmoded retribution as a penal philosophy. Pragmatically speaking, the mechanistic outlook has proved itself one support for democratic morality.

But its blessings acknowledged, may it not be that so potent an instrument as analytical science in the hands of those who have had no adequate philosophy of science may also have begun to produce negative values? Like nuclear physics with its atomic products, it may be possible also that mechanistic human science can kill as under other conditions it can cure; that it may destroy him on whom it is used, as well as burn the hands of him who uses it. There is, at least, the theoretical possibility that the teacher could become so thoroughly imbued with the analytical spirit that his pupils would assume, in his mind, the form of objects for scientific probing and manipulation, rather than real personalities demanding direct personal interest and regard. Again, theoretically, there is the possibility that the reflexive effect on the teacher himself might be loss of faith in the reality of his own freedom.

Should such a development involve many teachers it would be a very serious matter for education. That the problem is as yet only a cloud on the horizon is not the fault of our champions of educational science. It is due rather to three situations, as the writer sees the matter: namely, (1) the slow progress of the psychological sciences as they bear upon education; (2) the healthy circumstance that most persons who go into the teaching of children, whether due to temperament or previous experience, are not highly inclined to abstraction and analysis; and (3) the probability that the abundant contacts which experienced teachers have had with the absorbing personalities of living children have built up an immunity to the mechanistic bias in personal relations. One might speculate that the present stress by thoughtful educators on close personal relations between teacher and learner is based on a growing intuitive fear of the impersonality of the scientific approach to teaching. That teaching is more than conscious scientific manipulation has long been sensed by those who hold that teaching is an art. . . .

There is a second reason why all pedagogical knowledge cannot readily be made common scientific property. That is, what the teacher observes in dealing with children is their particular reactions to the impact of his own peculiar personality. Much of the intuitive skill picked up by the teacher is, therefore, his own private brand, valid only in relations between himself and his pupils, and largely incommunicable to other teachers. Even a commonly accepted principle of teaching when applied by different teachers takes on a variety of guises because of personality factors. Indeed, a few teachers seem to succeed well enough apparently violating good principles. But the violation is, of course, only apparent. It is made so by the highly personal ways in which such teachers carry out the principles, ways quite obscure to observers. It is because of this inimitable character of a teacher's methods with a child that merely seeing him at work does not yield an onlooker much pedagogical insight.

Further, considering the place of science in the realm of personal relations . . . the very great need of a deeper personalistic wisdom is also evidenced by problems that have accompanied the current intense concern with group process in education. The bizarre form taken by some inquiries is illustrated by a group of students engaged in investigating "group dynamics" by analysing themselves while discussing group dynamics! This introverted probing might be likened to the efforts of a scientific mole burrowing within its own digging machinery to observe its inner workings while burrowing! Whether or not it ends in destruction of the self-integrity of the investigator, such inquiry can, at the most, never yield full self-knowledge. For the self, studying the active self, must go on to studying the studying self, and so endlessly on! For the human self is never a static thing. It is subject to change, even under the impact of scientific observation of itself, by itself or by others.

What has been said is not to be interpreted as depreciation of self study. "Know thyself" is still a wise dictum. But it must be remembered that such study can yield only "historical" knowledge of the self, that is, only retrospective knowledge, knowledge of the person only in terms of past behavior. To the extent that past behavior is an index to future behavior (it must always be considered the basic index) historical knowledge of the person is indispensable. But this knowledge must be tempered by the understanding that the future can never be quite the past, and that neither will the self ever be quite like its past. For if nothing else changes the self, the very act of self-analysis (or awareness of analysis by others) will do so. . . .

Briefly, and in conclusion, what is needed by those who would use scientific knowledge of themselves or others is wisdom, that is, a more generous science—a philosophy which would properly evaluate analytical science within the whole picture of the human struggle for understanding. Up to recent years, the mechanistic postulate has been held up as both the beginning and the end of wisdom. The paralysing effect on the will of a person or a society of hyperanalytical self-scrutiny is a danger long known to social scientists and historians. Applying this warning to education, no science or supporting philosophy may be pursued to the point where it threatens the child's own consciousness of freedom and responsibility, or the teacher's own faith in the worth and freedom of the child as a person, or faith in his own free self. Nor may we entertain among us as a people the spirit of mechanistic science to the point where determinism threatens to become a part of our normal thinking. It is conceivable that such a habit may foster within our culture the deadening philosophy that "we are in the grip of history," an outlook which has long infected the thinking of other parts of the world. If we let this beast into our ideological tents, we are doomed as a free culture. Neither faith in an encompassing historical dialectic nor conviction of an inner mechanical necessity must be permitted to dull our sense of self-determination and responsibility, either as persons or as a society.

The writer thus contends that only a personalistic and at the same time naturalistic outlook can provide a philosophical framework adequate for the wholesome ordering of all experience, both moral and scientific.

Further reading

Green, T. F., "Teaching, Acting, and Behaving," *Harvard Educational Review,* 34 (Winter, 1964), 507–524.

Henderson, K. B., "Abstracting, Generalizing, and Explaining—Processes or Relations?" *Mathematics Teacher,* 54 (December, 1961), 600–605.

McClellan, J. E., "Skinner's Philosophy of Human Nature," *Studies in Philosophy and Education,* 4 (Spring, 1966), 307–332.

Mays, W., "A Philosophical Critique of Intelligence Tests," *Educational Theory,* 16 (October, 1966), 318–332.

Peters, R. S., "The Psychologist and the Teacher," in *Authority, Responsibility, and Education* (London: Allen and Unwin, 1959), pp. 119–137.

Schwab, J. J., "On the Corruption of Education by Psychology," *School Review,* 66 (Summer, 1958), 169–184.

Vandenberg, D., "On the Ground of Education," *Educational Theory,* 17 (January, 1967), 60–66.

DISCIPLINING THE MIND

When it is stipulated that the pupil's learning should also discipline his mind, i.e., when teaching and learning activities are intended to develop his mind and it is thought desirable to take noncognitive factors into account, then the educational problems involved become the philosophical issues of metaphysics. What is the nature of the mind? What is the relation of mind and body? What is the place of mind in man's whole being? What is the nature of human nature? What is the relation of man to the universe? What is the nature of the universe?

The archaic-sounding words *disciplining the mind* are meant to be vague, general, and all-inclusive. For example, when Skinner's view is applied to the classroom, it loses its status as a scientific theory that attempts to unify and explain some data and becomes a metaphysical view because the teacher's actions presume that the pupils have no minds. In this materialistic metaphysic, her efforts at operant conditioning discipline the pupil's "thinking," his "mind," as these terms would be defined within Skinnerian terminology. In practice operant conditioning becomes one form of mental discipline.

The procedures indicated in Part One to insure to the pupil that his learning constituted knowing in order to develop his mind might be considered as ways of disciplining his thinking, his mind. Disciplining the mind, however, can be distinguished from developing it. Dewey, for instance, maintains that mind is coextensive with body and is therefore "disciplined" through activities that embody the pupil's purposes but in which there are problems that cause him to stop and think. His "mind" undergoes the disciplinary action of experience as his desires, purposes, and ideas are modified to reëstablish harmony with the environment. Because the disciplinary action of the environment upon the mind and body suffices when pupils are engaged in purposeful activities, no problems of classroom management arise. In Dewey's view the teacher can be said to be disciplining the pupil's mind when she arranges conditions in ways conducive to engaging the pupil in worthwhile activities, i.e., when she employs procedures that are related to the conception of the nature of the mind that Dewey formulated: as coextensive with body, as central to human nature in the form of reflective thinking, and as continuous with the world around one.

Similarly, each of the following selections suggests a procedure to enable the pupil's mind to undergo some sort of disciplinary action. The educational recommendations differ as the metaphysical views of the nature of the mind differ. How an author thinks the mind can be disciplined depends upon what he thinks the mind is. To distinguish the views in one's mind, one might look for the authors' argument concerning (a) the role of the teacher in disciplining the pupil's mind; (b) the nature of the mind; (c) the relation of mind to body and to the whole of human nature; (d) the relation of mind to nature, the world, and the universe; and (e) the relation of disciplining to developing the mind.

The last item is a reminder of the relation of metaphysics to epistemology, particularly when they are "applied" to a common problem such as the development of mind. The previous statements about this relation can now be enlarged upon. Is metaphysics dependent upon epistemology? Must one first decide how one can know anything in order to speak intelligibly to metaphysical questions? Or is epistemology dependent upon metaphysics? Must one first decide upon the nature of the mind before one can speak meaningfully to the epistemological question of how the mind can know anything?

Strict allegiance to the scientific method of knowing, for example, eliminates metaphysics. The metaphysical realm, if there be one, is then beyond the realm of knowledge, is that of which one knows nothing and on which it behooves one to say nothing. But why should one say, "nothing"? And does this "solution" to the epistemological question involve a nonscientific conception of the nature of mind? Does it involve an unacknowledged metaphysics? Dewey, for example, clearly had a conception of the nature of mind behind his method of knowing. Was that conception obtained by using the scientific method? Can Dewey's version of the scientific method really establish that mind emerges as an evolutionary product of the interaction of the biological organism and the environment? Can scientific method really establish that man is a biological organism—and nothing more—without engaging in circular reasoning? If one maintains that we can know only through this method of knowing, that there is nothing beyond the realm that can be studied by scientific method, and that mind must be what it is when studied by scientific method because there is nothing beyond this realm, then what does he say to someone who insists that there are things beyond the scope of scientific method? That there is nothing more to be known? What about this "nothing"? Why is it so difficult to speak of the limits of scientific inquiry without referring to "nothing"? [1]

Soderquist spoke to these questions. Their relevance can be indicated in another question. Are the ideas in the readings of this section more important, more fundamental, than those of Section Two of Part One, or are the epistemological considerations of teaching and learning more fundamental? The question is not which seems to be more relevant to the specific tasks of teaching. This question has its own validity and indicates the reason for the order of appearance in this volume. The question is, rather, which issues, epistemological or metaphysical, have to be settled first in order to think adequately about teaching and learning activities as they relate to the development of the pupil's mind. If mind is what Horne says it is, then Dewey's answers to the epistemological questions are beside the point. Conversely, if knowing is what Dewey says it is, then Horne's answers to the metaphysical questions are beside the point.

The last item of the topics for study, the relation of disciplining to developing the mind, is, in other words, a suggestion to keep the relatedness of the epistemological and metaphysical considerations of teaching and learning in view. Its significance is that crucial and controversial philosophical issues are settled at one stroke when one decides whether metaphysics or epistemology should take precedence. So too are many educational issues settled at one stroke. Any answer, however, is only a point of view. It is educatively useful to keep this an open question as the following selections are read.

[1] To catch the full import of the significance of this "nothing" and this line of questioning, see Martin Heidegger, "What is Metaphysics?" in *Existence and Being* (Chicago: Regnery, 1949), pp. 355–392.

LEARNING AS EXPERIENCING

John Dewey

The nature of experience can be understood only by noting that it includes an active and a passive element peculiarly combined. On the active hand, experience is *trying*—a meaning which is made explicit in the connected term experiment. On the passive, it is *undergoing*. When we experience something we act upon it, we do something with it; then we suffer or undergo the consequences. We do something to the thing and then it does something to us in return: such is the peculiar combination. The connection of these two phases of experience measures the fruitfulness or value of the experience. Mere activity does not constitute experience. It is dispersive, centrifugal, dissipating. Experience as trying involves change, but change is meaningless transition unless it is consciously connected with the return wave of consequences which flow from it. When an activity is continued *into* the undergoing of consequences, when the change made by action is reflected back into a change made in us, the mere flux is loaded with significance. We learn something. It is not experience when a child merely sticks his finger into a flame; it is experience when the movement is connected with the pain which he undergoes in consequence. Henceforth the sticking of the finger into flame *means* a burn. Being burned is a mere physical change, like the burning of a stick of wood, if it is not perceived as a consequence of some other action.

Blind and capricious impulses hurry us on heedlessly from one thing to another. So far as this happens, everything is writ in water. There is none of that cumulative growth which makes an experience in any vital sense of that term. On the other hand, many things happen to us in the way of pleasure and pain which we do not connect with any prior activity of our own. They are mere accidents so far as we are concerned. There is no before or after to such experience, no retrospect nor outlook, and consequently no meaning. We get nothing which may be carried over to foresee what is likely to happen next, and no gain in ability to adjust ourselves to what is coming—no added control. Only by courtesy can such an experience be called experience. To "learn from experience" is to make a backward and forward connection between what we do to things and what we enjoy or suffer from things in consequence. Under such conditions, doing becomes a trying, an experiment with the world to find out what it is like; the undergoing becomes instruction—discovery of the connection of things.

Two conclusions important for education follow. (1) Experience is primarily an active-passive affair; it is not primarily cognitive. But (2) the *measure of the value* of an experience lies in the perception of relationships or continuities to which it leads up. It includes cognition in the degree in which it is cumulative or amounts to something, or has meaning. In schools, those under instruction are too customarily looked upon as acquiring knowledge as theoretical spectators, minds which appropriate knowledge by direct energy of intellect. The very word pupil has almost come to mean one who is engaged not in having fruitful experiences but in absorbing knowledge directly. Something which is called mind or consciousness is severed from the physical organs of activity. The former is then thought to be purely intellectual and cognitive, the latter to be an irrelevant and intruding physical factor. The intimate union of activity and undergoing its consequences which leads to recognition of meaning is broken; instead we have two fragments: mere bodily action on one side, and meaning directly grasped by 'spiritual' activity on the other.

It would be impossible to state adequately the evil results which have flowed from this dualism of mind and body, much less to exaggerate them. Some of the more striking effects may, however, be enumerated. (*a*) In part bodily activity becomes an intruder. Having nothing, so it is thought, to do with mental activity, it becomes a distraction, an evil to be contended with. For the pupil has a body and brings it to school along with his mind. And the body is, of necessity, a wellspring of energy; it has to do something. But its activities, not being utilized in occupation with things which yield significant results, have to be frowned upon. They lead the pupil away from the lesson with which his 'mind' ought to be occupied; they are sources of mischief. The chief source of the 'problem of discipline' in schools is that the teacher has often to spend the larger part of the time in suppressing the bodily activities which take the mind away from its material. A premium is put on physical quietude; on silence, on rigid uniformity of posture and movement; upon a machine-like simulation of the attitudes of intelligent interest. The teacher's business is to hold the pupils up to these requirements and to punish the inevitable deviations which occur.

The nervous strain and fatigue which result with both teacher and pupil are a necessary consequence of the abnormality of the situation in which bodily activity is divorced from the perception of meaning. . . .

(*b*) Even, however, with respect to the lessons which have to be learned by the application of 'mind,' some bodily activities have to be used. The senses—especially the eye and ear—have to be employed to take in what the book, the map, the blackboard, and the teacher say. The lips and vocal organs, and the hands, have to be used to reproduce in speech and writing what has been stowed away. The senses are then regarded as a kind of mysterious conduit through which information is conducted from the external world into the mind; they are spoken of as gateways and avenues of knowledge. To keep the eyes on the book and the ears open to the teacher's words is a mysterious source of intellectual grace. Moreover, reading, writing, and figuring—important school arts—demand muscular or motor training. The muscles of eye, hand, and vocal organs accordingly have to be trained to act as pipes for carrying knowledge back out of the mind into external action. For it happens that using the muscles repeatedly in the same way fixes in them an automatic tendency to repeat.

The obvious result is a mechanical use of the bodily activities which (in spite of the generally obtrusive and interfering character of the body in mental action) have to be employed more or less. For the senses and muscles are used not as organic participants in having an instructive experience, but as external inlets and outlets of mind. Before the child goes to school, he learns with his hand, eye, and ear, because they are organs of the process of doing something from which meaning results. The boy flying a kite has to keep his eye on the kite, and has to note the various pressures of the string on his hand. His senses are avenues of knowledge not because external facts are somehow 'conveyed' to the brain, but because they are *used* in doing something with a purpose. The qualities of seen and touched things have a bearing on what is done and are alertly perceived; they have a meaning. But when pupils are expected to use their eyes to note the form of words, irrespective of their meaning, in order to reproduce them in spelling or reading, the resulting training is simply of isolated sense organs and muscles. It is such isolation of an act from a purpose which makes it mechanical. It is customary for teachers to urge children to read with expression, so as to bring out the meaning. But if they originally learned the sensory-motor technique of reading—the ability to identify forms and to reproduce the sounds they stand for—by methods which did not call for attention to meaning, a mechanical habit was established which makes it difficult to read subsequently with intelligence. The vocal organs have been trained to go their own way automatically in isolation, and meaning cannot be tied on at will. Drawing, singing, and writing may be taught in the same mechanical way, for, we repeat, any way *is* mechanical which narrows down the bodily activity so that a separation of body from mind—that is, from recognition of meaning—is set up. . . .

(c) On the intellectual side, the separation of 'mind' from direct occupation with things throws emphasis on *things* at the expense of *relations* or connections. It is altogether too common to separate perceptions and even ideas from judgments. The latter are thought to come after the former in order to compare them. It is alleged that the mind perceives things apart from relations, that it forms ideas of them in isolation from their connections—with what goes before and comes after. Then judgment or thought is called upon to combine the separated items of 'knowledge' so that their resemblance or casual connection shall be brought out. As a matter of fact, every perception and every idea is a sense of the bearings, use, and cause, of a thing. . . . Judgment is employed in the perception; otherwise the perception is mere sensory excitation or else a recognition of the result of a prior judgment, as in the case of familiar objects.

Words, the counters for ideas, are, however, easily taken for ideas. And in just the degree in which mental activity is separated from active concern with the world, from doing something and connecting the doing with what is undergone, words, symbols, come to take the place of ideas. The substitution is the more subtle because *some* meaning is recognized. But we are very easily trained to be content with a minimum of meaning, and to fail to note how restricted is our perception of the relations which confer significance. We get so thoroughly used to a kind of pseudo-idea, a half-perception, that we are not aware how half-dead our mental action is, and how much keener and more extensive our observations and ideas would be if we formed them under conditions of a vital experience which required us to use judgment: to hunt for the connections of the thing dealt with.

There is no difference of opinion as to the theory of the matter. All authorities agree that that discernment of relationships is the genuinely intellectual matter, hence, the educative matter. The failure arises in supposing that relationships can become perceptible without *experience*—without that conjoint trying and undergoing of which we have spoken. It is assumed that 'mind' can grasp them if it will only give attention, and that this attention may be given at will irrespective of the situation. Hence the deluge of half-observations, of verbal ideas, and unassimilated 'knowledge' which afflicts the world. An ounce of experience is better than a ton of theory simply because it is only in experience that any theory has vital and verifiable significance. An experience, a very humble experience, is capable of generating and carrying any amount of theory (or intellectual content), but a theory apart from an experience cannot be definitely grasped even as theory. It tends to become a mere verbal formula, a set of catchwords used to render thinking, or genuine theorizing, unnecessary and impossible. Because of our education we use words, thinking they are ideas, to dispose of questions, the disposal being in reality simply such an obscuring of perception as prevents us from seeing any longer the difficulty.

Thought or reflection, as we have already seen virtually if not explicitly, is the discernment of the relation between what we try to do and what happens in consequence. No experience having a meaning is possible without some element of thought. But we may contrast two types of experience according to the proportion of reflection found in them. All our experiences have a phase of 'cut and try' in them—what psychologists call the method of trial and error. We simply do something, and when it fails, we do something else, and keep on trying till we hit upon something which works, and then we adopt that method as a rule of thumb measure in subsequent procedure. Some experiences have very little else in them than this hit and miss or succeed process. We see *that* a certain way of acting and a certain consequence are connected, but we do not see *how* they are. We do not see the details of the connection; the links are missing. Our discernment is very gross. In other cases we push our observation further. We analyze to see just what lies between so as to bind together cause and effect, activity and consequence. This extension of our insight makes foresight more accurate and comprehensive. The action which rests simply upon the trial and error method is at the mercy of circumstances; they may change so that the act performed does not operate in the way it was expected to. But if we know in detail upon what the result depends, we can look to see whether the required conditions are there. The method extends our practical control. For if some of the conditions are missing, we may, if we know what the needed antecedents for an effect are, set to work to supply them; or, if they are such as to produce undesirable effects as well, we may eliminate some of the superfluous causes and economize effort.

In discovery of the detailed connections of our activities and what happens in consequence, the thought implied in cut and try experience is made explicit. Its quantity increases so that its proportionate value is very different. Hence the quality of the experience changes; the change is so significant that we may call this type of experience reflective—that is, reflective *par excellence*. The deliberate cultivation of this phase of thought constitutes thinking as a distinctive experience. Thinking, in other words, is the intentional endeavor to discover *specific* connections between something which we do and the consequences which result, so that the two become continuous. Their isolation, and consequently their purely arbitrary going together, is cancelled; a unified developing situation takes its place. The occurrence is now understood; it is explained; it is reasonable, as we say, that the thing should happen as it does.

Thinking is thus equivalent to an explicit rendering of the intelligent element in our experience. It makes it possible to act with an end in view. It is the condition of our having aims. . . .

These considerations may be generalized by going back to the conception of experience. Experience as the perception of the connection between something tried and something undergone in consequence is a process. Apart from effort to control the course which the process takes, there is no distinction of subject matter and method. There is simply an activity which includes both what an individual does and what the environment does. A piano player who had perfect mastery of his instrument would have no occasion to distinguish between his contribution and that of the piano. In well-formed, smooth-running functions of any sort—skating, conversing, hearing music, enjoying a landscape—there is no consciousness of separation of the method of the person and of the subject matter. In whole-hearted play and work there is the same phenomenon.

When we reflect upon an experience instead of just having it, we inevitably distinguish between our own attitude and the objects toward which we sustain the attitude. When a man is eating, he is eating *food*. He does not divide his act into eating *and* food. But if he makes a scientific investigation of the act, such a discrimination is the first thing he would effect. He would examine on the one hand the properties of the nutritive material, and on the other hand the acts of the organism in appropriating and digesting. Such reflection upon experience gives rise to a distinction of *what* we experience (the experienc*ed*) and the experienc*ing*—the *how*. When we give names to this distinction we have subject matter and method as our terms. There is the thing seen, heard, loved, hated, imagined, and there is the act of seeing, hearing, loving, hating, imagining, etc.

This distinction is so natural and so important for certain purposes that we are only too apt to regard it as a separation in existence and not as a distinction in thought. Then we make a division between a self and the environment or world. This separation is the root of the dualism of method and subject matter. That is, we assume that knowing, feeling, willing, etc., are things which belong to the self or mind in its isolation, and which then may be brought to bear upon an independent subject matter. We assume that the things which belong in isolation to the self or mind have their own laws of operation irrespective of the modes of active energy of the object. These laws are supposed to furnish method. It would be no less absurd to suppose that men can eat without eating something, or that the structure and movements of the jaws, throat muscles, the digestive activities of stomach, etc., are not what they are *because* of the material with which their activity is engaged. Just as the organs of the organism are a continuous part of the very world in which food materials exist, so the capacities of seeing, hearing, loving, imagining are intrinsically connected with the subject matter of the world. They are more truly ways in which the environment enters into experience and functions there than they are independent acts brought to bear upon things. Experience, in short, is not a combination of mind and world, subject and object, method and subject matter, but is a single continuous interaction of a great diversity (literally countless in number) of energies.

For the purpose of *controlling* the course or direction which the moving unity of experience takes, we draw a mental distinction between the how and the what. While there is no *way* of walking or of eating or of learning over and above the actual walking, eating, and studying, there are certain elements in the act which give the key to its more effective control. Special attention to these elements makes them more obvious to perception (letting other factors recede for the time being from conspicuous recognition). Getting an idea of *how* the experience proceeds indicates to us what factors must be secured or modified in order that it may go on more successfully. . . .

A consideration of some evils in education that flow from the isolation of method from subject matter will make the point more definite. (*i*) In the first place, there is the neglect (of which we have spoken) of concrete situations of experience. There can be no discovery of a method without cases to be studied. The method is derived from observation of what actually happens, with a view to seeing that it happen better next time. But in instruction and discipline, there is rarely sufficient opportunity for children and youth to have the direct normal experiences from which educators might derive an idea of method or order of best development. Experiences are had under conditions of such constraint that they throw little or no light upon the normal course of an experience to its fruition. "Methods" have then to be authoritatively recommended to teachers, instead of being an expression of their own intelligent observations. Under such circumstances, they have a mechanical uniformity, assumed to be alike for all minds. Where flexible personal experiences are promoted by providing an environment which calls out directed occupations in work and play, the methods ascertained will vary with individuals—for it is certain that each individual has something characteristic in his way of going at things.

(*ii*) In the second place, the notion of methods isolated from subject matter is responsible for the false conceptions of discipline and interest already noted. When the effective way of managing material is treated as something ready-made apart from material, there are just three possible ways in which to establish a relationship lacking by assumption. One is to utilize excitement, shock of pleasure, tickling the palate. Another is to make the consequences of not attending painful; we may use the menace of harm to motivate concern with the alien subject matter. Or a direct appeal may be made to the person to put forth effort without any reason. We may rely upon immediate strain of "will." In practice, however, the latter method is effectual only when instigated by fear of unpleasant results.

(*iii*) In the third place, the act of learning is made a direct and conscious end in itself. Under normal conditions, learning is a product and reward of occupation with subject matter. Children do not set out, consciously, to learn walking or talking. One sets out to give his impulses for communication and for fuller intercourse with others a show. He learns in consequence of his direct activities. The better methods of teaching a child, say, to read, follow the same road. They do not fix his attention upon the fact that he has to learn something and so make his attitude self-conscious and constrained. They engage his activities, and in the process of engagement he learns; the same is true of the more successful methods in dealing with number or whatever. But when the subject matter is not used in carrying forward impulses and habits to significant results, it is just something to be learned. The pupil's attitude to it is just that of having to learn it. Conditions more unfavorable to an alert and concentrated response would be hard to devise. Frontal attacks are even more wasteful in learning than in war. This does not mean, however, that students are to be seduced unaware into pre-occupation with lessons. It means that they shall be occupied with them for real reasons or ends, and not just as something to be learned. This is accomplished whenever the pupil perceives the place occupied by the subject matter in the fulfilling of some experience.

(*iv*) In the fourth place, under the influence of the conception of the separation of mind and material, method tends to be reduced to a cut and dried routine, to following mechanically prescribed steps. No one can tell in how many schoolrooms children reciting in arithmetic or grammar are compelled to go through, under the alleged sanction of method, certain pre-ordained verbal formulae. Instead of being encouraged to attack their topics directly, experimenting with methods that seem promising and learning to discriminate by the consequences that accrue, it is assumed that there is one fixed method to be followed. It is also naïvely assumed that if the pupils make their statements and explanations in a certain form of "analysis," their mental habits will in time conform. Nothing has brought pedagogical theory into greater disrepute than the belief that it is identified with handing out to teachers recipes and models to be followed in teaching. Flexibility and initiative in dealing with problems are characteristic of any conception to which method is a way of managing material to develop a conclusion. Mechanical, rigid woodenness is an inevitable corollary of any theory which separates mind from activity motivated by a purpose.

In brief, the method of teaching is the method of an art, of action intelligently directed by ends. But the practice of a fine art is far from being a matter of extemporized inspirations. Study of the operations and results of those in the past who have greatly succeeded is essential. There is always a tradition. . . .

Such matters as knowledge of the past, of current technique, of materials, of the ways in which one's own best results are assured, supply the material for what may be called *general* method. There exists a cumulative body of fairly stable methods for reaching results, a body authorized by past experience and by intellectual analysis, which an individual ignores at his peril. . . . There is always a danger that these methods will become mechanized and rigid, mastering an agent instead of being powers at command for his own ends. But it is also true that the innovator who achieves anything enduring, whose work is more than a passing sensation, utilizes classic methods more than may appear to himself or to his critics. He devotes them to new uses, and in so far transforms them.

Education also has its general methods. And if the application of this remark is more obvious in the case of the teacher than of the pupil, it is equally real in the case of the latter. Part of his learning, a very important part, consists in *becoming* master of the methods which the experience of others has shown to be most efficient in like cases of getting knowledge.[1] These general methods are in no way opposed to individual initiative and originality—to personal ways of doing things. On the contrary they are reinforcements of them. For there is radical difference between even the most general method and a prescribed rule. The latter is a *direct* guide to action; the former operates indirectly through the enlightenment it supplies as to ends and means. It operates, that is to say, through intelligence, and not through conformity to orders externally imposed. Ability to use even in a masterly way an established technique gives no warranty of artistic work, for the latter also depends upon an animating idea.

If knowledge of methods used by others does not directly tell us what to do, or furnish ready-made models, how does it operate? What is meant by calling a method intellectual? Take the case of a physician. No mode of behavior more imperiously demands knowledge of established modes of diagnosis and treatment than does his. But after all cases are *like,* not identi-

---

[1] This point is developed below in a discussion of what are termed psychological and logical methods, respectively.

cal. To be used intelligently, existing practices, however authorized they may be, have to be adapted to the exigencies of
particular cases. Accordingly, recognized procedures indicate to
the physician what inquiries to set on foot for himself, what
measures to *try*. They are standpoints from which to carry on
investigations; they economize a survey of the features of the
particular case by suggesting the things to be especially looked
into. The physician's own personal attitudes, his own ways
(individual methods) of dealing with the situation in which he is
concerned, are not subordinated to the general principles of
procedure, but are facilitated and directed by the latter. The
instance may serve to point out the value to the teacher of a
knowledge of the psychological methods and the empirical devices found useful in the past. When they get in the way of his
own common sense, when they come between him and the
situation in which he has to act, they are worse than useless. But
if he has acquired them as intellectual aids in sizing up the
needs, resources, and difficulties of the unique experiences in
which he engages, they are of constructive value. In the last
resort, just because *everything* depends upon his own methods
of response, *much* depends upon how far he can utilize, in
making his own response, the knowledge which has accrued in
the experience of others.

As already intimated, every word of this account is directly
applicable also to the method of the pupil, the way of learning.
To suppose that students, whether in the primary school or in
the university, can be supplied with models of method to be
followed in acquiring and expounding a subject is to fall into a
self-deception that has lamentable consequences. . . .

One must make his own reaction in any case. Indications of
the standardized or general methods used in like cases by others
—particularly by those who are already experts—are of worth
or of harm according as they make his personal reaction more
intelligent or as they induce a person to dispense with exercise
of his own judgment. . . .

LEARNING AS ACTING

William James

The most general elements and workings of the mind are all that the teacher absolutely needs to be acquainted with for his purposes.

Now the *immediate* fact . . . is also the most general fact. It is the fact that in each of us, when awake (and often when asleep), *some kind of consciousness is always going on.* There is a stream, a succession of states, or waves, or fields (or of whatever you please to call them), of knowledge, of feeling, of desire, of deliberation, etc., that constantly pass and repass, and that constitute our inner life. The existence of this stream is the primal fact; the nature and origin of it form the essential problem. . . . So far as we class the states or fields of consciousness, write down their several natures, analyze their contents into elements, or trace their habits of succession, we are on the descriptive or analytic level. So far as we ask where they come from or why they are just what they are, we are on the explanatory level. . . . For our present purposes I shall . . . turn to mere description. . . .

We have thus fields of consciousness—that is the first general fact; and the second general fact is that the concrete fields are always complex. They contain sensations of our bodies and of the objects around us, memories of past experiences and thoughts of distant things, feelings of satisfaction and dissatisfaction, desires and aversions, and other emotional conditions, together with determinations of the will, in every variety of permutation and combination.

In most of our concrete states of consciousness all these different classes of ingredients are found simultaneously present to some degree, though the relative proportion they bear to one another is very shifting. One state will seem to be composed of hardly anything but sensations, another of hardly anything but memories, etc. But around the sensation, if one consider care-

Reprinted from *Talks to Teachers* (New York: Holt, Rinehart, and Winston, 1892), pp. 7–9, 11–15, 17–19. By permission of the publisher.

fully, there will always be some fringe of thought or will, and around the memory some margin or penumbra of emotion or sensation. . . .

In the successive mutations of our fields of consciousness, the process by which one dissolves into another is often very gradual, and all sorts of inner rearrangements of contents occur. Sometimes the focus remains but little changed, while the margin alters rapidly. Sometimes the focus alters, and the margin stays. Sometimes focus and margin change places. Sometimes, again, abrupt alterations of the whole field occur. There can seldom be a sharp description. All we know is that, for the most part, each field has a sort of practical unity for its possessor, and that from this practical point of view we can class a field with other fields similar to it, by calling it a state of emotion, of perplexity, of sensation, of abstract thought, of volition, and the like.

Vague and hazy as such an account of our stream of consciousness may be, it is at least secure from positive error and free from admixture of conjecture or hypothesis. . . .

I wish now to continue the description of the peculiarities of the stream of consciousness by asking whether we can in any intelligible way assign its *functions*.

It has two functions that are obvious: it leads to knowledge, and it leads to action.

Can we say which of these functions is the more essential?

An old historic divergence of opinion comes in here. Popular belief has always tended to estimate the worth of a man's mental processes by their effects upon his practical life. But philosophers have usually cherished a different view. "Man's supreme glory," they have said, "is to be a *rational* being, to know absolute and eternal and universal truth. The uses of his intellect for practical affairs are therefore subordinate matters. 'The theoretic life' is his soul's genuine concern." Nothing can be more different in its results for our personal attitude than to take sides with one or the other of these views, and emphasize the practical or the theoretical ideal. In the latter case, abstraction from the emotions and passions and withdrawal from the strife of human affairs would be not only pardonable, but praiseworthy; and all that makes for quiet and contemplation should be regarded as conducive to the highest human perfection. In the former, the man of contemplation would be treated as only half a human being, passion and practical resource would become once more glories of our race, a concrete victory over this earth's outward powers of darkness would appear an equivalent for any amount of passive spiritual culture, and conduct would remain as the test of every education worthy of the name.

It is impossible to disguise the fact that in the psychology of our own day the emphasis is transferred from the mind's purely rational function, where Plato and Aristotle, and what one may call the whole classic tradition in philosophy had placed it, to the so long neglected practical side. The theory of evolution is mainly responsible for this. Man, we now have reason to believe, has been evolved from infra-human ancestors, in whom pure reason hardly existed, if at all, and whose mind, so far as it can have had any function, would appear to have been an organ for adapting their movements to the impressions received from the environment, so as to escape the better from destruction. Consciousness would thus seem in the first instance to be nothing but a sort of superadded biological perfection—useless unless it prompted to useful conduct, and inexplicable apart from that consideration.

Deep in our own nature the biological foundations of our consciousness persist, undisguised and undiminished. Our sensations are here to attract us or to deter us, our memories to warn or encourage us, our feelings to impel, and our thoughts to restrain our behavior, so that on the whole we may prosper and our days be long in the land. Whatever of transmundane metaphysical insight or of practically inapplicable aesthetic perception or ethical sentiment we may carry in our interiors might at this rate be regarded as only part of the incidental excess of function that necessarily accompanies the working of every complex machine. . . .

In the learning of all matters, we have to start with some one deep aspect of the question, abstracting it as if it were the only aspect; and then we gradually correct ourselves by adding those neglected other features which complete the case. No one believes more strongly than I do that what our senses know as 'this world' is only one portion of our mind's total environment and object. Yet, because it is the primal portion, it is the *sine qua non* of all the rest. If you grasp the facts about it firmly, you may proceed to higher regions undisturbed.

. . . Mental action is conditioned by brain action, and runs parallel therewith. But the brain, so far as we understand it, is given us for practical behavior. Every current that runs into it from skin or eye or ear runs out again into muscles, glands, or viscera, and helps to adapt the animal to the environment from which the current came. It therefore generalizes and simplifies our view to treat the brain life and the mental life as having one fundamental kind of purpose.

. . . The inessential 'unpractical' activities are themselves far more connected with our behavior and our adaptation to the environment than at first sight might appear. No truth, however abstract, is ever perceived, that will not probably at some time influence our earthly action. You must remember that, when I talk of action here, I mean action in the widest sense. I mean speech, I mean writing, I mean yeses and noes, and tendencies 'from' things and tendencies 'toward' things, and emotional determinations; and I mean them in the future as well as in the immediate present. As I talk here, and you listen, it might seem as if no action followed. You might call it a purely theoretic process, with no practical result. But it *must* have a practical result. It cannot take place at all and leave your conduct unaffected. If not to-day, then on some far future day, you will answer some question differently by reason of what you are thinking now. Some of you will be led by my words into new veins of inquiry, into reading special books. These will develop your opinion, whether for or against. That opinion will in turn be expressed, will receive criticism from others in your environment, and will affect your standing in their eyes. We cannot escape our destiny, which is practical; and even our most theoretic faculties contribute to its working out.

These few reasons will perhaps smooth the way for you to acquiescence in my proposal. As teachers, I sincerely think it will be a sufficient conception for you to adopt of the youthful psychological phenomena handed over to your inspection if you consider them from the point of view of their relation to the future conduct of their possessor—sufficient at any rate as a first conception and as a main conception. You should regard your professional task as if it consisted chiefly and essentially in *training the pupil to behavior,* taking behavior, not in the narrow sense of his manners, but in the very widest possible sense, as including every possible sort of fit reaction in the circumstances into which he may find himself brought by the vicissitudes of life.

The reaction may, indeed, often be a negative reaction. *Not* to speak, *not* to move, is one of the most important of our duties, in certain practical emergencies. "Thou shalt refrain, renounce, abstain!" This often requires a great effort of will power, and, physiologically considered, is just as positive a nerve function as is motor discharge. . . .

In our foregoing talk we were led to frame a very simple conception of what an education means. In the last analysis it consists in the organizing of *resources* in the human being, of powers of conduct which shall fit him to his social and physical world. An 'uneducated' person is one who is nonplussed by all but the most habitual situations. On the contrary, one who is educated is able practically to extricate himself, by means of the examples with which his memory is stored and of the abstract conceptions which he has acquired, from circumstances in which he never was placed before. Education, in short, cannot be better described than by calling it *the organization of acquired habits of conduct and tendencies to behavior.* . . .

If all this be true, then immediately one general aphorism emerges which ought by logical right to dominate the entire conduct of the teacher in the classroom.

No reception without reaction, no impression without correlative expression—this is the great maxim which the teacher ought never to forget.

An impression which simply flows in at the pupil's eyes or ears, and in no way modifies his active life, is an impression gone to waste. It is physiologically incomplete. It leaves no fruits behind it in the way of capacity acquired. Even as mere impression, it fails to produce its proper effect upon the memory; for, to remain fully among the acquisitions of this latter faculty, it must be wrought into the whole cycle of our operations. Its *motor consequences* are what clinch it. Some effect due to it in the way of an activity must return to the mind in the form of the *sensation of having acted,* and connect itself with the impression. The most durable impressions are those on account of which we speak or act, or else are inwardly convulsed.

The older pedagogic method of learning things by rote, and reciting them parrot-like in the schoolroom, rested on the truth that a thing merely read or heard, and never verbally reproduced, contracts the weakest possible adhesion in the mind. Verbal recitation or reproduction is thus a highly important kind of reactive behavior on our impressions; and it is to be feared that, in the reaction against the old parrot-recitations as the beginning and end of instruction, the extreme value of verbal recitation as an element of complete training may nowadays be too much forgotten.

When we turn to modern pedagogics, we see how enormously the field of reactive conduct has been extended by the introduction of all those methods of concrete object teaching which are the glory of our contemporary schools. Verbal reactions, useful as they are, are insufficient. The pupil's words may be right, but the conceptions corresponding to them are often direfully wrong. In a modern school, therefore, they form only a small part of what the pupil is required to do. He must keep notebooks, make drawings, plans, and maps, take measurements, enter the laboratory and perform experiments, consult authorities, and write essays. He must do in his fashion what is often laughed at by outsiders when it appears in prospectuses under the title of 'original work', but what is really the only possible training for the doing of original work thereafter. The most colossal improvement which recent years have seen in secondary education lies in the introduction of the manual training schools; not because they will give us a people more handy and practical for domestic life and better skilled in trades, but because they will give us citizens with an entirely different intellectual fibre. Laboratory work and shop work engender a habit of observation, a knowledge of the difference between accuracy and vagueness, and an insight into nature's complexity and into the inadequacy of all abstract verbal accounts of real phenomena, which, once wrought into the mind, remain there as lifelong possessions. They confer precision, because, if you are *doing* a thing, you must do it definitely right or definitely wrong. They give honesty, for, when you express yourself by making things, and not by using words, it becomes impossible to dissimulate your vagueness or ignorance by ambiguity. They beget a habit of self-reliance; they keep the interest and attention always cheerfully engaged, and reduce the teacher's disciplinary functions to a minimum. . . .

No impression without expression, then—that is the first pedagogic fruit of our evolutionary conception of the mind as something instrumental to adaptive behavior. But a word may be said in continuation. The expression itself comes back to us, as I intimated a moment ago, in the form of a still further impression—the impression, namely, of what we have done. We thus receive sensible news of our behavior and its results. We hear the words we have spoken, feel our own blow as we give it, or read in the bystander's eyes the success or failure of our conduct. Now this return wave of impression pertains to the completeness of the whole experience, and a word about its importance in the schoolroom may not be out of place.

It would seem only natural to say that, since after acting we normally get some return impression of result, it must be well to let the pupil get such a return impression in every possible case. Nevertheless, in schools where examination marks and 'standing' and other returns of result are concealed, the pupil is frustrated of this natural termination of the cycle of his activities, and often suffers from the sense of incompleteness and uncertainty; and there are persons who defend this system as encouraging the pupil to work for the work's sake, and not for extraneous reward. Of course, here as elsewhere, concrete experience must prevail over psychological deduction. But, so far as our psychological deduction goes, it would suggest that the pupil's eagerness to know how well he does is in the line of his normal completeness of function, and should never be balked except for very definite reasons indeed.

Acquaint them, therefore, with their marks and standing and prospects, unless in the individual case you have some special practical reason for not so doing.

LEARNING AS FEELING

Harry S. Broudy

Does Whitehead's metaphysics have any special relevance for educational philosophy? Does this question justify an inquiry into the nature of the actual entity, concrescence, and the other concepts central to his system? In one sense, the answer would have to be "No," for one might argue that his *Aims of Education* has rendered further speculation on this topic unnecessary. That the import of his total metaphysical outlook, the philosophy of organism, should favor certain attitudes toward life and education is hardly surprising. Yet the tone and content of these essays, while not incompatible with the metaphysics of *Process and Reality,* unmistakably reflect the culture, values, and institutions of the England in which Whitehead was educated, as indeed all essays on the aims of education at this (molar) level must. Does the doctrine of the actual entity—the most general metaphysical formula of Whitehead—enable us to say anything about the ultimate unit-act of education, viz., learning, that is not emphasized in Whitehead's remarks on education?

This question touches on the more general question as to the relation of metaphysics to the philosophy of education. Theoretically, one would expect that a metaphysical formula would have variables for which educational terms could be substituted. In other words, if learning is an instance of actualizing a potentiality, approximating the Absolute, participating in the Forms, or the like, then the analysis of the former would apply to the latter. For example, Dewey's description of how an indeterminate situation is made determinate, how discontinuities and conflicts are transmuted into continuity and harmony, is a formula in which one can substitute for certain variables and come out with a theory of learning that interprets the formula. Froebel performed such an interpretation on the Hegelian formula, and associationistic learning theories can be regarded as inter-

Reprinted from "Actual Entities and the Learning Process," *Educational Theory,* 11 (October, 1961), 217–219, 225–227 f. By permission of the author and the editor of *Educational Theory.*

pretations of a metaphysical-epistemological scheme in which atomic sensations are the sole and somewhat frustrating avenues to reality. Is concrescence, as used by Whitehead to describe the creation of an actual entity, such a formula? If so, what interpretations do we get by substituting learning components in the formula? . . .

The most basic ingredient of the real world for Whitehead is an "actual entity," in some circumstances called an "actual occasion." The word "actual" emphasizes that these entities are not appearances of something more fundamental than themselves. They are what they are, when and where they are (113, 122).[1] Not only are they the stuff out of which all that is is made, but like Plato's Idea of the Good they are the means by which all being is explained. To search for a reason, remarks Whitehead, is to search for one or more actual entities (37).

The word "entity" needs a somewhat more extended observation. First of all, it is not an atom in the sense of being a simple, impenetrable, imperishable particle. It is complex and all of *Process and Reality* is devoted to its analysis. It is an entity, however, in the sense of being a process with a beginning, middle, and end; it has a unity of character that makes it one. There is a sense in which its existence is for its own individual sake, although it is what the entire universe has made it.

Actual entities are not what in ordinary language are called physical things. Physical things, in Whitehead's language, would be a related set of actual entities (nexus). A "nexus" is a connected set of actual entities and when all of these entities share a common form by virtue of having inherited it from other members of the nexus, it is a society. When inheritance of the form is such that we get a series of ancestors and progeny, then the order is said to be personal (51).

Thus what we call an individual thing Whitehead would call an enduring object. This means that an actual entity is not a substance in the Aristotelian sense of the word. It is not that which perdures through a series of qualitative changes, although an enduring object does have a repeatedly reproduced form which Whitehead identifies with the Aristotelian "substantial

[1] All page references unless otherwise indicated are to *Process and Reality*.

form" (51). Nor is an actual entity quite the same as an event. "An event is a nexus of actual occasions. An actual occasion is an event with only one member. Thus a molecule is an event not an actual occasion. Change is the difference between actual occasions comprised in some determinate event" (113–114).

The model of a substance shedding and acquiring qualities throughout a period of time is so firmly rooted in our language that to find an alternate is not easy, and the task is not made easier by Whitehead's distinction between genetic and coordinate division of the actual entity. An actual entity in its becoming goes through certain phases, and the identification of these phases Whitehead calls genetic division. It is an account of the actual entity's adventure of becoming as "seen" from the inside. It is an internal adventure; the actual entity as a whole never changes or moves (124). On the other hand, once it has become, the actual entity is a constituent of other actual entities; it is a "cause" of other entities. The way in which it operates as a cause is discovered by "coordinate" division (448).

So the metaphor we seek should help us visualize a world that is in everlasting process yet made up of entities that themselves never change or move. Perhaps no one model can adequately do the trick.

Let us, however, suggest that an actual entity considered in its subjective immediacy, from the inside, so to speak, is like a tiny electric bulb that receives its impulse with varying degrees of intensity from all other actual entities, but especially from those in its own neighborhood or nexus. As it appropriates this energy, it glows and this glow reflects not only the influences upon it, but also the peculiar perspective from which this particular bulb received the energy. As it achieves its full intensity and brightness, it perishes, but in doing so it transmits its character as a pulse of feeling to be objectified in other actual entities that inherit it.

This is its internal adventure, but what does it mean to say that an actual entity comes into being and perishes but never changes? Only perhaps that there is no "it" until the becoming is over.

If, on the other hand, one considers the actual entity as it "causes" other entities, or as it becomes a component in a strand or society of entities, then the metaphor suggested is more like that of a complex electric sign made up of individual bulbs which glow in various time orders and thereby give rise to the illusion of motion in the sign. The motion can be analyzed into different states at successive moments, but this will be an analysis of the entities as they *have become and objectified themselves,* not as they were in the process of their becoming.

I am sure that these metaphors are inaccurate; my only defense is that we have no process language that can speak only in verbs, and that the moment one uses a noun, he is open to the charge that he is talking substance language, precisely what Whitehead wanted to avoid.

As to why Whitehead calls his philosophy organism, the simplest answer, I suppose, is that the basic process constituting an actual entity is the organizing of a multiplicity into a unity, the past into a present and future, potentialities into one actuality. "The ultimate metaphysical principle is the advance from disjunction to conjunction, creating a novel entity other than the entities given in disjunction. . . . The many become one, and are increased by one" (32). Moreover, the role of inheritance and novelty give high plausibility to organization as the basic activity of the real. "Concrescence" as the production of novel togetherness is an apt description of how living things inherit from their ancestors, develop their individual traits, and, in turn, become ancestors themselves. Cultures succeed each other via inheritance plus novelty, and works of art likewise transform the given by novel modes of ordering. . . .

Whitehead says this in many ways in numerous contexts. Creativity, novelty, creative advance, and self-determination are as characteristic of the actual entity as giveness and determination. "It is to be noted that every actual entity, including God, is something for its own sake; and thereby transcends the rest of actuality . . . every actuality, including God, is a creature transcended by the creativity which it qualifies" (135).

This uniqueness has two sources. Because each actual entity is what it is, when and where it is, it receives or prehends the world through its own perspective, i.e., through the filter of those actual entities from which it inherits its data directly. Thus no two actual entities receive the world in precisely the same way. But whereas for low-grade occasions little is added to what is inherited, for high-grade occasions with mentality, the realm of the possible offers freedom via thought and imagination—the freedom to combine and recombine the eternal objects into all degrees of complexity, intensity, and vividness.

Because there can be integrations of integrations of feeling, because there can be no end of the diversities to be unified, the creative advance of novelty is assured, with each new actual entity contributing by its own becoming an ingredient to which all other actual entities must somehow conform.

In the last analysis, it is significance for itself that measures the reality of the entity. It is the number of diversities or contrasts that it can unify that gives it intensity and vividness, breadth as well as depth. In short, the world process and a work of art are to be judged by the same criteria.

What does the doctrine of the actual entity suggest as to the nature of the educative process? The two quotations which follow, it seems to me, indicate emphases that call for about as much change in educational perspective as they do in metaphysical perspectives.

If we are considering the society of successive actual occasions in the historic route forming the life of an enduring object, some of the earlier actual occasions may be without knowledge, and some of the later ones may possess knowledge. In such a case, the un-knowing man has become knowing. . . . Every actual entity has the capacity for knowledge, but in general, knowledge seems to be negligible apart from a peculiar complexity of some actual occasion. When we survey the chequered history of our own capacity for knowledge, does common sense allow us to believe that the operations of judgment, operations which require definition in terms of conscious apprehension, are those operations which are foundational in existence either as an essential attribute for an actual entity, or as final culmination where unity of experience is attained! (244–245).

And a bit later Whitehead again says:

The primitive form of physical experience is emotional—blind emotion—received as felt elsewhere in another occasion and conformally appropriated as a subjective passion. In the language appropriate to the higher stages of experience, the primitive element is *sympathy,* that is, feeling the feeling *in* another and feeling conformally *with* another. We are so used to considering the high abstraction, 'the stone is green,' that we have difficulty in eliciting into consciousness the notion of 'green' as the qualifying character of an emotion. Yet, the aesthetic feelings, whereby there is pictorial art, are nothing else than products of contrasts latent in a variety of colours qualifying emotion, contrasts which are made possible by their patterned relevance to each other. The separation of the emotional experience from the presentational intuition is a high abstraction of thought (246–247).

The most general statement of the educational import of these quotations is the primacy of the aesthetic dimension of experience. Although every actual entity has the capacity for knowledge, to know, in the ordinary sense of that term, is neither the essential attribute of the real nor its goal. This takes Whitehead far into the camp of James and Bergson and far out of the camp of Plato and Aristotle. This follows if the real is self-significance and if selfhood grows as higher and higher integrations of feeling come about. Clear conceptualized experience is a later, more derivative, more episodic phase of the real than is the creative advance of nature through the entities that it ejects on the way. Had not John Dewey so overstressed the scientific skills in constructing practically advantageous continuities within nature, his closeness to Whitehead would be more apparent. Despite *Art as Experience* the learning paradigm for Dewey is problem-solving whereas for Whitehead it is more akin to artistic production of selfhood.

If the human career is regarded as a growth of selfhood, this brings Whitehead into a long tradition of regarding learning as a means or form of growth, a view more in the spirit of Froebel than in that of the associationism of Locke and Hume.

Two sub-observations, it seems to me, are important for educational theory and they follow from the primacy of the aesthetic.

1. If reality and significance are measured by the diversity of data integrated in feeling, then a premium is placed on furnishing the pupil of the widest spectrum of values possible as data for unification. This would be trite and trivial were it not for the fact that contrary philosophies of education are the rule rather than the exception. It would be safe to say that the schooling fostered by a culture in any epoch will stress those values that

secure success. It may stress rhetoric at one time, physics at another, and social psychology at still another. Our own time is no exception in this regard; if Whitehead is right, much of our formal schooling is dead wrong, even in intent. The role of the aesthetic mode of experience as the matrix out of which emerge the cognitive and the practical is grossly undervalued, and the appreciative learnings are about as far on the periphery of formal schooling as they can get without falling over the edge altogether.

2. The other observation has to do with the general doctrine of prehensions and the remarks in the quotation above referring to sympathy: ". . . the primitive element is *sympathy,* that is, feeling the feeling *in* another and feeling conformally *with* another." Is it possible that learning is also fundamentally the feeling of a feeling *in* another and *with* another? Where would these feelings be? In the learning task? In the teacher? In the task as it is felt by the teacher? Do we have a phenomenology of learning that can cope with this notion of learning?

When Pupil P is assigned a lesson L by Teacher T, it is assumed that L is presented by T for apprehension and mastery by P. But this is a highly abstract and schematized account of the situation. In Whiteheadian language, clusters of different data are given for prehension. Actual entities, eternal objects, and propositions usually constitute L, and included among them are the entities constituting the body of the teacher, his voice, his appearance, and his mode of feeling the content of the lesson. The pupil P is asked to abstract from the welter of data only those constituting L. From the concrete experience and modes of feeling that make up his own self, he is asked to disengage all but attention to L and only those memories and attitudes relevant to L.

That pupil and teacher do carry this off on occasion is true, but it is equally true that these occasions are rare enough to be remarkable, and they are remarkable precisely because in the first instance, the pupil prehends the data by way of feeling, and he prehends all the data emanating from T as well as L and from his own experience. The pupil's datum is the lesson "as felt by the teacher in his own prehensions," more like Dewey's total situation, and the pupil feels it as conforming with values and purposes that constitute his subjective aim. It is therefore not surprising that the pupil learns not L as such but rather L as felt by T and prehended by P.

If, however, we follow the paradigm of concrescence of the actual entity, there are in the learning act conceptual feelings of eternal objects and propositional feelings as well as physical feelings. Depending on the learning task, clarity, definiteness, and abstraction on the one hand, and concreteness, vividness, and immediacy on the other, vary in importance.

The teaching act, accordingly, is, in large part, the strategy used to select and fashion the data which are to be prehended by the pupil in the act of learning. Part of the strategy involves decisions about how much of the teacher's and the pupil's subjective aims and forms shall be allowed to function in the learning act. In mathematics and science the more we can abstract from the total existential involvement of the participants the better. The study of literature and the humanities in general without a considerable existential involvement of both teacher and pupil seems ill advised. The proper mixture of concreteness and abstraction, of involvement and disengagement are the concern of the arts of teaching and studentship respectively.

Art in any form is hard and long and therefore the golden fleece of educational theory is a scheme whereby one method of teaching, one curriculum, one type of school organization would make unnecessary this *ad hoc* blending of concreteness and definiteness, coherence and inclusiveness, intellectual competence and sensitive sympathy. No scheme has as yet been able to pull this off. As a result, the concrete and intellectual poles tend to pull apart into different curricula and often into different types of schools. To achieve unity one may try to house them under one roof, a notoriously unreliable method of producing compatibility in either domestic or scholastic arrangements.

The Whitehead formula for the actual entity is more useful in pointing out with some precision some of the tasks that still confront learning theory rather than in giving new answers to them. How, for example, does abstraction, conceptualization, thinking of various sorts, supervene upon the concrete welter of feeling that is not yet conceptually structured? How can pedagogy guide the learner to attend to propositional feelings about truth and falsity when other modes of integration are more urgent? How can facility in abstraction be prevented from attenuating the fullness of experience? How can the teacher evaluate the kind and degree of integration of feelings going on in the pupil at a given time?

These are perhaps not new problems, but the Whitehead formula puts them into the same frame as problems of epistemology, metaphysics, cosmology, and value theory; for educational philosophy this is a great advantage. The notion that the teaching art immortalizes itself as an act of learning is in itself an impressive way of pointing to its significance.

LEARNING AS CO-DISCLOSURE

Donald Vandenberg

The more honorable partners of recent protest movements in society and on campus have attempted to rectify abuses of power through opposing them with nonviolent power. The extent of these protest movements raises the question concerning the use and development of nonviolent power in education. Although much thinking and research in education can be construed as attempting to render the educative process less violent, little attention has been given to the phenomenon of nonviolent power as such in education. This is rather astounding, for much has been written about education for freedom, for brotherhood, and for democracy, but these cannot be achieved apart from the nonviolent use of power. In the words of Paul Ricoeur, "I can conceive of an authority which would propose to educate the individual to freedom, which would be a power without violence; in short, I can imagine the difference between power and violence. . . . This imagination liberates the essence; and this essence governs all efforts to transform power into an education to freedom. . . . In making himself foreign and alienated from this sense of nonviolent power, man becomes alienated from himself." [1]

A recent attempt to come to grips with education and power fails to distinguish violent and nonviolent power. Recasting his classification of educational theories in terms of power, Theodore Brameld [2] advocated that the schools should try to become powerful, dominant institutions, but by having more concern with the power of schools in their societal role than with the essence of the educative process, he imagined the possible power *of* education rather than the power possible *in* educating. Concern with the power available consequent upon schooling made Brameld's conception of the essence of power come closer to the conception of the view he calls "essentialism" than to

[1] Paul Ricoeur, *Fallible Man* (Chicago: Henry Regnery Co., 1965), pp. 182–183.
[2] Theodore Brameld, *Education as Power* (New York: Holt, Rinehart, and Winston, 1966).

146

either of the views he calls "perennialism" and "progressivism." The latters' concern with the powers of reason and intelligence, respectively, is with a mode of power to be found within the educative process (according to the views at any rate) and with a nonviolent power, whereas Brameld's conception of the nature of power partakes of the violence of societal power struggles. Although his view opposes "essentialism" for doing precisely this, Brameld's own concern for education and power is related to the same power struggles, albeit on the opposing side. By partaking of the violence that is inherent in societal power structures because these "structures" are reducible to dominance and submission patterns, i.e., to commanding/obeying relations, and thus to the corrective but coercive use of power, and thus to force,[3] Brameld's conception of power would, like "essentialism," bring the forms of power found in society into the schooling process so that their violence would permeate the educative process.[4]

It is not the intent of this paper to quarrel with Brameld's classification and interpretation of educational theories nor with his educational recommendations or goals. Nor is it the intent to quarrel with the societal necessity of institutionalized (i.e., objectified and inauthentically human) relations wherein man's power over man is solidified into forms of corrective and thereby acceptable coercive and violent power. The intent, rather, stems from the respect for the chastity of the educative relation which prompts one to say, "A plague on both your

[3] Cf.: "The objectification of man's power over man in an institution is the new *object* which can serve us as a guide in an immense world of feelings which manifest affectively the diverse modalities of human power according to which it is exercised, opposed, courted, or undergone. All the social roles that a man may exercise initiate situations which political institution consolidates into an object. Affectivity interiorizes these situations as inter-subjective feelings which modulate indefinitely on the theme of commanding/obeying." Ricoeur, *op. cit.,* p. 180.

[4] In the last chapter of *Education as Power,* entitled "World Civilization: The Galvanizing Purpose of Public Education," Brameld advocates the mythologizing of a utopian goal such that the mythology would not only permeate but become the driving force of education through the use of symbols, drama, and so on. Not only is this tantamount to the "forms of power" through which societal power groups achieve and maintain their "power," i.e., through their "propaganda literature," but it is a forceful and total mystification of the pupil.

houses," and is to attempt to articulate a nonviolent power that belongs to the educative process. After trying to indicate why the use of violent power prohibits educating, it will proceed to an existential, phenomenological description of educative action in order to delineate the nonviolent and authentically human power that is constitutive of the pedagogic relation. Then nonviolent ways in which "pupils" can be led to the pedagogic encounter will be indicated.

The major difficulty with allowing various forms of commanding/obeying, or coercive force, into the teacher/pupil relation is the simultaneous transformation of the relation from a pedagogic to a dominance/submission "relation" in which it is never clear as to who is dominating whom. The alleged inferior dominates the alleged superior by determining the kind of person he is going to have to become in order to dominate successfully as surely as the reverse. In dominance/submission relations both parties have their being for the other such that the "inferior" decides what conduct is going to be necessary before he will "submit": he alters the conduct and hence the being of the "superior" as much as the lady sets the course the pursuing male has to run and the price he has to pay. Letting courtship patterns be what they will, the consequence for the teacher/pupil relation when it is transformed into a dominance/submission "relation," when teacher and pupil fall into having their being for others, is that neither party has his attention focused primarily on the matter at hand, "task-centered."

Whatever form commanding/obeying takes in the classroom, whether it is taking attendance, surprise quizzes, reward and punishment (or "reinforcement") examinations, use of "peer group" pressure, propaganda, oratory, eloquence, scoldings, and so on, including explicit, verbal commands, its very use indicates that the people who are having their being as pupils are already alienated from the work of the classroom, from the person who is having her being as a teacher, or from the school itself, and find themselves there only through some externally compelling, coercive, and inauthentic reason. Further moves on the part of the person who is having her being as a teacher involving coercive force of any kind, however subdued, increases the alienation of the person who is having his being as a pupil. Ontologically, increasing the pressure of a dominance/ submission relation increases the depth in which the participants have their being for others. Then the use of commanding/ obeying tactics on the part of the 'teacher' [5] increase the extent of the 'pupil's' having his being for others, which increases his alienation from the world, which makes him more inauthentically there, i.e., more alienated from himself and from the 'teacher'; rather than contributing to his clarification over his situation, it increases his mystification as it promotes the illusion that the reasons of other people are his own, and it does not help him establish his own reasons for being there. As it happens, however, the 'pupil', in each and every case, is always in class precisely because he wants to be there. Exactly like everyone else, the 'pupil' is where he is because of a perfectly gratuitous choice to be there, *all things considered,* and his problems center in living up to his condition as a student fully, in living in harmony with previous choices and their consequences of which he is unaware. No form of commanding/ obeying can clarify his situation for him because commanding/ obeying makes him situationless in its pushing him into having his being for others.

On the other hand, so too is the 'teacher' there of her own gratuitous choice to be there as a teacher, all things considered. She too may be there for inauthentic reasons stemming from having her being for others rather than for herself, rather than simply to be as a teacher, but no use of what is ordinarily called power will assist her in her own clarification of why she is there; on the contrary, it will further the alienation from herself, from her authentically human possibilities as a teacher, because its use alienates the 'teacher' from the 'pupil's' own possibilities of being in her attempt to displace them with her own in forms of commanding, i.e., through some use of violent power. If the 'pupil' is his future, i.e., if he has his being in his possibilities of being, which extend outward to the "world" and forward to the "future" only insofar as he can spatialize and temporalize from his own origin, and if he has his being to be, i.e., if he has to

---

[5] Hereafter 'teacher' will stand for "the person who is having her being as a teacher" and 'pupil' will stand for "the people who are having their being as students."

bring his own possibilities into existence by projecting from the null basis that he is into them in order to be, then all attempts to coerce him into the pedagogic relation essentially remove him from his own possibilities of being, from his project of being, and alienate him from these possibilities of being, i.e., from himself and others, including the 'teacher.' This use of power alienates the 'teacher' from the 'pupil' because within it he can no longer be seen in his projecting toward his future, in his being. Because the 'teacher' can no longer see the 'pupil' as who he essentially is within any form of commanding, the intrusion of this mode of power is precisely an avoidance and destruction of the authentically human pedagogic relation as an encounter between two people. It is precisely opposed to what can bring the 'pupil' into a pedagogic relation with the 'teacher.'

The intrusion of various forms of commanding/obeying into the teacher/pupil relation, in other words, is an attempt to relieve the manifestations of the 'pupil's' alienation from the 'teacher' (at its best) and could be allowed only by 'teachers' who are inauthentically there as teachers, who are alienated from the pupil in their alienation from their own being as teachers. No use of what is ordinarily called power can relieve the 'teacher's' anxiety over the fact that when "symptoms" of the 'pupil's' alienation from the pedagogic relation manifest themselves, her own being as a teacher is in question in its being, over the fact that the 'pupil's' refusal of her proffered help is a venture in his very being that challenges her in her very being. These refusals place the 'teacher's' being as a teacher, her power of being, on trial. The power of being, however, depends upon the amount of nonbeing that can be accommodated.[6] Then the use of what is ordinarily called power, i.e., power in the sociological or political sense, is a manifestation of the lack of the power of being, of weakness, for its use in the classroom betrays the incapacity to accommodate the threat of nonbeing that manifestations of the 'pupil's' venturings away from the 'teacher' bring to her. Its use cannot restore the pedagogic relation in which the 'teacher' helps the 'pupil' to become a person in his own right because it encourages him to hide

[6] Paul Tillich, *Love, Power, and Justice* (New York: Oxford University Press, 1954), p. 48.

behind appearances in his seeming to be whatever or whoever will pacify this arrogant, violent power.

In this seeming to be other than who he is in order to pacify this "power," the 'pupil's' actions lose their quality of action. They become gestures that no longer disclose who he is. Without this disclosure, his speech becomes so much free-floating talk even when it uses the "correct" words. It becomes the means to achieve his own preconceived ends that he keeps concealed, perhaps even from himself, and it does not disclose his situation, his world, or what he has learned either to the 'teacher' or to himself. It becomes his own retaliatory use of force against the 'teacher', however concealed and subdued it may be. It is, rather, an essential powerlessness because it does not allow for the emergence of the power of being that arises only when people create a space for their appearance by disclosing who they really are.[7] The power of being does not arise whenever any of the various forms of commanding/obeying enter the teacher/pupil relation. It cannot because the 'teacher' does not rely on the power of being to establish a genuinely pedagogic relation in which authentically human learnings can occur.

Within the 'pupil's' experiencing (from his viewpoint), learnings do not happen to him at all. They happen to his world as part of his outgoing explorations: dark areas around him become lightened as the possibilities therein become disclosed, "opened up," to him. With genuine learnings his world becomes increasingly brighter, richer, more complex, and more fully articulated and interrelated as more and more possibilities are disclosed to him. The possibilities disclosed in educating belong both to the 'pupil' and to his world because he exists his world. Likewise do they also belong to the 'teacher' and to her world, for she exists her world. Within the authentically human pedagogic relation, then, action that is educating simultaneously (a) projects the 'teacher' into the possibilities she is disclosing; (b) brings the possibilities into the 'teacher's' being; (c) projects the 'pupil' into the possibilities that are disclosed; (d) brings those possibilities into the 'pupil's' being; (e) brings the possibilities disclosed into the 'teacher's' and 'pupil's' being; (f) projects the 'teacher's' and 'pupil's' being into the possibilities disclosed in the co-disclosure, thereby bringing them to coexist in the disclosures; (g) co-discloses possibilities in the world where the "referents" to the "words" of the 'teacher' are; (h) brings the possibilities of the world into being; (i) brings the possibilities of being into being in clearing a place for their appearance; and (j) lets the possibilities of being be, thereby allowing being to clear a space for itself.

If, by disclosing possibilities of being, educating action allows being to clear a space for itself, this signifies that it allows being to be. But what can let being be except the power of being? And what lets the power of being emerge within the pedagogic encounter? To answer these questions a closer explication of what has already been said is necessary.

Educating action brings the possibilities of the world into being through the mutual participation in their disclosure. 'Teacher' and 'pupil' project into them in order to become conscious of them. By becoming conscious of them as possibilities of the world, they become those possibilities. Educating action thus brings possibilities of later action into awareness for the 'pupil,' into being for him, at the same time that they are brought back into the 'teacher's' being by her renewed awareness of them, which remembrance is her projection into them. Educating action, however, can occur only when the 'pupil' implicitly understands that he requires help in the disclosure of possibilities of being, for only then does he project into the disclosure with his whole being and only then is he able to coexist with the 'teacher' in the possibility opened up. This coexistence occurs only when both 'teacher' and 'pupil' are authentically there in the classroom, i.e., only when both are aware of their gratuitous choices to be there and are living up to the conditions of those choices by being authentically as a teacher and being authentically as a pupil. This in turn occurs only when the 'teacher' understands that her being as a teacher is in question in its being, for the 'pupil' can always turn away from her, and only when the 'pupil' understands that his being is in question, for otherwise he would not be there as a student.

To avoid reifying the person who has his being as a student, the subject matter, or the language through which educating action occurs, and to avoid an analytic reduction of the phenomena involved to something else, the way to describe the coexistence that occurs in the educating action of the pedagogic encounter is the *co-disclosure of possibilities of being*. The "language" of the classroom that "serves" as a "medium" of the interhuman is no self-subsisting entity and cannot be considered as such without omitting the being of the speaker and the listeners. The "language" places both the speaker and the hearers into the situation "referred" to by the "words" spoken in the locus of their "referents," imaginatively, as it were.[8] The designations "words" and "referents," however, still reify words, for one can ask for the "referent" for the "word" *word*. Thus the nonreductive way of saying that both 'teacher' and 'pupil' "have the same referents for the teacher's words" is to say that they *coexist in projecting into possibilities that are speakingly disclosed*. That is to say that educating action is the co-disclosure of being.[9]

When the 'teacher' speaks authentically with the 'pupil', the whole world is created anew each moment: the horizons of both 'teacher' and 'pupil' are under constant co-creation. Otherwise (in inauthentic speech) the talking goes into mid-air, not quite understood, dead language, a mere intrusion of the past into the present that voids the present by eliminating it (almost). Then the 'pupil' remains aloof, a spectator of what is said. Authentically pedagogic speech, on the contrary, transcends the present by plunging into the future that is so close it hardly seems to require the plunge but that does like the spoken "sentence" that

[8] This "sentence" has been expressed ontologically by Martin Heidegger: ". . . it is only language that affords the very possibility of standing in the openness of the existent. Only where there is language is there world. . . . Only where world predominates is there history. Language is a possession in a more fundamental sense. It is good for the fact that (*i.e.,* it affords a guarantee that) man can *exist* historically. Language . . . is that event which disposes of the supreme possibility of human existence. . . . The being of man is founded in language." "Hölderlin and the Essence of Poetry," in *Existence and Being* (Chicago: Henry Regnery, 1949), pp. 276–277.

[9] This is close to what Arendt meant by the development of the political realm, the *polis,* or the space of appearance when people disclose themselves, except that it includes the intentionality of human existence. See *The Human Condition,* pp. 198–200.

is a sally into the future, requiring not a little courage because it is a leaping into what does not yet exist. Nevertheless, the nothingness "contains" possibilities of being that can be brought into being by completing the "sentence" in any one of a myriad of ways; in this transcending of the present by futuring, authentically pedagogic speech makes the present moment luminous.[10] When the present moment becomes luminously present, when 'teacher' and 'pupil' coexist in the possibilities disclosed, when the possibilities of being are brought into being in the pedagogic clearing of the space for their appearance, then the 'teacher' has authoritativeness in the perspective of the 'pupil' because the disclosures are "accepted" as genuine disclosures because they are revealed as such to him. Then there is no need for the use of violent power because the pedagogic encounter within which the power of being arises has established itself.

The power of being, authentically human and nonviolent power, forms itself within the pedagogic relation as the 'teacher' reveals possibilities of being, i.e., as possibilities of being prompt their revelation.[11] Her power, the power that permits 'teacher' and 'pupil' to be authentically there together in the disclosures, does not come from her own being as if it were cut off from the world but from the possibilities disclosed, from the opening into the world revealed by her "words" that the 'pupil' was implicitly searching for.[12] Her power comes from the opening into being that is simultaneously an opening out of being into the disclosing speaking to each other that constitutes the pedagogic encounter.

[10] Compare Heidegger on "the single conversation," *op. cit.,* pp. 276–279.

[11] Cf. Heidegger: "But the gods can acquire a name only by addressing and, as it were, claiming us. The word which names the gods is always a response to such a claim." *Ibid.,* p. 279.

[12] In his elucidation of this power, Paul Tillich indicates the centrality of the phenomenon of power: "But the self is self only because it has a world, a structured universe. . . . Self and world are strictly correlated, and so are individualization and participation. . . . To understand the highly dialectical nature of participation it is necessary to think of power instead of in terms of things. . . . The identity of participation is an identity in the power of being. In this sense the power of being of the individual self is partly identical with the power of being of his world, and conversely." *The Courage to Be* (New Haven: Yale University Press, 1952), pp. 87–89.

If the co-disclosures are viewed anthropocentrically, they are openings into being, but if they are viewed nonanthropocentrically to include the initiation of the disclosures by the possibilities of being of the world, then they are the opening out of being into the pedagogic relation. This opening out of being that is generated "equally" by the 'teacher' and by the possibilities themselves is the power of being to be. This nonviolent power forms itself within the pedagogic encounter insofar as genuine possibilities of being are disclosed: insofar as the 'teacher' lets being be. Authentically human power emerges where there are genuine disclosures, i.e., insofar as the 'teacher' establishes being, insofar as she is a guardian of being. The 'teacher' can be a guardian of being only insofar as she lets being be her guardian by refusing to surrender herself to the anonymous "power" objectified in the schooling relation in the "role" of the "teacher." Only when she has the courage to be, is able to disclose herself, and is someone herself, can being be her guardian. When being is the guardian of the teacher, the power of being emerges in the pedagogic encounter as possibilities of being are disclosed, for being is the power of being. Being is the power of being.[13] Increasing the possibilities of being through educative disclosures increases the power of being. Education becomes powerful as possibilities of being are disclosed in educating action within the authentically human pedagogic encounter. No encounter, pedagogic or otherwise, can occur, however, within any form of commanding/obeying.

The problem of developing power in education consequently becomes the problem of clearing the way for the establishment of the pedagogic encounter. There are three aspects to the founding of the pedagogic relation that parallel the three aspects of the encounter: (1) leading the 'pupil' back to himself in a return to the origin of his being to enable him to want to be someone himself so he can be authentically there as a student; (2) leading the 'pupil' to an encounter with "subject matter" within his explorations of the world that constitute his being as a student; (3) leading the 'pupil' to an encounter with the person

[13] In fact, when seeking for a concept to furnish a fundamental description of being as being, Tillich chose the concept of power as it is used here. See *Love, Power, and Justice*, p. 35.

who is a teacher in the classroom, because he requires help in his explorations of the world in the regions thereof constituted by so-called subject matter. These are not three separate "processes" that are only afterwards interrelated, but correspond to three features of the encounter: (1) In any encounter there has to be someone there to encounter. The 'pupil' who has let himself fall into having his being for others, into the anonymous "role" of being a pupil, cannot enter into an encounter with the 'teacher', even though he may be more capable of a surface sociability and cleverness that does not disclose himself, nor clear a space for his appearance, because there is no one there to disclose. (2) Someone who is becoming himself has to continue exploring the world because of the dissatisfaction with any being that may have been achieved, dissatisfaction that grows with the awareness that he still has his being to be, still outstanding in the realization of further possibilities of being, such that there is always more "research" to do as part of one's explorations. (3) People who have their being as teachers can facilitate explorations and eliminate blunderings into inauthentic possibilities that the 'teacher' and her 'teachers' and their 'teachers' have had to explore and eliminate as being inauthentic. But their perspectives are available only to those 'pupils' who accept what they say as authoritative, only to those 'pupils' who want to be independently but who explore so intensively they become aware that they require help.

The first dimension of creating the pedagogic relation possesses pedagogic priority, for the 'pupil's' wanting to be someone himself is the fundamental means of educating. If the 'pupil' is alienated from the pedagogic relation, it is because he is first of all alienated from his world and his own authentic possibilities of being in it. He no longer wants to be independently, to be someone himself, to take up for himself his having to be, despite appearances to the contrary. He lacks the power of being. Then all forms of commanding/obeying, i.e., the use of violent "power," rather than establishing the conditions that make an encounter possible, further convince him of his powerlessness. Leading him to the pedagogic encounter requires "methods" that re-establish his power of being someone himself, that give him the courage to be himself in participation. Among these nonviolent "means" are the admonition, the provocation, the summons, the challenge, the request, the invitation, the beckoning, and the appeal.

A phenomenological explication of these ways of letting the 'pupil' be is beyond the scope of this paper.[14] Suffice it to say that they differ from all forms of commanding/obeying, especially from those that contain some "reinforcement," in that (a) they are future-oriented, enabling the 'pupil' to hear the call of conscience and take up responsibility for his own being, which is the beginning of his gaining power over his own existence; (b) they can arise within action without premeditation and its accompanying alienating manipulation, enabling the 'pupil' to experience the power of the 'teacher's' being in direct confrontation; (c) they confine themselves to different ways of awakening the 'pupil', enabling the 'teacher' to depend upon the power of being; (d) they acknowledge the hazardous character of educating, enabling the person who chooses to have her being as a teacher to be authentically there as a teacher by enabling her to respect the 'pupil' as the person he is; and (e) they invoke the nonviolent power of being, enabling authentic coexistence to be established in the classroom and possibly enabling the subsequent achievement of the kind of social reconstruction that Brameld had in mind.

[14] For explication of the admonition and the appeal and their contrast with commanding and reward and punishment, see my "Educating for Authenticity," *Journal of Existentialism,* forthcoming.

LEARNING AS BECOMING

Giovanni Gentile

First of all, no one has ever conceived the possibility of separating discipline from education. What is often done is to distinguish discipline from that part of education which is called instruction, and to consider the two as integrating the total concept of education. Mention is often made of the educational value of discipline. But this kind of co-ordination of the two forms of education—discipline and instruction—and their subordination to the generic concept of education are more easily formulated than comprehended. For if we should distinguish them simply on the grounds that one is the necessary antecedent of the other, we should have a relationship similar to that which connects any part of instruction with the part which must be presupposed before it as an antecedent moment in the same process of development. But the relationship which exists between any two parts of instruction cannot serve to distinguish from instruction a thing which is different from it.

We might wish, perhaps, to consider as characteristic of this absolute antecedence the establishment of the authority without which teaching, properly so called, cannot begin. But the objection to this would be that every moment of the teaching process presupposes a new authority, which can never be considered as definitely acquired, which is constantly being imposed anew, and which must proceed at every given instance from the effective spiritual action exercised by the teacher upon the pupil. In other words, I mean to say that no teacher is able independently of the merits of his teaching to maintain discipline simply and solely on the strength of his personal prestige, of his force of character, or any other suitable qualification. For whoever he may be, and whatever the power by which at the start he is able to attract the attention of his pupils and to keep it riveted on his words, the teacher as he begins to impart information ceases to

Abridged from *The Reform of Education,* trans. D. Bigongiari (New York: Harcourt, Brace, and World, 1922), pp. 171–177, 179–181, 184–191. By permission of the publisher.

be what he was immediately before, and becomes to the eyes of his pupils an ever changing individual—bigger or smaller, stronger or weaker, and therefore more or less worthy of that attention and that respect of which boys are capable in their expectance of spiritual light and joy. The initial presentation is nothing more than a promise and an anticipation. In the course of teaching this anticipation must not be disappointed, this promise must be constantly fulfilled and more than fulfilled by the subsequent developments. The teacher's personality as revealed at the beginning must be borne out by all that he does in the course of the lesson. Experience confirms this view, and the reason of it is to be found in the doctrine now familiar to us of the spirit that never *is* definitely, but is always constituting itself, always *becoming*. And every man is esteemed and appreciated on the strength of what he shows himself to be at any given moment, and in virtue of the experience which we continue to have of his being—a being which is the development in which he realises himself.

So, then, discipline is never enforced definitely and in such a way that the teacher may proceed to build on it as on a firm basis without any further concern. And it is therefore difficult to see how we could possibly sever with a clean cut the task of keeping discipline from the duty of imparting instruction.

Nor is it any more plausible to maintain that discipline, though it may not chronologically precede instruction, is its logical antecedent, in the sense that there are at every instant of the life of the school both discipline and instruction, the former as a condition of the latter. The difficulty here is that if we assumed this, we ought to be able to indicate the difference between the condition and the conditioned, which difference, unless we rest content with vague words, is not forthcoming, and cannot be found. I maintain that were it possible for the teacher definitely to enthrone, so to speak, discipline in his school, all his work were done. He would have fulfilled his entire duty, acquitted his obligation, and achieved the results of his mission, whether we look upon this mission in the complex of its development, or whether we consider it ideally in the instant of its determined act, which is yet a process and therefore a development. For what, in fact, is discipline? Is it established authority? But this authority is the whole of education. For authority cannot be, as I have explained before, a mere claim: it must become actual in the effective action performed by the educating personality, and this action *is* education. And when this education consists, for example, in the imparting of a rule of syntax, education becomes actual when the pupil really apprehends that rule from his instructor exactly as it is taught to him, and thus appropriates the teacher's manner of thinking and his intellectual behaviour on that special subject, and acts and does as the teacher wants him to. And from the point of view of discipline, this is all we want at that moment.

If in the course of education, considered as a whole or at any particular moment of it, we should separate discipline from instruction, now turning our attention to the one and now to the other, we know from experience that we should never get anywhere. As a matter of fact, the distinction thrusts itself to the fore only when the problem of discipline is erroneously formulated by treating it abstractly. For who is it that worries over discipline as such, and as though it were a thing different from teaching? Who is it that looks upon this problem as an insoluble one? Only the teacher who, unable to maintain discipline, frets over it and failing to discover it where it is naturally to be found, desperately looks for it where it is not, where it could not possibly be. . . .

The real teacher, the naturally gifted teacher, never bothers about these puzzling questions of pedagogical discipline. He teaches with such devotion; he is so close spiritually to his pupils, so sympathetic with their views; his work is so serious, so sincere, so eager, so full of life, that he is never compelled to face a recalcitrant, rebellious personality that could only be reduced by resorting to the peculiar means of discipline. The docility of the pupils in the eyes of the able teacher is neither an antecedent nor a consequent of his teachings; it is an aspect of it. It originates with the very act by which he begins to teach, and ceases with the end of his teaching. Concretely, the discipline which good teachers enforce in the classroom is the natural behaviour of the spirit which adheres to itself in the seriousness and inwardness of its own work. Discipline, authority, and respect for authority are absent whenever it is impossible to establish that unique superior personality, in which the spiritual life of the pupils and of the teachers are together fused and united. Whenever the students fail to find their ideal in the teacher, when they are disappointed by his aspect, his gaze, his words, in the complex concreteness of his spiritual personality, which does not rise to the ideal which at every moment is present in their expectations, then the order of discipline is lacking. But when this actual unity obtains—this unity which is the task of the teacher, and the aim of all education—then discipline, authority, and respect are present as never failing elements.

This pedagogical problem of discipline would never have arisen if immature reflection had not distinguished two empirically different aspects of human personality, the practical and the theoretical, whereby it would appear that man, when he does things, should not be considered in the same light as when he thinks and understands, knows and learns. From this point of view, discipline of deportment is to be referred to the pupil as practical spiritual activity, while teaching aims at his theoretic activity. The former should guide the pupil, regulate his conduct as a member of that special community which we call the school, and facilitate the fulfillment of the obligations which he has toward the institution, toward his fellow-pupils, and toward himself. The latter, on the other hand, assuming the completion of this practical edification, proceeds to the mental formation of the personality, considered as progressive acquirement of culture. Discipline in this system appears to be the morals of the school. I use the word morals in a very broad sense—just as morality might be considered as the discipline of society and of life in general. For everybody, it is argued, distinguishes between the character of man and his intelligence, between his conduct and his knowledge. The two terms may indeed be drawn together, but they also exist quite apart. So that a man devoid of character, or possessed with an indomitable will for evil, may nevertheless be extremely learned and shrewd, or as subtle as the serpent; whereas a moral man, through lack of understanding, may become the sport of rogues, and remain illiterate, devoid of all, even of the slightest accomplishments. For will is one thing, they say, and the intellect is another.

The question of the abstractness of discipline impels us now to examine the legitimacy of this broader distinction, which does not simply concern the problems of the school, but extends to the fundamental principles of the philosophy of the spirit. Under its influence, contemporary thought attacks all the surviving forms of this ancient distinction between will and intellect. . . . So we must conclude that the life of the spirit is never mere contemplation. What seems to be contemplation—that consciousness which the spirit acquires of itself, and, acquiring which, realises itself—is a creation: a creation not of things but of its own self. For what are things but the spirit as it is looked at abstractly in the multiplicity of its manifestations?

We shall more easily understand that our knowing and our doing are indiscernible, if we recall that our doing is not what is also perceived externally, a motion in space caused by us. This external manifestation is quite subordinate and adventitious. The essential character of our doing is the internal will, which does not, properly speaking, modify things, but does modify us, by bringing out in us a personality which otherwise would not have been. This is the substance of the will, which we cannot deny to thought, if thought is, as I have shown, development, and therefore continuous self-creation of the personality.

If intellect then and will are one and the same thing, to such an extent that there is no intellect which in its development is not development of personality, formation of character, realisation of a spiritual reality, we shall be able to understand that the ideas of two distinct spiritual activities, as the basis of the ordinary distinction between moral and intellectual training, are mere abstractions that tend to lead us away from the comprehension of the living reality of the spirit. This distinction appears to me exceedingly harmful, nothing being more deplorable, from the moral point of view, than to consider any part of the life we have to live as morally indifferent, and nothing being more harmful to the school than the conviction that the moral formation of man is not the entire purpose of education, but only a part of its content. It is indispensable, I maintain, that the educator have the reverent consciousness of the extremely delicate moral value of every single word which he addresses to his pupils and of the profoundly ethical essence of the instruction which he imparts to them. For the school which gives instruction with no moral training in reality gives no instruction at all. All the objections voiced on this score against education, which we try to meet by adding on to instruction all that ought to integrate the truly educational function, are the result of this abstract way of looking upon instruction solely as the culture of an intellect which in some way differs from the will, from character, and from moral personality. . . .

The moment the child begins reading, he must of necessity read *something*. There is no mere instrument without the material to which it is to be applied. The infant who opens his eyes and strives to look cannot but see something. The "picture," insignificant for the teacher, has its own special colouring for the child's mind. He fixes his gaze on it; he draws it within himself, cherishes it, and fosters it with his fancies. Such is the law of the spirit! It may be violated, but the consequences of transgression are commensurate with the majesty of this law.

Grammars too, like spelling primers and rhetorics and logic and every kind of preceptive teaching, may be assumed as a form separated from its contents, as something empty and abstract. The child is taught for instance that the letter *m* in *mamma* does not belong to that word (we call it a "word," and forget that to him at least it is not a word but his own mother). That letter *m,* we tell him, is found in other words, *mat, meat,* etc. We show him that it is in all of them, and yet in none of them. We therefore can and must abstract it from all concrete connections, isolate and fix it as that something which it is in itself—the letter *m.* In the same manner we abstract the rule of grammar from a number of individual examples. We exalt it over them, and give it an existence which is higher, and independent of theirs. And so for rhetoric, and so for logic.

But in this process of progressive abstraction, in this practice of considering the abstract as something substantial, and of reducing the concrete and the particular to the subordinate position of the accessory, life recedes and ebbs away. The differences between this and that word, between two images, two thoughts, two modes of thinking, of expressing, of behaving, at first become slight, then negligible, then quite inexistent, and the soul becomes accustomed to the generic, to the empty, to the indifferent. It knows no longer how to fix the peculiarities of things, how to notice the different traits of men's characters, their interests, their diverse values, until finally it becomes indifferent and sceptical. Words lose their meaning; they no longer smack of what they used to; their value is gone. Things lose their individuality, and men their physiognomies. This scepticism robs man of his own faith, of his character and personality. The fundamental aim of education ceases to exist. Abstract education is no education at all. It is not even instruction. . . .

Instruction then which is not education is not even instruction. It is a denuded abstraction, violently thrust like other abstractions into the life of the spirit where it generates that monstrosity which we have described as material culture, mechanical and devoid of spiritual vitality. That culture, being material, has no unity, is fragmentary, inorganic, capable of growing indefinitely without in any way transforming the recipient mind or becoming assimilated to the process of the personality to which it simply adheres extrinsically. This mechanical teaching is commensurate with things, and grows proportionately with them; but it has no intimate relation with the spirit. He who knows one hundred things has not a greater nor a different intellectual value from him who knows ten, since the hundred and the ten are locked up in both in exactly the same way that two different sums of money are deposited in two different vaults. What merit is there in the safe which contains the greater sum? The merit would belong to the man who had accumulated the greater amount by a greater sum of labour, for it would then be commensurate with work, which is the developing process itself and the life of the human personality to which we must always have recourse when we endeavour to establish values. For as we have seen, nothing is, properly speaking, thinkable except in relation to the human spirit.

Whether one reads a single book or an entire library, the result is the same, if what is read fails to become the life of the reader—his feelings and his thoughts, his passions and his meditation, his experience and the extolment of his personality. The poet Giusti has said: "Writing a book is worse than useless, unless it is going to change people." Reading a book with no effect is infinitely worse. Of course the people that have to be transformed, both for the writer and for the reader (who are not two very different persons after all), are not the others, but first of all the author himself. The mere reading of a page or even a word inwardly reconstitutes us, if it does consist in a new throb of our personality, which continuously renews itself through the incessant vibrations of its becoming. This then is the all-important solution—that the book or the word of a teacher arouse our souls and set them in motion; that it transform itself into our inner life; that it cease to be a thing, special and determinate, one of the many, and become transfused into our personality. And our personality in its act, in the act, I say, and not in the abstract concept which we may somehow form of it—is absolute unity: that moving unity to which education can in no wise be referred, unless it is made identical with its movement, and therefore entirely conformant to its unity.

The man whose culture is limited, or, rather, entirely estranged from the understanding of life, is called *homo unius libri*. We might just as well call him *homo omnium librorum.* For he who would read all books need have a leaking brain like the perforated vessels of the daughters of Danaus—a leak through which all ideas, all joys, all sorrows, and all hopes, everything that man may find in books, would have to flow unceasingly, without leaving any traces of their passage, without ever forming that personality which, having acquired a certain form or physiognomy, reacts and becomes selective, picks what it wants out of the congeries, and chooses, out of all possible experiences, only what it requires for the life that is suited to it. We should never add books upon books *ad infinitum!* It is not a question of quantity. What we need is the ability to discover our world in books—that sum total of interests which respond to all the vibrations of our spirit, which assuredly . . . has a multiplicity of interests, but all of them radiating from a vital centre. And everything is in the centre, since everything originates there.

Education which strives to get at the centre of the personality, the sole spot whence it is possible to derive the spiritual value of a living culture, is essentially moral, and may never be hemmed in within the restricted bounds of an abstract intellectual training. There is in truth a kind of instruction which is not education, not because it is in no way educative, but because it gives a bad education and trains for evil. This realistic education, which is substantially materialistic, extinguishes the sentiment of freedom in man, debases his personality, and stifles in him the living consciousness of the spirituality of the world, and consequently of man's responsibility.

The antithesis between instruction and education is the antithesis between realistic and idealistic culture, or again, that existing between a material and a spiritual conception of life. If the school means conquest of freedom, we must learn to loathe the scrappiness of education, the fractioning tendency which presumes to cut off one part from the rest of the body, as if education, that is, personality, could have many parts. We must learn to react against a system of education which, conceiving its rôle to be merely intellectualistic, and such as to make of the human spirit a clear mirror of things, proceeds to an infinite subdivision to match the infinite multiplicity of things. Unity ought to be our constant aim. We should never look away from the living, that is, the person, the pupil into whose soul our loving solicitude should strive to gain access in order to help him create his own world.

LEARNING AS WORKING

Herman Horne

The discussion must be limited to the self-consciousness of man, so as to exclude the body, the problems of which belong to the natural sciences.

First, as to the origin of man. . . .

(*a*) Education, as a human process with a meaning to spell concerning the truth, seizes upon *mind* as the final useful append-age to the organism in its upward evolution. That which nature by spontaneous variation, the struggle for existence, and the survival of the fit, bestows as its last best gift to the organism, education seizes upon to improve, thus raising evolution from the unconscious natural to the conscious mental plane. The highest type of selective agency of man—education—lays hold upon the highest selected product of nature—mind—for further improvement, thereby indicating mind as the highest type of temporal reality. . . . The school and also the other more general educative agencies of civilization lay all their stress upon mind as the most valuable, the most useful, the most real, element in life. Chosen last as the result of an incalculably long, prehistoric process of natural selection, mind is become first. Education may be pardoned its ontological boldness if it questions reflectively whether the reality it selects as ultimate is not the ultimate reality. Is not reality mental?

(*b*) . . . Education shows us a development, the unrealized powers of mind through exercise becoming actualized. But what in the nature of things is the possibility of development? Can something develop from nothing? . . . Can mind come from something not itself mental? . . . Can maturity of mind develop out of simple immaturity? . . . Can that develop in the tem-poral process which is not eternally realized? . . . Education finds itself unable to understand how the development of unreal-ized mind which it secures can occur without implying that, underneath its whole process and giving power at every point, is the one realized mind. Not a first cause in a temporal series of events does education reflectively and vainly seek, but an adequate cause of its great central fact of development. This it satisfactorily finds only in the existence of a mind which needs no development itself, and so can guarantee the fruitfulness of all educational efforts for development. Thus education upon reflection is forced to hold that the reality it declares mental it must also declare actual.

(c) Man is the only educable being. The horse, the dog—the lower animals—are trained, not educated. Apparently the lower creature frames to himself no goal to be reached, no moral or intellectual end to be attained, no development to be secured. There is direction, but not self-direction; consciousness, but not self-consciousness; inherited instinct, but not conceptual reasoning. Such intelligences are trained, through processes of associative memory, but not educated, through the pursuit of rational ends self-consciously conceived. The dividing line between training and education is uncertain but real. In the field of animal intelligence least of all is the modern psychologist permitted to dogmatize. He only finds man with a history, literature, science, and the arts of civilization which the lower animal lacks. He knows man's works are due to his powers of symbolic thinking. He must suspect then that this is the distinguishing characteristic of man, differentiating him from the lower animals. . . . The lower creation seems to lack that power of self-directed pursuit of consciously conceived ends which makes education possible. This power we have already named, in brief, self-activity. Man is the only educable being because only he has a sufficient measure of self-activity to attain by effort rational ends. . . .

Second, as to the nature of man. . . .

(a) Education is the product of the mind's effort. The development of mind is from within out, not from without in. No teacher and no curriculum can educate the youth who will not respond. The teacher may lead the pupil to the founts of learning, but he cannot make him drink. The teacher's art, as some one has said, consists in making the pupil so thirsty that he will want to drink. Teaching is not so much the cause of learning, which is so frequently asserted, as it is the occasion or condition of learning. The cause of learning is the pupil himself and his effort. The teacher, the curriculum, the apparatus, the school buildings—these all are but the stimulating environment of the pupil. The teacher is like the gardener who digs about and nourishes the plant which grows of its own impulse. The pupil is like the plant so stimulated in so far as his response is his own, but he is unlike the plant in that his response may be withheld. There is a possible willful obstinacy in pupils that does not appear in plants. If they do not become educated in the day of their visitation from the teacher, it is because they would not. The ultimate responsibility for winning an education rests with the will of the pupil. We try to teach, train, instruct, and discipline him, but we cannot educate him; he must educate himself. Every educated man is self-educated; the only difference is that in some cases the stimulating and nourishing environment was lacking, unfortunately so for both the man and his self-education, while in the other cases the man had good assistance. The pupil's ultimate power to make himself work must be acknowledged by teachers. Their function is not to make pupils learn but to make learning so attractive and compelling in interest that pupils will want to learn; not theirs to hector over and be-lecture pupils, but to provide a happy occupation for their free individualities. Not in me, not in me, sayeth the teacher, but the kingdom of education is within you. Education, all this means to say, is the result of the effort of the self-active mind to assimilate the incoming stimuli from the school, is free individuality expressing itself.

(*b*) Education presents us with results proportionate to effort expended. The degree of effort put forth by the pupil in response to his educative environment determines his educational attainment. The same school stimuli received different responses from different individuals; the educational process is not so much the stimulus shaping the individual, as the individual responding to the stimulus. The same school sends forth pupils with a diversity of attainments, because the same stimuli have received individual responses. Just as the natural world, though one, has produced a variety of organisms through their individual reactions upon its stimuli, so the unitary environment of the school produces a variety of achievements through the individual responses of the pupils. The greater the effort expended, within the natural limits of health, the greater the amount of knowledge and the degree of development secured. One pupil puts forth more effort than another, he thereby secures a greater return. . . . Not simply the prior question of whether he will work or not, but also the present question of how much he will work, seems subject to the free decision of his own personality. Will I give attention at all? How much attention will I give? These two ultimate questions are answerable only by the individual pupil himself, and upon their momentous answers hang the weight of his present and future education. Every pupil is the keeper of his own educational results.

(c) Through the energy of effortful attention man becomes in his education what he is intended to be; he realizes his nature; develops his natural potentialities; attains his mental majority; declares his intellectual independence; is emancipated from the slavery of ignorance, superstition, fear, and evil; becomes a free being. That which is cramped, dwarfed, and hidden within the chambered recesses of his own personal nature is manifested in full fruition in the light. The word of educational development, "I become," is partially exchanged for the word of real existence, "I am."

Putting these matters together concerning the nature of man, we may say that education means that through his own effort, helped by an invigorating environment, man becomes what he is intended to be; but to become through one's own effort, through response to stimuli, what one is intended to be is to be free. The nature of man is freedom.

Education does not imply a freedom of acting with an unmotived will, the so-called liberty of indifference, for the stimulating educational environment is present, presenting motives to consciousness to which to respond; neither does it imply a freedom of will to respond to the strongest motive, which is determinism, for education observes the inequality of response of different pupils to the same stimuli, and of the same pupil at different times. These observations do not prove, but they are indicative of, the presence of an independent variable in the conscious response of the pupil to educational motives. But in contrast to the liberty of indifference and determinism, education implies the freedom of consciousness to realize in some measure, through effort of attention, its own selected ends. Such freedom alone is the adequate possibility of education, for only such a free being has a rational end to be self-actively attained; only such freedom permits the self-realization of one's rational destiny. This is not an absolute freedom to do anything at any time; it is a limited freedom to do something at some time. It permits man to utilize his world to attain his own rational ends; it prevents his being the puppet of circumstances, the creature of environment, and the slave of the strongest impulse. It is a freedom, not of the will as a part of consciousness, but of consciousness itself to direct its own thoughts, to attend to selected ideas, thereby inhibiting others, and so to enact its own purposes in conduct. The will is free because the consciousness is free. My ability to direct my thoughts is my ability to act as I will. As a man thinketh in his mind, so is he in his life.

Since the mind is a unity, though its operations are many, the question concerning the freedom of the will is really a question concerning the freedom of mind.

Third, the destiny of man. There are two notable things about education that bear on this far-reaching question, and that go together. (*a*) Man's education as an empirical process is never completed; (*b*) the possibility of man's development seems infinite.

No man is ever all he can be. At any point in his development he has a growing future. His purposes are not ended with his life, nor does he live in a spent world. Neither does the race in its development discover any waning intellectual possibilities; rather a growth in attainment, if not in capacity. Age does not wither, nor custom stale, the philosopher's love of truth, the artist's love of beauty, or the saint's love of virtue. These ideals of the human reason flee us as we pursue them in time. There is always more to know, and to love, and to do. With these fundamental demands on the universe from the great deeps of man's nature, the incident in life called death seems apparently to have nothing to do. Man does not limit his will to know, to enjoy, and to achieve, to his life's unknown term of years. His plans bridge the chasm of death; they call for an unending time in which their execution may be effected. . . .

Given this unlimited demand by man upon his world, what of it? Man has a nature to realize to which any amount of time assignable is inadequate. What follows? Either the universe is irrational, with a good work begun which could not be continued, or man has the power of an endless life. . . .

CONCOMITANT LEARNING

The following article deals with the nature of the mind as it becomes structured through learning. It is one view of "attitudes" of mind that result concomitantly with desirable learning. The selection invites four kinds of questions. First, Dewey is often criticized for not having read Freud and for not being able to account for the phenomena of depth psychology, i.e., for the "unconscious." What is there in the selection to indicate otherwise? Second, how does Dewey's view of these attitudes compare with other views? With Wirth's? With authenticity as it is discussed in existential literature of which Buytendijk and Gusdorf are examples? Third, what is the difference between traits of individual method and moral virtues? If one agrees with the desirability of the attitudes of mind, does one have to agree with the method of learning to which they apparently belong? What methods other than Dewey's might promote their formation? And finally, what other attitudes of mind are pedagogically desirable? What methods of teaching might promote their development?

To compare this selection with Kilpatrick's view when the latter is concerned with personality structures, see "The Project Method" in *Teachers College Record,* 19 (September, 1918), 319–335. Another metaphysical consideration, the pupil's experiencing of different levels of reality in the learning situation, can be examined in Holton's "Conveying Science by Visual Presentation" in *Education of Vision,* ed. G. Kepes (New York: Braziller, 1965), pp. 50–77.

ATTITUDES OF MIND

John Dewey

Methods remain the personal concern, approach, and attack of an individual, and no catalogue can ever exhaust their diversity of form and tint.

Some attitudes may be named, however, which are central in effective intellectual ways of dealing with subject matter. Among the most important are directness, open-mindedness, single-mindedness (or whole-heartedness), and responsibility.

1. It is easier to indicate what is meant by directness through negative terms than in positive ones. Self-consciousness, embarrassment, and constraint are its menacing foes. They indicate that a person is not immediately concerned with subject matter. Something has come between which deflects concern to side issues. A self-conscious person is partly thinking about his problem and partly about what others think of his performances. Diverted energy means loss of power and confusion of ideas. Taking an attitude is by no means identical with being conscious of one's attitude. The former is spontaneous, naïve, and simple. It is a sign of whole-souled relationship between a person and what he is dealing with. The latter is not of necessity abnormal. It is sometimes the easiest way of correcting a false method of approach, and of improving the effectiveness of the means one is employing—as golf players, piano players, public speakers, etc., have occasionally to give especial attention to their position and movements. But this need *is* occasional and temporary. When it is effectual a person thinks of himself in terms of what is to be done, as one means among others of the realization of an end—as in the case of a tennis player practicing to get the "feel" of a stroke. In abnormal cases, one thinks of himself not as part of the agencies of execution, but as a separate object—as when the player strikes an attitude thinking of the impression it will make upon spectators, or is worried because of the impression he fears his movements give rise to.

Reprinted from *Democracy and Education,* by permission of Macmillan Company. Copyright 1916 by Macmillan Company, renewed 1944 by John Dewey. Pp. 204–210.

Confidence is a good name for what is intended by the term directness. . . . It denotes the straightforwardness with which one goes at what he has to do. It denotes not *conscious* trust in the efficacy of one's powers but unconscious faith in the possibilities of the situation. It signifies rising to the needs of the situation.

We have already pointed out the objections to making students emphatically aware of the fact that they are studying or learning. Just in the degree in which they are induced by the conditions to be so aware, they are *not* studying and learning. They are in a divided and complicated attitude. Whatever methods of a teacher call a pupil's attention off from what he has to do and transfer it to his own attitude towards what he is doing impair directness of concern and action. Persisted in, the pupil acquires a permanent tendency to fumble, to gaze about aimlessly, to look for some clew of action beside that which the subject matter supplies. . . .

2. Open-mindedness. Partiality is, as we have seen, an accompaniment of the existence of interest, since this means sharing, partaking, taking sides in some movement. All the more reason, therefore, for an attitude of mind which actively welcomes suggestions and relevant information from all sides. . . . Openness of mind means accessibility of mind to any and every consideration that will throw light upon the situation that needs to be cleared up, and that will help determine the consequences of acting this way or that. Efficiency in accomplishing ends which have been settled upon as unalterable can coexist with a narrowly opened mind. But intellectual growth means constant expansion of horizons and consequent formation of new purposes and new responses. These are impossible without an active disposition to welcome points of view hitherto alien, an active desire to entertain considerations which modify existing purposes. Retention of capacity to grow is the reward of such intellectual hospitality. The worst thing about stubbornness of mind, about prejudices, is that they arrest development; they shut the mind off from new stimuli. Open-mindedness means retention of the childlike attitude; closed-mindedness means premature intellectual old age.

Exorbitant desire for uniformity of procedure and for prompt external results are the chief foes which the open-minded attitude meets in school. The teacher who does not permit and encourage diversity of operation in dealing with questions is imposing intellectual blinders upon pupils—restricting their vision to the one path the teacher's mind happens to approve. Probably the chief cause of devotion to rigidity of method is, however, that it seems to promise speedy, accurately measurable, correct results. The zeal for "answers" is the explanation of much of the zeal for rigid and mechanical methods. Forcing and overpressure have the same origin, and the same result upon alert and varied intellectual interest. But there is a kind of passivity, willingness to let experiences accumulate and sink in and ripen, which is an essential of development. Results (external answers or solutions) may be hurried; processes may not be forced. They take their own time to mature. Were all instructors to realize that the quality of mental process, not the production of correct answers, is the measure of educative growth, something hardly less than a revolution of teaching would be worked.

3. Single-mindedness. So far as the word is concerned, much that was said under the head of "directness" is applicable. But what the word is here intended to convey is *completeness* of interest, unity of purpose, the absence of suppressed but effectual ulterior aims for which the professed aim is but a mask. It is equivalent to mental integrity. Absorption, engrossment, full concern with subject matter for its own sake, nurture it. Divided interest and evasion destroy it.

Intellectual integrity, honesty, and sincerity are at bottom not matters of conscious purpose but of quality of active response. Their acquisition is fostered of course by conscious intent, but self-deception is very easy. Desires are urgent. When the demands and wishes of others forbid their direct expression they are easily driven into subterranean and deep channels. Entire surrender and whole-hearted adoption of the course of action demanded by others are almost impossible. Deliberate revolt or deliberate attempts to deceive others may result. But the more frequent outcome is a confused and divided state of interest in which one is fooled as to one's own real intent. One tries to serve two masters at once. Social instincts, the strong desire to please others and get their approval, social training, the general sense of duty and of authority, apprehension of penalty, all lead to a half-hearted effort to conform, to "pay attention to the lesson," or whatever the requirement is. Amiable individuals want to do what they are expected to do. Consciously the pupil thinks he is doing this. But his own desires are not abolished. Only their evident exhibition is suppressed. Strain of attention to what is hostile to desire is irksome; in spite of one's *conscious* wish, the underlying desires determine the main course of thought, the deeper emotional responses. The mind wanders from the nominal subject and devotes itself to what is intrinsically more desirable. A systematized divided attention expressing the duplicity of the state of desire is the result.

One has only to recall his own experiences in school or at the present time when outwardly employed in actions which do not engage one's desires and purposes, to realize how prevalent is this attitude of divided attention—double-mindedness. We are so used to it that we take it for granted that a considerable amount of it is necessary. It may be; if so, it is the more important to face its bad intellectual effects. Obvious is the loss of energy of thought immediately available when one is consciously trying (or trying to seem to try) to attend to one matter, while unconsciously one's imagination is spontaneously going out to more congenial affairs. More subtle and more permanently crippling to efficiency of intellectual activity is a fostering of habitual self-deception, with the confused sense of reality which accompanies it. A double standard of reality, one for our own private and more or less concealed interests, and another for public and acknowledged concerns, hampers, in most of us, integrity and completeness of mental action. Equally serious is the fact that a split is set up between conscious thought and attention and impulsive blind affection and desire. Reflective dealings with the material of instruction is constrained and half-hearted; attention wanders. The topics to which it wanders are unavowed and hence intellectually illicit; transactions with them are furtive. The discipline that comes from regulating response by deliberate inquiry having a purpose fails; worse than that, the deepest concern and most congenial enterprises of the imagination (since they center about the things dearest to desire) are casual, concealed. They enter into action in ways which are unacknowledged. Not subject to rectification by consideration of consequences, they are demoralizing.

School conditions favorable to this division of mind between avowed, public, and socially responsible undertakings, and private, ill-regulated, and suppressed indulgences of thought are not hard to find. What is sometimes called "stern discipline," i.e., external coercive pressure, has this tendency. Motivation through rewards extraneous to the thing to be done has a like effect. Everything that makes schooling merely preparatory works in this direction. Ends being beyond the pupil's present grasp, other agencies have to be found to procure immediate attention to assigned tasks. Some responses are secured, but desires and affections not enlisted must find other outlets. Not less serious is exaggerated emphasis upon drill exercises designed to produce skill in action, independent of any engagement of thought—exercises having no purpose but the production of automatic skill. Nature abhors a mental vacuum. What do teachers imagine is happening to thought and emotion when the latter get no outlet in the things of immediate activity? Were they merely kept in temporary abeyance, or even only calloused, it would not be a matter of so much moment. But they are not abolished; they are not suspended; they are not suppressed— save with reference to the task in question. They follow their own chaotic and undisciplined course. What is native, spontaneous, and vital in mental reaction goes unused and untested, and the habits formed are such that these qualities become less and less available for public and avowed ends.

4. Responsibility. By responsibility as an element in intellectual attitude is meant the disposition to consider in advance the probable consequences of any projected step and deliberately to accept them: to accept them in the sense of taking them into account, acknowledging them in action, not yielding a mere verbal assent. Ideas, as we have seen, are intrinsically standpoints and methods for bringing about a solution of a perplexing situation: forecasts calculated to influence responses. It is only too easy to think that one accepts a statement or believes a suggested truth when one has not considered its implications, when one has made but a cursory and superficial survey of what further things one is committed to by acceptance. Observation

and recognition, belief and assent, then become names for lazy acquiescence in what is externally presented.

It would be much better to have fewer facts and truths in instruction—that is, fewer things supposedly accepted—if a smaller number of situations could be intellectually worked out to the point where conviction meant something real—some identification of the self with the type of conduct demanded by facts and foresight of results. The most permanent bad results of undue complication of school subjects and congestion of school studies and lessons are not the worry, nervous strain, and superficial acquaintance that follow (serious as these are), but the failure to make clear what is involved in really knowing and believing a thing. Intellectual responsibility means severe standards in this regard. These standards can be built up only through practice in following up and acting upon the meaning of what is acquired.

Intellectual *thoroughness* is thus another name for the attitude we are considering. There is a kind of thoroughness which is almost purely physical: the kind that signifies mechanical and exhausting drill upon all the details of a subject. Intellectual thoroughness is *seeing a thing through*. It depends upon a unity of purpose to which details are subordinated, not upon presenting a multitude of disconnected details. It is manifested in the firmness with which the full meaning of the purpose is developed, not in attention, however "conscientious" it may be, to the steps of action externally imposed and directed. . . .

CREATIVITY

Several metaphysical issues are involved in the inquiry concerning the educational phenomena of creativity. The most important may be the question of determinism. If either the universe or human nature is mechanistic, there is little room for genuine and worthwhile creative, novel action in education. Ever since Heisenberg formulated the principle of uncertainty, however, it has been difficult to say that there are more than statistical laws operative in the universe. This is not to deny mechanism, but it is to say that asserting its existence in the universe goes beyond physics into metaphysics.

On the other hand, the social or behavioral scientist is almost forced to assume a methodological principle of determinism in order to gather warrantable knowledge; many remain content with statistical correlations rather than hoping to find laws of behavior. In either of these cases creativity remains possible because principles adopted to facilitate inquiry into human nature say nothing about the nature of human nature, and because statistical correlations say nothing about particulars (i.e., statistical laws do not determine individual events). Again, this is not to deny mechanism in human nature, but it is to say that asserting its existence goes beyond the testable, i.e., is a metaphysical assertion.

It is possible, moreover, to have different answers to the question of freedom versus determinism for different segments of the universe, particularly for nature and human nature. Just as man is the only entity that speaks and writes, so too might one maintain that man is the only entity that is undetermined. Again, human events may be radically different from natural events. Not so in the following selection. For Whitehead, as Dunkel indicates, creativity permeates the entire universe including man and human education. Whitehead sees everything, including man, condemned to creativity. He can be seen as giving the support of a complete metaphysical and cosmological system to the suspicions of Aschner and Soderquist concerning the mechanistic sciences of man.

For explicit demonstrations that the possibility of creativity lies in the metaphysical basis of a view of man, see Ernest Bayle's chapter entitled "Existence, Causation, and Intelligence" in his *Democratic Educational Theory* (New York: Harper, 1960), pp. 93–102; Hallman's "Can Creativity Be Taught?" *Educational Theory,* 14 (January, 1964), 15–23, and his "Creativity and Educational Philosophy," *Educational Theory,* 17 (January, 1967), 3–13, and Shaw's response to the latter in *Educational Theory,* 18 (Spring, 1968), 164–168; and also Morland's "The Doctrine of Natural Law—Its Implications for Education," also in *Educational Theory,* 11 (January, 1961), 168–173 f.

THRUST TOWARD NOVELTY

Harold B. Dunkel

Whitehead sees the task of speculative philosophy as that of framing "a coherent, logical, necessary system of general ideas in terms of which every element of our experience can be integrated" [1] or "all those generic notions adequate for the expression of any possible interconnection of things." [2] "Creativity" is a major member of this set of ideas or notions. In contrast to Whitehead's habit of sometimes using different words to symbolize the same term or his occasional belief that some parts of his system might be recast, "creativity" remains constant throughout his cosmological writings. On the various occasions when Whitehead specifies his major terms, [3] "creativity" always appears and is used in the same sense.

Since no member of this major network of terms is to be understood apart from the others, [4] a comprehensive discussion of creativity would demand an equally comprehensive discussion of the other members of the set. But the exigencies of space and of desirable emphasis necessitate our doing much less than full justice to this theoretical demand. The following discussion of some other members of the set is, therefore, cursory, sufficient merely to locate creativity within the network of terms and to show how the metaphysical principles to which they refer affect creativity as it operates in the Whiteheadian universe.

In one of the simplest presentations of his metaphysical system, [5] Whitehead divides his major terms into two categories: (a) those referring to the actual temporal world, and (b) those

Reprinted from "Creativity and Education," *Educational Theory*, 11 (October, 1961), 209, 211–216. By permission of the author and the editor of *Educational Theory*.

[1] Alfred N. Whitehead, *Process and Reality* (New York: Social Science Bookstore, 1941), p. 4.

[2] *Ibid.*, p. vii.

[3] *Ibid.*, ch. II; see also his *Adventures of Ideas* (New York: Macmillan, 1935), ch. XV; *Religion in the Making* (New York: Macmillan, 1926), ch. III.

[4] *Process and Reality*, p. 5.

[5] *Religion in the Making*, pp. 89 ff.

referring to the elements which contribute to the formation of that world. In the first group fall "actual entity," "prehension," and "nexus"; into the second fall "eternal objects," "God," and "creativity."

For Whitehead the actual world is a process, and this process is the becoming, the self-creation, or "concrescence" of actual entities.[6] These are the final, real things of which the world is made up, the smallest elements into which the events of experience may be analyzed. These are "drops of experience, complex and interdependent."[7] They are interdependent because they involve each other by reason of their prehensions of each other. These prehensions are the "feelings" which each entity has, the account it takes, of the rest of the universe. Since Whitehead holds the doctrine of internal relations (that an entity is constituted by its relations and not by its substance or essence, which first exists and then is externally related in various ways), these prehensions constitute the actual entity. Or from the other point of view, it is by its prehensions of the rest of the universe that the entity constitutes itself and makes itself what, in fact, it is. . . .

The entire universe, in a sense, lies before the actual entity for prehension. But the universe as such is a mere multiplicity. Its elements are scattered and are partly conflicting. For the actual entity to come into being, this warring diversity must be transformed into a harmonious unity, since a discordant multiplicity is essentially chaos. Creativity is "that ultimate principle by which the many, which are the universe disjunctively, become the one actual occasion, which is the universe conjunctively."[16] Thus God in his primordial nature, as the primordial, non-temporal accident of creativity, imposes some limitations on the realm of eternal objects by his original conceptual evaluation of them, his initial prehensions of them.[17] Then, as an entity, He serves as a "lure for feeling," as a datum offered for prehension by actual entities, and each actual entity

[6] *Process and Reality,* p. 33.

[7] *Ibid.,* p. 28.

[16] *Ibid.,* pp. 31, 325–326; see also his *Science and the Modern World* (New York: Macmillan, 1948), pp. 250–251.

[17] *Process and Reality,* pp. 344, 374, 528.

is further defined by the demands of its own subjective form, the data offered by preceding actual entities, and the other limitations imposed upon indeterminate creativity by the rest of Whitehead's system.

Thus any examination of creativity as actualized must carry us into the full stream of Whitehead's system. For the cosmological scheme may be said to be fundamentally a detailed study of the transformations of creativity; and anything which can be said about any part of this process is relevant to a discussion of creativity as actualized. . . .

At the very general level of abstraction, certain important characteristics of creativity as an abstract principle are evident without our becoming involved in the specific details.

First, as a metaphysical principle, it will be all-pervasive. We can find no corner of the universe, no occasion of experience, where creativity and the other metaphysical principles are not operative.[18] As an ultimate universally immanent in the universe, it will appear everywhere, though any given appearance finds it conditioned in an extensive and complicated fashion by the other principles and elements.

Second, this drive which is built into the universe is an urge toward novelty. Strictly speaking, in regard to creativity alone "novelty may mean 'new creatures' " merely in the sense of "more creatures to replace the old." Thus an enduring object like Castle Rock at Edinburg or Cleopatra's needle on the Thames Embankment (to use Whitehead's examples) requires a vast succession of new actual entities of about the same kind merely to maintain itself persistently as it is. And creativity accounts for this succession of similar creatures.[19] But other elements in Whitehead's system show that "novelty" is also meant to include the sense "something of a new kind." The consequent nature of God, the function of the untrue proposition as an ideal, and other parts of the system clearly produce novelty in this latter sense of the term.[20] Whitehead is not a believer in life or experience in a rut. Adventure, the entertain-

[18] *Ibid.*, p. 7.
[19] *Ibid.*, pp. 74–76.
[20] *Ibid.*, p. 529; *Science,* pp. 228, 290; *Adventures of Ideas,* pp. 249–250.

ment of new possibilities, the achievement of new types of experience, all play too large a part in his system for that. Creativity does not merely keep the existing cosmological wheels turning. It is a thrust toward what has not been felt, conceived, or actualized before.

Third, creativity is rhythmic. It is cyclical or periodic. That process which is the actual world of experience is not a flow but a series of pulsations. At bottom it is constituted by the actual entities which, as quanta, have their day and cease to be. Creativity as actualized is a continuous cycle of births and deaths.[21]

To characterize creativity in these respects as a universally immanent, rhythmic thrust toward novelty is to give a fairly exhaustive description of creativity prior to its modification by other principles or elements. So major and pervasive a force must leave its mark so clearly on the structure of the White-headian universe and on the role of man within that universe that its effects on educational theory and practice should be readily apparent. Three are clear though they appear in varied aspects.

Probably no feature of Whitehead's educational thought is more characteristically his than his view concerning the rhythmic nature of education. As two of his major essays ("The Rhythm of Education" and "The Rhythmic Claims of Freedom and Discipline") and other less extensive statements have made familiar, Whitehead sees education as properly moving in certain great cycles. Not only does each major cycle in education begin with an exploratory Stage of Romance, which grows into the Stage of Precision, which, in turn, develops into the Stage of Generalization; each minor cycle or eddy which constitutes it should follow the same pattern.[22] As Whitehead puts it, there is continual consummation and continual starting afresh.[23]

Though Whitehead could have arrived at this view by various routes, there seems more than a coincidental relation between

[21] *Process and Reality*, p. ix.
[22] Alfred N. Whitehead, *The Aims of Education* (London: Williams and Norgate, 1932), p. 49.
[23] *Ibid.*, p. 30.

this feature of the educational process and that creativity which lies at the base of the universe.

The way of rhythm pervades all life, and indeed all physical existence. This common principle of Rhythm is one of the reasons for believing that the root principles of life are, in some lowly form, exemplified in all types of physical existence. In the Way of Rhythm a round of experiences forming a determinate sequence of contrasts attainable within a definite period, are codified so that the end of one such cycle is the proper antecedent stage for the beginning of another such cycle. . . .

At the level of human experience we do find fatigue arising from the mere repetition of cycles. The device by which this fatigue is again obviated takes the form of the preservation of the fundamental abstract structure of the cycle, combined with the variation of the concrete details of succeeding cycles. . . . Thus the Rhythm of life is not merely to be sought in simple cyclical recurrence. The cycle element is driven into the foundation, and variations of cycles, and of cycles of cycles, are elaborated.[24]

In the preceding passage Whitehead is actually speaking of the cosmic processes, of creativity as it finds manifestation in the entities of the actual temporal world. But the description could serve almost equally well as a general description of the rhythmic structure of education. Education is rhythmic because the cosmos is rhythmic. The universe is a process. "There is a rhythm of process whereby creation produces natural pulsation, each pulsation forming a natural unit of historic fact." [25]

Thus the rhythmic nature of creativity at least in its manifestations in actuality is one characteristic of creativity which seems clearly perceptible at even a fairly detailed level of Whitehead's education program.

The second sort of trace which creativity seems to leave on Whitehead's educational thought arises from the fact that creativity is a *thrust* into novelty. The manifestation of creativity in actuality consists of the ceaseless self-creation of actual entities. Because creativity is inherent in the nature of things, concrescence is a natural process. Entities naturally evolve through concrescence because creativity is immanent in them. A human

---

[24] Alfred N. Whitehead, *The Function of Reason* (Princeton, N.J.: Princeton University Press, 1929), pp. 16–17.

[25] Alfred N. Whitehead, *Modes of Thought* (New York: Macmillan, 1938), p. 120.

person is for Whitehead a very complex organization of such entities into what he terms a "complex personal society," and education is a very special kind of development for such highly complicated organisms. But it seems more than a mere analogy that Whitehead sees education as fundamentally a natural process. It is not one foreign to the student's nature, something that must be imposed upon him because of social necessity. On the contrary, Whitehead sees the great educational cycles developing as a result of "natural cravings," "rhythmic cravings," or "the call of life within the child." [26] Hence Whitehead places little emphasis on extrinsic motivation or even immediate practical benefit, though he never denies the existence and desirability of the latter. The student is seen as enjoying the exercise of his powers and as having considerable internal motivation and persistence in reaching his intellectual goals. . . .

Another facet of this same point appears in Whitehead's views on teachers and educational institutions. Since education is at ground a natural process and since the student has an internal urge toward it, the student himself is to a considerable extent master of his educational fate and captain of his educational soul. There is a close parallel here, of course, with the process of concrescence. Though the concrescent entity cannot wholly avoid matters of brute fact, it can, through that patterning of the universe which it achieves through its positive and negative prehensions, control its own constitution to a considerable extent. Without this much control it could hardly be said to be self-creating. The educational process is similarly natural, and the student has analogous control over his educational development and similar responsibility for it. "The principle of progress is from within: the discovery is made by ourselves, the discipline is self-discipline, and the fruition is the outcome of our own initiative." [27]

If, then, education is such a natural process, why schools and teachers? Some of Whitehead's reasons are appropriate here, and we shall come to another one in connection with a later

[26] *Aims of Education,* pp. 31, 43, 51; Alfred N. Whitehead, *Essays in Philosophy and Science* (New York: Philosophical Library, 1948), p. 127.

[27] *Aims of Education,* pp. 51, 55, 62.

point. Certainly the function of teachers and institutions is only ancillary, though teachers often forget this fact and over-estimate the importance of their function.[28] They aid the natural bent of the student in several ways. One is by preventing waste.[29] Nature, particularly at the lower stages of existence, is prodigal. The teacher helps make the educational process more efficient by selecting the proper materials and procedures,[30] by pruning out the unessential stuff [31] (which will inevitably become inert [32]), by focusing on the important, leading ideas,[33] and by simplifying them.[34] This later function is the reason for Whitehead's famous dictum: "A certain ruthless definiteness is essential in education." [35]

A second way in which the teacher assists the natural thrust of creativity is by eliciting enthusiasm. Though the student may have a natural urge toward his own education, there are inevitably dull spots.[36] For example, in the educational cycles, it is hard to proceed very far into the Stage of Precision without some loss of enthusiasm.[37] Here, by "eliciting enthusiasm by resonance from his personality" and by creating "the environment of a larger knowledge and a firmer purpose," [38] the teacher can supplement, if it flags, that drive which the student has within him because of the immanence of creativity.

Thus creativity as an undifferentiated drive which moves the universe seems to reappear in a rather specialized form at the higher, human, levels of life as the basic motive power of the educational process.

The third fundamental characteristic of creativity before it is conditioned by other principles in the system is that it is a thrust, not merely toward the continuance of things as they have been, but towards new entities, new ideas, and new types of

---

[28] *Ibid.*, p. 53.
[29] *Ibid.*, p. 62.
[30] *Ibid.*, pp. 7–8, 119; *Essays*, pp. 133–139, 159.
[31] *Aims of Education*, pp. 56, 119.
[32] *Ibid.*, pp. 1–2, 121–122; *Essays*, p. 147.
[33] *Aims of Education*, p. 123.
[34] *Ibid.*, pp. 51–52.
[35] *Ibid.*, p. 57.
[36] *Essays*, p. 128.
[37] *Aims of Education*, pp. 55–56, 144, 146; *Process and Reality*, p. 514.
[38] *Aims of Education*, p. 62.

experience—"the infinite variety of specific instances which rest unrealized in the womb of nature." [39] This aspect of creativity so pervades Whitehead's whole system that to cite instances of it in its varied forms seems almost to be a random quoting of Whitehead's remarks on almost any topic. "No generation can merely reproduce its ancestors. You may preserve the life in a flux of form, or preserve the form amid an ebb of life. But you cannot permanently enclose the same life in the same mold." [40] Or, to put essentially the same point more positively, "the attainment of that last perfection of any finite realization depends on freshness. Freshness provides the supreme intimacy of contrast, the old with the new." [41] Thus if we consider God and the World, we find that neither reaches static completion; "both are in the grip of the ultimate metaphysical ground, the creative advance into novelty." [42] Or in regard to tolerance, we find that our duty toward it is in part our "finite homage to the abundance of inexhaustible novelty which is awaiting the future." [43]

This emphasis on the creative advance into novelty is no less characteristic of Whitehead's educational doctrine than it is of his cosmological one, and in education too its trace appears in different forms. One such manifestation is Whitehead's continual emphasis on the importance of imagination. Imagination is another major contribution which the teacher makes to the educative process. Without imagination, learning becomes stale (like yesterday's fish).[44] To transmit the old patterns, the old perspectives are not enough. Unless "learning is lighted up with imagination," universities, with schemes of orthodoxies, "will stifle the progress of the race." [45] "A university is imaginative or else it is nothing" because "the proper function of a university is the imaginative acquisition of knowledge." [46] This emphasis on imagination and "suggestiveness" marks almost every sentence in which he discusses the higher levels of education.

[39] *Process and Reality*, p. 26.
[40] *Science and the Modern World*, p. 269.
[41] *Essays*, p. 90.
[42] *Process and Reality*, p. 529.
[43] *Adventures of Ideas*, p. 65.
[44] *Aims of Education*, p. 147.
[45] *Ibid.*, p. 146; *Essays*, pp. 23–24.
[46] *Aims of Education*, p. 145.

But it is fundamentally the same force which motivates his famous diatribes against "inert" ideas at all educational levels, those ideas which are not utilized, tested, or thrown into *fresh* combinations.[47] For similar reasons he sometimes worries about professional education, which, though it should be a source of suggestiveness,[48] often tends to produce "minds in a groove," [49] or those which have no fertility of thought.[50]

That the creative advance into novelty rests on the entertainment of novel ideas and ideals has both a social and an individual side, for, after all, "the human being is inseparable from its environment in each occasion of its existence." [51] On the social side, in order to be effective such ideas must be "sustained, disentangled, diffused, and coordinated with background" before they can ultimately pass into exemplification in action.[52] Here a social function for formal education is clear. Yet "the worth of any social system depends on the value experience it promotes among individual human beings." [53] In this aspect we have education for personal development. But viewed in either perspective, this educational advance is the particularized simulacrum of undifferentiated, ultimate creativity.

In sum, the rhythmic surge of creativity, which is the motive power of the universe, is the ultimate source of educational growth, and the formal processes of education are one complex means by which the creative advance into novelty is, in the case of mankind, rendered more efficient and more fruitful.

[47] *Ibid.*, pp. 1–2.
[48] *Essays*, p. 162.
[49] *Science and the Modern World*, p. 282.
[50] *Aims of Education*, p. 82.
[51] *Adventures of Ideas*, p. 80.
[52] *Ibid.*, p. 81.
[53] *Essays*, p. 52.

AXIOLOGICAL CONSIDERATIONS

AXIOLOGY VERSUS SOCIOLOGY

By indicating how the philosophical concern for the teaching and learning of values differs from the concerns of the clinical psychologist, social psychologist, and sociologist, the following two articles serve to define the axiological dimension of education.

By distinguishing psychological adjustment from social adjustment, adjustability, and adaptability, Lawson attempts to indicate how much the teacher should be concerned with the pupil's adjustment while indicating that directions for the teaching and learning of values cannot be taken from the psychology of adjustment. Nor do other senses of the term *adjustment* yield valid directions for education in values. How well does Lawson argue the case for intelligent adaptability?

Arnstine both disagrees and agrees with Lawson. By taking social adjustment much more seriously, he seems to say that sociologists are perhaps right when they point to the power of enculturating forces in shaping the individual's values. In borrowing Dewey's distinction concerning values and evaluating, he also illustrates a primary concern of axiology: defining the nature of values. Using this distinction, he indicates the difficulties of teaching values if they are learned "unconsciously" through the processes of enculturation. Values can be, rather, unlearned as they are gradually replaced with conscious evaluations. Arnstine agrees with Lawson, however, if it is granted that the "values" of a person capable of constructive adaptability are precisely evaluations, for then the people who refuse to adjust to some things (Lawson) are those who dare to be different in important respects (Arnstine). In either case these are the people who have been successfully educated in values, whose learning of values amounted to evaluating.

This point can be clarified by drawing the parallel with epistemology. As Green distinguishes instructing from training, conditioning, etc., on the basis of the degree of intelligence required of the pupil, so too do Lawson and Arnstine distinguish the teaching of values from inculcating, etc., on the basis of degree of intelligence and conscious awareness required of the pupil. As the epistemological concern is to enable the pupil's learning to constitute knowing (Maccia), so too is the axiological concern to enable the pupil's valuing to constitute evaluating. These two selections present the problems that are involved.

CONCERNING THE TERM ADJUSTMENT

Douglas E. Lawson

The argument presented here is an attempt to meliorate some of the sharpness of disagreement noted among those who speak of adjustment of the student as an aim or supposed aim of education, as a function or supposed function of the school. The belief held here is that much of this disagreement is the unfortunate result of the variety of meanings which the term *adjustment* conveys to various people. Three distinct meanings are involved:

a. *adjustment* as a condition of the student who "fits into" his group, has a close identification with its interests and activities, and is thought of, both by the group and by himself, as "belonging," as sharing in its decisions, and as accepting the group and being accepted by it;

b. *adjustment* in the clinical sense of inner personality integration requisite for consistent emotional-intellectual balance, self evaluation, self control, and effective ability to distinguish between reality and fantasy;

c. *adjustment* in the sense of being sufficiently adjustable or adaptable to be capable of modifying one's attitudes, behavior, habits, and beliefs when circumstances make such modification desirable. It is in this sense that the term perhaps has been most misunderstood and probably should not have been used. *Adjustment* is apt as a term implying a status (adjusted-ness) rather than a potential (ability to adjust). A better term probably would be *adjustability*.

. . . I do not believe that many of America's leading educators accept any doctrine which would place primary emphasis upon the learner's adjustment *per se*. But many of them do place emphasis upon the adjustment of the school's requirements to the individual's needs and potential abilities; and many believe that in a changing world it becomes vital for one to be

Reprinted from "Suggestions Concerning the Term Adjustment," *Educational Forum,* 25 (January, 1961), 175–179. By permission of Kappa Delta Pi, An Honor Society in Education, owner of the copyright.

capable of adjusting where intelligent assessment of the situation indicates such adjustment.

The unfortunate fact is that we have rather thoughtlessly used the term *adjustment* when, at times, we should have used a different term—*adjustability*.

By adjustability I mean an ability to evaluate a situation, make intelligent choices, and then adjust to those things to which we should adjust. Adaptability or adjustability (rather than adjustment) implies the ability of the individual to modify his responses and improve their effectiveness. It implies educability. And without such adjustability there is no growth.

When we say that a child is well adjusted we usually are trying merely to say that *at the moment and within the given environment* he is making responses that are consistent with the demands for survival (here using the term *survival* in a very broad context). But we do not use the term by way of suggesting that intelligent and imaginative organisms, capable of modifying the environment, should uncritically accept and adjust to whatever predominantly characterizes an environment or any aspect of it.

For example, such an interpretation would mean that when blind intolerance, superstition, cruelty, false values, and stupidity characterize the time and place in which one lives, one should adjust himself to an acceptance of the herd's mores. Few educators so recommend. Such a doctrine is not the prevailing doctrine of American education, either in theory or in practice, either in the classroom advocacy found in the words of professors of education or in the practical efforts of teachers in the public schools.

A concept which would advocate adjustment as an aim of education without specifying the nature of that to which one should adjust would be a denial of all melioristic philosophy, a philosophy which has characterized American education rather consistently throughout its recent history. We believe with Lester F. Ward that "the environment transforms the animal; man transforms the environment."

One does not transform an environment nor meliorate its adversities if one is adjusted to it. Nor, of course, should one. The characteristic of intelligent man is his ability to make wise decisions; and in so doing he must "weigh all things" and "hold fast that which is good." That which is bad, he rejects. Or he tries to modify it.

Should one, in an environment of squalor and moral depravity, be "adjusted" to his condition? If one lives in a time and place where cruelty is within the mode of human behavior, should he so adjust himself as to accept it with indifference?

Human progress has been made by those "unadjusted" spirits who were incapable of accepting the social mores, the conditions of living, the values of the herd, the entrenched doctrines, or what Bacon called "the tyranny of custom."

When I say that adjustability provides a better concept than adjustment, I mean a *selective adjustability*. It is of course essential that, on the basis of independent and intelligent choice, man shall be capable of adjusting where adjustment is wholesomely desirable. Rigid unadjustability may be, and often is, a sign of pathological conditions, of blind prejudice, or of non-educability. One who is intelligent and educable can and should adjust to certain circumstances and certain changes. For example, one finds himself for the first time living among people of other racial and religious backgrounds. Or, upon marrying, he finds that there must be adjustments in habits, routine, customs, and taste if the marriage is to be preserved. A student entering college often finds the need to readjust his concept of scholarship, objective thinking, and habits of study. Moving from one country to another, one is required to adjust to innumerable conditions, tastes, customs, and concepts.

To be able to meet such changing circumstances, one must be adjustable. At the same time one must be capable of effective choice, refusing to adjust where such adjustment would mean the abandonment of principle, the abnegation of responsibility, the loss of essential freedom, or the violation of another's basic rights.

A further misconception has been pointed out by Paul Woodring, who correctly notes that we sometimes mistake social conformity for psychological adjustment.[1] . . . Such a doctrine would be one of temporary expediency; something with

[1] Paul Woodring, *A Fourth of a Nation* (New York: McGraw-Hill Book Co., 1957), p. 188.

which to meet, or conform to, the prevailing social demands regardless of their worth, their significance, or their rightness.

But I do not believe that this is the doctrine of modern educational theory as taught in our colleges and universities. It is, of course, the doctrine of occasional teachers and occasional schools. For this doctrine some academicians blame John Dewey. They do so because they have not read him; for few writers have spoken more emphatically than did Dewey in his insistence upon the importance of independent choice and intellectual freedom, against "the inert, stupid" nature of the traditions or customs which "pervert learning into a willingness to follow" and into "conformity, constriction," and abandonment of the spirit of experiment and individual inquiry.[3]

Certainly it is desirable that the individual be adjusted in the sense of being effectively oriented to reality. But this orientation is not a necessary correlate of social adjustment which would require one to accept the values and standards of his time or place. To be adjusted socially in the sense that one complacently and uncritically gives assent to the mores and attitudes of his group may be, in fact, evidence of maladjustment to the larger society and its more humane needs. It even may mean that he lacks the ability to adjust constructively to the ethical or aesthetic demands of more universal scope since they would require his rejection of certain narrower group mores. It may be that, through adjustment to his group's patterns, he remains forever a contributor to that mass inertia which always drags against progress, purposeful change, and experimental inquiry.

Human progress in the intellectual and creative areas is dependent upon the spark of discontent which is struck when a creative and independent mind comes into contact with the hard crust of custom. It comes when the lone individual possessed of initiative and courage finds himself maladjusted to the pattern of social thought and has the gift of articulate and constructive dissent. His value to humanity lies in stubborn refusal to be adjusted to standards, beliefs, or values which he cannot conscientiously accept.

All of us have seen the thoroughly adjusted individual within

[3] John Dewey, *Human Nature and Conduct* (New York: Henry Holt and Co., 1922), p. 64.

some provincial circle of ignorance, narrowness, or prejudice. He conforms totally, loyally, or even fanatically to the traditions of his group. His conformity becomes blind partisanship which substitutes the strength of togetherness for the strength of rationality. As a loyal party man he may be so well adjusted to the requirements of his sub-group's conformity as to be incapable of any real vision that would embrace the needs of the total humanity. . . . For such partisanship is a type of localized *adjustment* which encourages one to abdicate his individual rights as a being capable of independent thought. It blinds him to the over-arching principles and value perspectives demanded by the free intellect.

The job of education is to help man to learn to philosophize and to do so in the fullest sense which the term implies. And philosophy is impossible for the man who has mortgaged his brain to secure a merely provincial status and approval within a massminded group of his contemporaries. It is impossible for the person who accepts the culturalistic fallacy and divests himself of individual responsibility for intellectual and ethical decision.

I believe that the majority of educators, when they plead the importance of adjustment on the part of the child, are speaking with reference to adjustment in the clinical sense of the child's inner personality integration. Concerning the need for this type of adjustment there can be no argument. Here we refer to the child's consistency of emotional-intellectual balance, his ability to exercise self control, to evaluate himself, to face reality. Failure in this regard may be traceable to various factors, physiological or environmental. An endocrinological imbalance, for example, may be at the root of a child's maladjustment. A too great sensitivity may be a factor. Attitudes and fears implanted by misinformed parents likewise may be responsible, as may extreme differences between the student's learning capacity and the capacities of his classmates. Emotional and mental disturbances are known to be involved in the maladjustment of some cases, and to result in extreme withdrawal, isolation, aggression, and other behaviors which bring many cases to the attention of clinical specialists. When educators speak of the importance of securing better adjustment of the child in these cases, they are speaking of the need for inner adjustment and personality integration. They are not speaking of adjustment as social conformity or blind acceptance of group standards or attitudes.

In summary, it is believed here that there is need for a more careful use of the term. One should neither praise nor condemn *adjustment* without specifying the meaning he intends the word to convey. And if he refers to the uncritical acceptance of the prevailing mores or the behavior patterns and attitudes of one's group, a better term probably would be *social conformity*. If he refers to inner balance and stability of a well-integrated personality whose emotional and intellectual responses are wholesome and conducive to constructive and creative activity, he perhaps is speaking of the individual's personality adjustment or *psychological adjustment*.

If, however, one is speaking of the personal modifiability of the individual, his ability to adapt to new circumstances, and to change his habits, beliefs, and attitudes as changing circumstances require, he is speaking of *adjustability*—not *adjustment*.

Finally, if one refers to the ability and tendency to adjust one's concepts, habits, beliefs, or attitudes intelligently and selectively through rational and independent choice, one is referring to what might be more specifically termed *intelligent, selective,* or *constructive adaptability*.

Constructive adaptability should be a trait that contrasts both with blind conformity and with a rigid, inflexible (often pathological) adherence to established personal response patterns. So long as the individual is capable of wholesome and constructive adaptation, the schools should encourage the student's independence and individuality. And if he is incapable of such change, he should be considered for possible guidance and specialized clinical study.

SOME PROBLEMS IN
TEACHING VALUES

Donald G. Arnstine

. . . When we teach values, we become deliberate. We attempt
to replace or supplant the incidental conditioning process called
enculturation. The agencies most commonly charged with the
deliberate teaching of values are the home, the church, and the
school. Since the schools constitute the focus of this discussion,
it might be noted in passing that many values presented by the
schools are not deliberately taught. The administrative organization (usually patterned on the model of military efficiency), the
social climate (usually authoritarian), and the total curriculum
pattern (usually oriented toward individual rather than group
efforts and goals) all present, in an incidental, non-deliberate
way, a particular set of values. However, since the school does
not deliberately *teach* these values, those responsible for and
involved in presenting them are often under the impression that
the values are therefore not *learned*. This would be an unjustifiable assumption. Pupils probably do learn the values manifested
in these elements of the school just as they learn other values by
enculturation. This aspect of the school's role in value learning
has already received some attention,[1] and while it is surely
worthy of further study, it falls outside the scope of this paper,
which focuses on the deliberate teaching of values.

By noting that the term "teaching" implies some sort of
deliberate act, we find that the scope of value *teaching* in
schools is rather drastically reduced. We are now ready to

Reprinted from "Some Problems in Teaching Values," *Educational
Theory*, 11 (July, 1961), 158–167. By permission of the author and the
editor of *Educational Theory*.

[1] See Willard Waller, *Sociology of Teaching* (New York: John Wiley
and Sons, 1932); W. W. Charters, "The School as a Social System,"
Review of Educational Research, 22 (February, 1952), 41–50; Hilda
Taba, *School Culture* (Washington: American Council on Education,
1955); Wilbur B. Brookover, *A Sociology of Education* (New York:
American Book Co., 1955); Anselm L. Strauss, "Sociological Approach
to Educational Organizations," *School Review*, 65 (Autumn, 1957),
330–338; Myles W. Rodehaver *et al.*, *Sociology of the School* (New
York: Crowell, 1957).

consider whether the classroom teacher [teaches] values, and if so, how he does it. . . . I shall mean by the term "teaching" a performance that influences a person to act in a certain way deliberately specified by someone else; furthermore, this performance must in some way enable that person to so act, when it is appropriate, on future occasions without being similarly prompted.

Let's try out the definition. Suppose I am seated at the dinner table and my five-year-old nephew, in passing me the succotash, spills it on my lap. "Arnold," I exclaim, "if you ever do that again, I'm going to warm your backside." If on future occasions Arnold doesn't spill any more succotash (or, preferably, anything else), then he has learned. And I have taught him. My method happened to be a threat of violence. Now suppose that after he had spilled the succotash I had said, "Well, Arnold, now haven't you made a prize fool of yourself." Again, if Arnold later succeeds in passing the succotash, he has learned and I have taught him—this time by embarrassing him in front of others. I might have said, "Arnold, aren't you sorry you've spilled the succotash on my new suit?" and by shaming him have taught him. Or I might have said, "It's all right, Arnold, I know that it must be awkward for you to handle that heavy bowl," and thus have taught him by accepting him. Or I might even have said, "Look, Arnold, if you pass the bowl with *both* hands—like this—you probably won't spill any more succotash." Thus I might have taught him by explaining, or demonstrating a method of operation. I might even have taught him by saying, "Pick up the bowl, Arnold, and see if you can figure out a safer way of passing it."

It might be noted that this leaves us with a rather broad meaning for teaching. It includes threatening, embarrassing, shaming, accepting, explaining, demonstrating, stimulating, and, it might be added, propagandizing, indoctrinating, and just plain telling. Our limiting conditions are, however, that the performance must be deliberate and must call forth some observable kind of behavior on the part of the learner that can be performed relatively independently by him at some later time. Thus we do not need to distinguish between teaching and "real" teaching. The definition would usually exclude commanding, since the recipient of the command would not be expected to repeat his act unless he received another similar command. Similarly, telling would not be teaching if whoever was told had to be told again in order to repeat the act. And, of course, enculturation would not be teaching, since enculturation ordinarily implies non-deliberate processes. If this definition of teaching still seems too broad, we shall shortly see that unless it is retained, we will have to abandon our present enterprise and agree that values cannot be taught. . . . When a learner, unaided, makes choices on the basis of certain values previously presented to him, then we shall say he has been taught those values. We shall not claim that those values have been taught if the learner has been enabled only to verbally enunciate those values.

Choices are guided by values, but not always directly. More accurately, it might be said that choices are usually guided by evaluations, and sometimes by valuations (or values). A value or valuation differs from an evaluation because it is immediate —it is the direct feeling of liking or disliking, of approving or disapproving. Evaluation, on the other hand, is a conscious, intellectual, discursive process in which consequences of choices or actions are consciously weighed.[2] When we make conscious evaluations we consider alternatives and weigh consequences, but these alternatives and consequences must ultimately be considered in the light of prior valuations or values. In evaluation, we ask if this is a right or a wrong, a good or a bad thing. We may next consider the consequences of this thing, and then ask whether these consequences are good or bad. But in any situation where choices are being justified, this elaboration and evaluation of consequences eventually comes to a halt. We may decide that voting is good because it leads to popular government, and popular government is good because it leads to individual self-determination, and this is good because psychologists say it produces mental health. But we do not ask whether or not mental health is good; rather than making a judgment on, or an evaluation of, mental health, we simply accept it as good for the same reason that we immediately consent to the judg-

[2] This categorization follows Dewey's; to be more precise, it might be said that valuation is the act of asserting a value.

ment that it is better to be healthy than not to be healthy. Such an acceptance of value, which is not thought-out or discursive, but is immediate, is a valuation. To simplify matters, it will be called a value. By means of this process people universally hold food to be valuable without ever bothering to assert that they must eat food in order to stay alive, and that living is better than not living.

Valuation may occur at any stage in the process of weighing consequences, and, generally speaking, the less given to discursive thought an individual is, the earlier will he make valuations. Thus many people insist that voting is good simply because voting is good—a tautology, perhaps, but a common one and one deliberately encouraged by propaganda. Or valuation may occur at the next stage: voting is good because it leads to popular government, and popular government is good because it is democracy. At the next level, voting may be held to be good because it leads to individual self-determination, and this is a "natural right," and all "natural rights" are good. Of course, voting may be held to be bad through a similar process of evaluations and valuations.

In the process of making a choice, evaluation obviously cannot be carried on infinitely. All evaluations must ultimately be based upon valuations or values—direct and immediate non-discursive apprehensions of the good or the bad, the right or the wrong, the just or the unjust quality of things. . . .

The educational consequences of the foregoing discussion become clear when the matter is put this way: whether a proposition is an assertion of a value or an evaluation depends upon the person who is uttering the proposition. And, generally speaking, propositions that are value assertions for less sophisticated and mature people are likely to have the status of evaluations for more sophisticated people. Looked at from the other side, this is to say that less sophisticated people (e.g., younger students) can be expected to have a bigger warehouse of values. This being the case, such people have more opportunity for inconsistency among these many values.

A less sophisticated person may say, "It is good to give charity to the poor," and hold this assertion to be obvious and self-evident; for him giving charity is a value. But a more sophisticated person may say, "It is good to give charity," and add, "because if you do, there is more chance of your getting charity later on." Hence, for this person, giving charity is not a value but an evaluation—it must be justified by a value—viz., "it is good for me to receive charity." It might be noted in passing that although this latter value could itself be easily turned into an evaluation, it appears on the face of things that the less sophisticated person is the more "moral" of the two. He does not consider consequences of acts, but simply asserts propositions as values. This is, in fact, a legacy of religious thought. Moral men are good men who do not question values, but simply act automatically. But this is also a legacy of fascism and Nazism. Indeed, this kind of behavior is appropriate for simple men and children. If we want people to act in this way, there is little need to educate them about values and evaluations. As a matter of fact, the level of sophistication of small children is so undeveloped that only the crudest of evaluations can be explained to them. Little more can be done than to teach them to act consistently on the basis of what the teacher thinks are appropriate values for them to hold. As children become more mature, they can be taught more refined methods of evaluation. The merit of this suggestion lies in this—adults so taught might be enabled to make choices consistent with the values they hold. This apparently simple ability might well lead to a social revolution. . . .

If there is any sense in being concerned with the consequences of acts, then it is always reasonable to ask, "Why is such and such a value?" If considering the consequences of acts is educative, then teaching values, which is an educational endeavor, must involve the questioning of values. Of course, to do so is to hypothesize that the value in question may not be a value at all, but may be an evaluation. It would be more correct, then, to say we would be teaching evaluations. It might be added, parenthetically, that in such teaching, the more practice that is afforded in questioning what are held to be values, the more facile will be the transit between the learner's warehouse of values . . . and his choices in practical situations. Such practice could be expected to have at least two virtues. With increasing sophistication, the inventory in that warehouse might be reduced (thus reducing the possibilities for inconsistency), and, the stops on the journey between values and choices becoming more familiar, the choices that eventuate might more quickly and consistently meet the demands faced in situations that do not allow time for extended reflection and inquiry.

But when we consider the teaching of *values,* we can legitimately ask if they can be taught at all. If teaching values presents any problem, it is precisely because we are not dealing with the teaching of evaluations. On the basis of the foregoing discussion, it is clear that evaluations can be made both logically and empirically; they are either valid or invalid, true or false. Evaluations, then, can be taught in the same way that English grammar, or history, or chemistry is taught. There is, to be sure, no dearth of problems involved in this kind of teaching, but such problems are not our present concern.

Values, as distinct from evaluations, are formed non-rationally. This being the case, values cannot be taught in the same way in which evaluations, or syllogisms, or facts of the world are taught. We may teach facts about the consequences of actions or entities, but even an acquaintance with all the consequences of any given thing will provide no values. The most direct way of teaching values, then, is to bash in the head of the learner until his values are those of his teacher's. While this method is still common practice among allegedly civilized people, a subtler kind of conditioned response is more often resorted to: the learner repeatedly meets misfortune by behaving in accordance with what his teacher considers the wrong values, and finds success in acting in accordance with his teacher's notion of the right values. This method is sometimes called "learning by experience." A variant of the use of experience in teaching values involves the deliberate use of the value norms of the student's peer group. In this case, the student's success is measured in terms of the degree of acceptance in the group he achieves by acting in accordance with the values of that group. By acting on the basis of different values, his being rejected or feeling rejected by the group constitutes failure.

Another way to teach values is through the constant verbal repetition of them. If violence is to be foregone, and the learner has no opportunity to behave in accordance with the values he is supposed to be learning, he may learn to behave at some future time in accordance with them by simply hearing them over and over again. This is called "learning by precept," and though its unaided use (without, for example, the support of aesthetic cues) has proved a dismal failure for three thousand years, it is still an immensely popular method of attempting to teach values in schools, in the home, and in religious institutions.

Finally, values can be taught by putting the learner into close social contact with an individual who behaves in accordance with what the teacher considers the right values (this person may be the teacher himself), and who is himself judged to be "good" by the learner. This is called "learning by example" or by imitation, and depends for its usefulness upon the learner's having made the prior valuation that the model provided for imitation is "good" or acceptable, and upon the availability of appropriate models. . . .

The method of teaching values that have been discussed—force, experience, precept, and imitation—are marked by serious limitations when they are employed in a school situation. While many parents still inculcate values in their children by means of force, the practice is publicly disapproved, and an occasional court case still appears in which a teacher is arraigned for laying hands on a student.

Teaching values by experience is an effective procedure, but it suffers from some drawbacks that limit its effective use in schools. Experience is not always conveniently generalized, and experiences tending to promote the inculcation of many kinds of important values cannot be had in the schools. . . . The football coach may bench a player for using his fists in a scrimmage, but it will come as no surprise to the basketball coach if that same player uses his elbows on the basketball court. And the English teacher would hardly expect disciplinary action on the athletic field to discourage that student from copying his neighbor's examination paper.

There is another serious drawback in teaching values by experience in the schools, for it must be allowed that many kinds of values, including several whose absence would lead to social chaos, can find no illustration in a school situation. Thus the school cannot easily afford opportunities for rewarding or punishing behavior involving values concerned with business economics, sex, many kinds of group memberships (especially the family), and so forth.

Finally, the use of group pressures to inculcate certain value choices in individuals presents some problems. If the values that the teacher wants to teach are already held by the overwhelming majority of students, then, of course, group pressures toward conformity will operate without any teaching. On the other hand, if the values the teacher wants to teach are not held by the majority of the group, then the teacher will have to resort to some other of the methods previously indicated in order to teach the values in question. In this case the efficacy of the pressures of group norms on individuals is at a minimum, and such norms only begin to operate on the more recalcitrant individuals after the group has begun to indicate acceptance of the desired values. Teaching values by experience in schools is possible, then, but it has its limitations, and cannot be depended upon as the school's sole means of value inculcation.

The fruitlessness of teaching values by precept has already been noted. Valuations are immediately felt and are not subject to truth or falsity in the way that logical or scientific statements are. For this reason values cannot be inculcated verbally as knowledge is dispensed: all that can be done is to dispense knowledge *about* values which, as has been seen, may have little to do with the subsequent behavior of the learner. . . . We would not be inclined to say that values have been taught if the only observable result on the learner's behavior were correct verbal responses on examination questions.

Teaching values by imitation is theoretically possible in the school where, presumably, the teacher would serve as the value model. However, the conditions of such learning are not easy to fulfill. First, the teacher must himself be an appropriate model. This is not always possible in view of the fact that teachers have as many personal shortcomings as anybody else. Furthermore, there is far from anything like agreement in the contemporary United States as to what constitutes an appropriate model. Finally, the teacher-as-model will not get an opportunity to demonstrate in the classroom many of the virtues which are of greatest importance for society.

The second condition making learning from a model difficult is that, even given a teacher who can serve as an appropriate model for imitation, the question as to whether the values demonstrated will be taught depends, ultimately, on whether that model accords with the students' prior valuations. Children have made many important valuations before they ever get to the school, against which they will compare, consciously or not, any model presented to them. The child who brings his racial prejudices to school with him is likely to disparage rather than imitate the teacher who is a model of racial tolerance in his equal treatment of white and Negro students. To take another illustration, the board of education may think that it's good to be neat, and the teacher may be a living model of such a value, but if the people whom his students have beforehand learned to respect and prize are not neat, there is little likelihood that the virtue of neatness will be learned.

Finally, there is another, broader problem that will make the teaching of values more difficult no matter which of the methods discussed is used. Obviously, if the teacher wishes to teach only those values already being learned by children through normal processes of enculturation, then there will hardly be any necessity for teaching at all. He can, at most, reinforce those enculturated values. If on the other hand the values to be taught in school are contradictory to those learned outside of school, some conflict must necessarily be engendered in the students. They may verbally accept values that oppose one another, but they cannot act on the basis of opposing values. In such cases of conflict, pupils must reject values learned through enculturation if they are to make choices on the basis of those taught by the school. This faces us with a rather imposing problem, for the out-of-school influences on value formation are strong, the more so because they usually operate without being noticed. This being the case, it would seem almost hopeless for any individual teacher to presume to teach, singlehanded, values opposed to any that are learned by the massive weight of culture. It would appear, in general, that little or no value teaching in these conflicting instances will take place unless most teachers are in general agreement about which values they want to teach. While this suggestion offers no guarantee that values will be taught, it seems a reasonable one if the assumption is correct that the influence of many teachers acting in concert is stronger than that of individual teachers acting at cross-purposes. With but few exceptions, one teacher standing alone is no match for the force of enculturation. To promote discussion of values among teachers thus becomes an important task of educational leadership.

A final point needs mentioning. It is probably not sufficient simply to teach one set of values as if they were superior to another set of values that has already been inculcated. If a value is to be taught positively, it is not enough that the force of its contrary be simply ignored. It will be necessary to point out why the value taught is in some way better than its opposite. But such a procedure involves the criticism of values held to be undesirable. As we have already seen, however, values as such cannot be criticized; they are immediately held, need no support, and brook no criticism. Criticism of values thought undesirable, then, is only possible by hypothesizing them to be evaluations, and examining and criticizing these. One last, rather crude example will serve to illustrate this point.

Suppose a pupil habitually avoids group work, and for the most part prefers to work by himself, often at rather outlandish projects that promise little success. Contemporary parents may recommend that such a child be encouraged in every way possible to join the group and participate in its projects. This recommendation will be based on a value, and while several different ones may be offered, one of them is sure to be that it isn't good for anyone to be too different. This proposition will be reflected in the behavior of their children, and may even be verbalized by many of them. Like their parents, they hold it to be a value; no need is felt to justify it. But if the teacher is to exert a contrary influence, he probably will have to do more than simply teach an opposing value. The entrenched value must be treated as hypothetical—as an evaluation. If the teacher opposes the belief that it isn't good for anyone to be different, he must ask himself, and his class, "Different in what respects?" And finally, he must ask, "Why not?"

Further reading

Champlin, N., "Value Inquiry and the Philosophy of Education," *Educational Leadership,* 13 (May, 1956), 467–473.

Dupuis, A. M., "Group Dynamics: Some Ethical Presuppositions," *Harvard Educational Review,* 27 (Summer, 1957), 210–219.

Ladd, E. T., "The Perplexities of the Problem of Keeping Order," *Harvard Educational Review,* 28 (Winter, 1958), 19–28.

Read, H., "The Aesthetic Basis of Discipline and Morality," in *Education Through Art* (London: Faber and Faber, 1943), pp. 265–278.

DEVELOPING CHARACTER

When it is demanded that learning should develop character, i.e., when teaching and learning activities are intended to develop the pupil's mind and when it is also deemed desirable to affect his future conduct and life in society, then the educational problems become the philosophical issues of value theory, ethics, esthetics, and social philosophy. What is value? What is valuable? What is beautiful? What is good? What is right? What is the good life? What is the good society?

A number of writers of major importance maintain that education is basically and most fundamentally a moral undertaking. All teaching and learning activities affect the pupil's conduct and life and the future society for better or for worse. Ascertaining which is better and which worse is the whole problem, they say, and it is a far more difficult problem than many would-be moralists imagine. It is more difficult than saying fine words and engaging in mutual approval and being self-righteous. The philosophers of education who maintain that education is essentially a moral endeavor have not been, by and large, militant, zealous missionaries, for they come to their conclusion as a result of evaluational thinking and mean it in a profound way.

This view of the primacy of the moral dimension of education would hold that both previously considered dimensions of education take direction from this one: epistemological and metaphysical considerations are of secondary importance to axiological considerations. The view says that regardless of disagreements that may exist about the nature of the good life and the good society and how to promote them through teaching and learning activities, nevertheless that is what the latter are all about. As Maccia suggests, determining the kind of learning that should be promoted in the classroom is first of all a matter of ethics and social philosophy, for it is in ethics that one decides in favor of logical goodness and truth and that the pupil's learnings should constitute knowings. And it is in social philosophy that one decides that the schools should promote the good life in the good society. These decisions are not as obvious as they may seem, for there are ethics that decide against logical goodness in favor of beauty or public opinion or economic advantage or faith, and there are social philosophies that decide against truth in favor of myth and propaganda. Finally, there are criteria of truth acceptable to contemporary epistemologists in philosophy of science that tend to equate logical goodness with beauty—beauty is truth and truth, beauty—when symmetry and simplicity of explanation and theory construction are major criteria of a scientific theory.

Be this as it may, the axiological dimension of teaching and learning is closely related to the epistemological and metaphysical dimensions. The previously noted difficulty of ascertaining which dimension is primary increases with the appearance of the third member of the trinity. Three in one, but which one? Does any answer merely yield a point of view? Perhaps, and perhaps the major differences between philosophies of education are related to the choice made about the relative significance to be attributed to the dimensions. Broudy, for example, tends to consider the epistemological dimension as primary, Gentile and Horne centralize the metaphysical dimension, and Dewey focuses upon the axiological dimension, particularly upon social philosophy.

The close connection between the cognitive and moral dimensions of teaching and learning is exemplified by the following selections. Perhaps they indicate as well that the cognitive and moral aspects of education are inseparable, and that consideration of the two as separate dimensions is wrong-headed. Perhaps this suggestion can be expanded to include the metaphysical dimension. Then instead of three in one, perhaps the solution to the problem of deciding which dimension should be considered primary is a matter of finding one in three. Perhaps instead of beginning with three dimensions of teaching and learning and then trying to estimate which is most important and can serve to unify the others, perhaps there is simply education, now considered from one facet, now considered from the other. Or would this be a metaphysical claim? If so, would it make the metaphysical dimension central? Or are there a number of ways of settling this matter, the philosophical being only one of them, and perhaps not the most decisive?

In the following selections, the progression is from Dewey's view that values, just like other learnings, should be learned experientially, to Gentile's view that values, just like other learnings, should be learned by spiritual activity. The progression is from centralizing the moral dimension of the teaching and learning situation to decentralizing the dimension in favor of another: it is from recommending the full participation of the pupil, through relying more and more on subject matter to transmit values, to a view legitimatizing the dominance of the teacher. The procedures recommended to enable the pupil to insure that his valuing constitutes evaluating vary accordingly. In addition to noting these procedures, the authors should be compared for their views on (a) the nature of values; (b) the nature of the good life and/or the good society; (c) the relation of moral and social values to intellectual values; (d) the relation of conduct in learning to conduct in later life; and (e) the relation of developing character to developing and disciplining the mind. The last item suggests the value of attempting to decide which of the three dimensions, if any, should be of primary concern.

An inability to resolve this problem, however, is no cause for dismay. It wreaks havoc with the very best minds. Should the ambiguity become too threatening to tolerate, one can always tear up the book—which won't solve the problem. Or one can follow the prevalent practice of thinking of something else, which won't solve the problem either. Or one can turn to the next section, which will also fail to solve the problem. It will, however, deepen the problematic insofar as the selection there enables one to see, from a certain perspective, the three dimensions functioning together.

LEARNING AS SOCIALIZING

John Dewey

I shall commence, however, with the old question of individual freedom and social control. . . .

It is often well in considering educational problems to get a start by temporarily ignoring the school and thinking of other human situations. I take it that no one would deny that the ordinary good citizen is as a matter of fact subject to a great deal of social control and that a considerable part of this control is not felt to involve restriction of personal freedom. Even the theoretical anarchist, whose philosophy commits him to the idea that state or government control is an unmitigated evil, believes that with abolition of the political state other forms of social control would operate: indeed, his opposition to governmental regulation springs from his belief that other and to him more normal modes of control would operate with abolition of the state.

Without taking up this extreme position, let us note some examples of social control that operate in everyday life, and then look for the principle underlying them. Let us begin with the young people themselves. Children at recess or after school play games. . . . The games involve rules, and these rules order their conduct. The games do not go on haphazardly or by a succession of improvisations. Without rules there is no game. If disputes arise there is an umpire to appeal to, or discussion and a kind of arbitration are means to a decision; otherwise the game is broken up and comes to an end.

There are certain fairly obvious controlling features of such situations to which I want to call attention. The first is that the rules are a part of the game. They are not outside of it. No rules, then no game; different rules, then a different game. As long as the game goes on with a reasonable smoothness, the players do not feel that they are submitting to external imposi-

Reprinted from *Experience and Education,* Collier Edition (New York: Macmillan, 1938), pp. 52–60, 67–72. By permission of Kappa Delta Pi, An Honor Society in Education, owner of the copyright.

tion but that they are playing the game. In the second place an individual may at times feel that a decision isn't fair and he may even get angry. But he is not objecting to a rule but to what he claims is a violation of it, to some one-sided and unfair action. In the third place, the rules, and hence the conduct of the game, are fairly standardized. . . . An element that is conventional is pretty strong. Usually, a group of youngsters change the rules by which they play only when the adult group to which they look for models have themselves made a change in the rules, while the change made by the elders is at least supposed to conduce to making the game more skillful or more interesting to the spectators.

Now the general conclusion I would draw is that control of individual actions is effected by the whole situation in which individuals are involved, in which they share, and of which they are co-operative or interacting parts. For even in a competitive game there is a certain kind of participation, of sharing in a common experience. Stated the other way around, those who take part do not feel that they are bossed by an individual person or are being subjected to the will of some outside superior person. When violent disputes do arise, it is usually on the alleged ground that the umpire or some other person on the other side is being unfair, in other words, that in such cases some individual is trying to impose his individual will on someone else.

It may seem to be putting too heavy a load upon a single case to argue that this instance illustrates the general principle of social control of the individuals without the violation of freedom. But if the matter were followed out through a number of cases, I think the conclusion that this particular instance does illustrate a general principle would be justified. Games are generally competitive. If we took instances of co-operative activities in which all members of a group take part, as for example in well-ordered family life in which there is mutual confidence, the point would be even clearer. In all such cases it is not the will or desire of any one person which establishes order but the moving spirit of the whole group. The control is social, but individuals are parts of a community, not outside of it.

I do not mean by this that there are no occasions upon which the authority of, say, the parent does not have to intervene and exercise fairly direct control. But I do say that, in the first place, the number of these occasions is slight in comparison with the number of those in which the control is exercised by situations in which all take part. And what is even more important, the authority in question when exercised in a well-regulated household or other community group is not a manifestation of merely personal will; the parent or teacher exercises it as the representative and agent of the interests of the group as a whole. With respect to the first point, in a well-ordered school the main reliance for control of this and that individual is upon the activities carried on and upon the situations in which these activities are maintained. The teacher reduces to a minimum the occasions in which he or she has to exercise authority in a personal way. When it is necessary, in the second place, to speak and act firmly, it is done in behalf of the interest of the group, not as an exhibition of personal power. This makes the difference between action which is arbitrary and that which is just and fair.

Moreover, it is not necessary that the difference should be formulated in words, by either teacher or the young, in order to be felt in experience. The number of children who do not feel the difference (even if they cannot articulate it and reduce it to an intellectual principle) between action that is motivated by personal power and desire to dictate and action that is fair, because in the interest of all, is small. I should even be willing to say that upon the whole children are more sensitive to the signs and symptoms of this difference than are adults. Children learn the difference when playing with one another. They are willing, often too willing if anything, to take suggestions from one child and let him be a leader if his conduct adds to the experienced value of what they are doing, while they resent the attempt at dictation. Then they often withdraw and when asked why, say that it is because so-and-so "is too bossy."

I do not wish to refer to the traditional school in ways which set up a caricature in lieu of a picture. But I think it is fair to say that one reason the personal commands of the teacher so often played an undue role and a reason why the order which existed was so much a matter of sheer obedience to the will of an adult was because the situation almost forced it upon the teacher. The school was not a group or community held together by participation in common activities. Consequently, the normal, proper conditions of control were lacking. Their absence was made up for, and to a considerable extent had to be made up for, by the direct intervention of the teacher, who, as the saying went, *"kept* order." He kept it because order was in the teacher's keeping, instead of residing in the shared work being done.

The conclusion is that . . . the primary source of social control resides in the very nature of the work done as a social enterprise in which all individuals have an opportunity to contribute and to which all feel a responsibility. Most children are naturally "sociable." Isolation is even more irksome to them than to adults. A genuine community life has its ground in this natural sociability. But community life does not organize itself in an enduring way purely spontaneously. It requires thought and planning ahead. The educator is responsible for a knowledge of individuals and for a knowledge of subject-matter that will enable activities to be selected which lend themselves to social organization, an organization in which all individuals have an opportunity to contribute something, and in which the activities in which all participate are the chief carrier of control.

I am not romantic enough about the young to suppose that every pupil will respond or that any child of normally strong impulses will respond on every occasion. . . . But it is certain that the general principle of social control cannot be predicated upon such cases. It is also true that no general rule can be laid down for dealing with such cases. The teacher has to deal with them individually. . . .

Exceptions rarely prove a rule or give a clew to what the rule should be. I would not, therefore, attach too much importance to these exceptional cases. . . . I do not think weakness in control when it is found in progressive schools arises in any event from these exceptional cases. It is much more likely to arise from failure to arrange in advance for the kind of work (by which I mean all kinds of activities engaged in) which will create situations that of themselves tend to exercise control over what this, that, and the other pupil does and how he does it. This failure most often goes back to lack of sufficiently thoughtful planning in advance. The causes for such lack are varied. The one which is peculiarly important to mention in this connection is the idea that such advance planning is unnecessary and even that it is inherently hostile to the legitimate freedom of those being instructed.

Now, of course, it is quite possible to have preparatory planning by the teacher done in such a rigid and intellectually inflexible fashion that it does result in adult imposition, which is none the less external because executed with tact and the semblance of respect for individual freedom. But this kind of planning does not follow inherently from the principle involved. I do not know what the greater maturity of the teacher and the teacher's greater knowledge of the world, of subject-matters, and of individuals is for, unless the teacher can arrange conditions that are conducive to community activity and to organization which exercises control over individual impulses by the mere fact that all are engaged in communal projects. Because the kind of advance planning heretofore engaged in has been so routine as to leave little room for the free play of individual thinking or for contributions due to distinctive individual experience, it does not follow that all planning must be rejected. On the contrary, there is incumbent upon the educator the duty of instituting a much more intelligent, and consequently more difficult, kind of planning. He must survey the capacities and needs of the particular set of individuals with whom he is dealing and must at the same time arrange the conditions which provide the subject-matter or content for experiences that satisfy these needs and develop these capacities. The planning must be flexible enough to permit free play for individuality of experience and yet firm enough to give direction towards continuous development of power. . . .

The principle that development of experience comes about through interaction means that education is essentially a social process. This quality is realized in the degree in which individuals form a community group. It is absurd to exclude the teacher from membership in the group. As the most mature member of the group he has a peculiar responsibility for the conduct of the interactions and intercommunications which are the very life of the group as a community. That children are individuals whose freedom should be respected while the more mature person should have no freedom as an individual is an idea too absurd to require refutation. The tendency to exclude the teacher from a positive and leading share in the direction of the activities of the community of which he is a member is another instance of reaction from one extreme to another. When pupils were a class rather than a social group, the teacher necessarily acted largely from the outside, not as a director of processes of exchange in which all had a share. When education is based upon experience, and educative experience is seen to be a social process, the situation changes radically. The teacher loses the position of external boss or dictator but takes on that of leader of group activities.

In discussing the conduct of games as an example of normal social control, reference was made to the presence of a standardized conventional factor. The counterpart of this factor in school life is found in the question of manners, especially of good manners in the manifestations of politeness and courtesy. The more we know about customs in different parts of the world at different times in the history of mankind, the more we learn how much manners differ from place to place and time to time. This fact proves that there is a large conventional factor involved. But there is no group at any time or place which does not have some code of manners as, for example, with respect to proper ways of greeting other persons. The particular form a convention takes has nothing fixed and absolute about it. But the existence of some form of convention is not itself a convention. It is a uniform attendant of all social relationships. . . .

It is possible, of course, for these social forms to become, as we say, "mere formalities." They may become merely outward show with no meaning behind them. But the avoidance of empty ritualistic forms of social intercourse does not mean the rejection of every formal element. It rather indicates the need for development of forms of intercourse that are inherently appropriate to social situations. Visitors to some progressive schools are shocked by the lack of manners they come across. One who knows the situation better is aware that to some extent their absence is due to the eager interest of children to go on with what they are doing. In their eagerness they may, for example, bump into each other and into visitors with no word of apology. One might say that this condition is better than a display of merely external punctilio accompanying intellectual and emotional lack of interest in school work. But it also represents a failure in education, a failure to learn one of the most important lessons of life, that of mutual accommodation and adaptation. Education is going on in a one-sided way, for attitudes and habits are in process of formation that stand in the way of the future learning that springs from easy and ready contact and communication with others. . . . It is, then, a sound instinct which identifies freedom with power to frame purposes and to execute or carry into effect purposes so framed. Such freedom is in turn identical with self-control; for the formation of purposes and the organization of means to execute them are the work of intelligence. Plato once defined a slave as the person who executes the purposes of another, and, as has just been said, a person is also a slave who is enslaved to his own blind desires. . . . There is no defect in traditional education greater than its failure to secure the active co-operation of the pupil in construction of the purposes involved in his studying. . . . The more their educational importance is emphasized, the more important it is to understand what a purpose is, how it arises, and how it functions in experience.

A genuine purpose always starts with an impulse. Obstruction of the immediate execution of an impulse converts it into a desire. Nevertheless neither impulse nor desire is itself a purpose. A purpose is an end-view. That is, it involves foresight of the consequences which will result from acting upon impulse. Foresight of consequences . . . involves (1) observation of surrounding conditions; (2) knowledge of what has happened in similar situations in the past, a knowledge obtained partly by recollection and partly from the information, advice, and warning of those who have had a wider experience; and (3) judgment which puts together what is observed and what is recalled to see what they signify. A purpose differs from an original impulse and desire through its translation into a plan and method of action based upon foresight of the consequences of acting under given observed conditions in a certain way.

The crucial educational problem is that of procuring the postponement of immediate action upon desire until observation and judgment have intervened. Unless I am mistaken, this point is definitely relevant to the conduct of progressive schools. Overemphasis upon activity as an end, instead of upon *intelligent* activity, leads to identification of freedom with immediate execution of impulses and desires. This identification is justified by a confusion of impulse with purpose, although, as has just been said, there is no purpose unless overt action is postponed until there is foresight of the consequences of carrying the impulse into execution—a foresight that is impossible without observation, information, and judgment. Mere foresight, even if it takes the form of accurate prediction, is not, of course, enough. The intellectual anticipation, the idea of consequences, must blend with desire and impulse to acquire moving force. It then gives direction to what otherwise is blind, while desire gives ideas impetus and momentum. An idea then becomes a plan in and for an activity to be carried out. . . .

Traditional education tended to ignore the importance of personal impulse and desire as moving springs. But this is no reason why progressive education should identify impulse and desire with purpose and thereby pass lightly over the need for careful observation, for wide range of information, and for judgment if students are to share in the formation of the purposes which activate them. In an *educational* scheme, the occurrence of a desire and impulse is not the final end. It is an occasion and a demand for the formation of a plan and method of activity. Such a plan, to repeat, can be formed only by study of conditions and by securing all relevant information.

The teacher's business is to see that the occasion is taken advantage of. Since freedom resides in the operations of intelligent observation and judgment by which a purpose is developed, guidance given by the teacher to the exercise of the pupils' intelligence is an aid to freedom, not a restriction upon it. Sometimes teachers seem to be afraid even to make suggestions to the members of a group as to what they should do. . . . But what is more important is that the suggestion upon which pupils act must in any case come from somewhere. It is impossible to understand why a suggestion from one who has a larger experience and a wider horizon should not be at least as valid as a suggestion arising from some more or less accidental source.

It is possible of course to abuse the office, and to force the activity of the young into channels which express the teacher's purpose rather than that of the pupils. But the way to avoid this danger is not for the adult to withdraw entirely. The way is, first, for the teacher to be intelligently aware of the capacities, needs, and past experiences of those under instruction, and, secondly, to allow the suggestion made to develop into a plan and project by means of the further suggestions contributed and organized into a whole by the members of the group. The plan, in other words, is a co-operative enterprise, not a dictation. The teacher's suggestion . . . is a starting point to be developed into a plan through contributions from the experience of all engaged in the learning process. The development occurs through reciprocal give-and-take, the teacher taking but not being afraid also to give. The essential point is that the purpose grow and take shape through the process of social intelligence.

LEARNING AS LOVING

F. J. J. Buytendijk

No other word has so much power to divert the mind of man from the fatigues of toil, from cares, from the hazards of emotional involvements, from all selfishness and meanness, as the word freedom. The magic power of this word is so great that the burning desire for freedom is not merely an appeal to a well-determined concept, but it opens a door to another climate. In the name of freedom the most sublime sacrifices and the most revolting injustices have been committed. No one knows exactly what freedom is, but all consider it as the sovereign good. Humanity's history and each particular man's history are exclusively determined by their relation to freedom.

When Bergson declares: "Freedom is a fact, and among the facts we know, there is none more clear," [1] the word "clear" does not here mean the clarity of an intellectual thought, but that of a cloudless sky. It is the clarity of pure spirituality, which does not let itself be grasped nor fixed by any concept. If freedom is the supreme good, if it is man's dignity and his ultimate goal, we may easily understand that any educator must of necessity set for himself the problem of learning how the child may be made to participate in this supreme good.

The aims and ideals of education have changed in vain—the tendency to give to man his most noble form remains invariable. That means our aim is to give him a free existence. However, the ethic and the pathetic of education are threatened with losing their animating force if we ignore the conditions which must be fulfilled in order to bring about true freedom, moral freedom.

In order to know the general and basic nature of these conditions, we must examine the development of the consciousness of freedom in the child. That is why I take the liberty of

Reprinted from "Experienced Freedom and Moral Freedom in the Child's Consciousness," *Educational Theory,* 3 (January, 1953), 1–13. By permission of the author and the editor of *Educational Theory.*

[1] Henri Bergson, *Essai sur les données immediates de la conscience* (Paris: P. U. F., 43° edition, 1944), p. 166.

drawing attention to the relation of experienced freedom and moral freedom. To this end, we need to answer coherently the following questions.

In what situations does the consciousness of freedom appear for the first time in the child? How is this primary experienced freedom anchored and rooted in the unconscious life? Can experienced freedom be changed by itself into moral freedom? Is the basis of the latter also in the original relations of the child with his environment? How can education reinforce moral freedom so that it becomes a life experience of the child, integrated to the totality of his personal development; that is to say, by what means will moral freedom be vitalized or life entirely humanized? . . . I wish only to try to clarify the relationship between experienced freedom and moral freedom, in the light of the questions posed above, starting from the essential character of the child's existence. Thus I hope to be able to contribute, in some small measure, to a clarification of the theoretical basis of education in true freedom.

But first we must state how, in our sense, the problem is related to the sciences and to philosophy. The positive sciences as well as philosophy often present a serious danger for education, a danger which is far from imaginary. The proof is seen in the way the fundamental principles of education have been fought and contested. We have had, of course, in this discussion often to depend on the authority of results in biology and physiology; but it has often not been well understood that the child—although he differs very much from the adult—must be considered, first of all, as a human being. That means that he is not merely an example of a natural species, but the representative of an historical idea.[2]

In any case, the child is specifically human from the moment when he first turns his gaze toward people and objects and when he expresses the blossoming of his human nature in his first smile. Already, in that hesitant response, the child is building for himself the beginning of his being, and at that moment he surpasses the limits of unconscious life and the laws of nature.[3]

[2] Maurice Merleau-Ponty, *Phénoménologie de la perception* (Paris: N. R. F., 1945).
[3] F. J. J. Buytendijk, "Das erste Lacheln des Kindes," *Zeitschrift "Psyche,"* II (1947), p. 57.

Only the teacher who takes account of the human nature of the child, expressing itself in his existence from the beginning, will be protected against the danger of biologism and naturalism. The positive sciences will never be able to convince such a teacher that the human being, in his earliest years, is only an organism which develops and reacts to the stimulations of the environment.

From the moment we discover human reality in the child, we also meet the irreducible phenomenon of limited freedom. From the moment when consciousness is aroused, there is a choice of world, a projection of world. "To be born, is to be born *of* the world and *to* the world at the same time. . . ." "Thus there is never determinism," but on the other hand there is "never absolute choice.". . . "The idea of situation excludes absolute freedom at the beginning of our operations.". . . "We choose our world and the world chooses us." [4]

Modern education should take these thoughts on the essence of human reality as directives, in order to be able to approach, at a more favorable time, the old problem of free education, of freedom. Now the result of this way of doing is threatened not only by the inadmissible parallel between the development of the child and animal life, but also by the danger of an unnecessary confusion of pedagogy and metaphysical problems. Although we should recognize that philosophy is capable of discovering the "essentia abstracta" of man, the "essentia concreta" never precedes existence. Man is always what he does and what he has done in his intentional relations with the world.

Philosophy can of course acquaint us with human possibilities, but it can never reveal the reality of the existence of a concrete man. And it is precisely this reality of existence which we must know if we are called upon to aid the development of a child to his true dignity as a human being. Thus we may see why the problem of education directed toward freedom cannot be clarified by a metaphysical discussion of arbitrary freedom or determinism or indeterminism. All philosophic speculation is sterile in an investigation of the relation of experienced freedom to moral freedom. We must rather be oriented toward the concreteness of the child's existence.

[4] Merleau-Ponty, *loc. cit.,* pp. 517–518.

Concerning this existence we may state that it is formed by autonomous activity, the initiative of the mind. The child, like all mankind—of whatever age or condition—is essentially characterized by the fact that, through the manifestation of his freedom, he is given his nature as well as his grasp of the world, his ethical principles, and consequently his system of values.

At the same time that the child is forming his own world, he is giving a direction to his physical being and lending it a power which the body does not naturally possess. The choice which the child of necessity makes in the different situations which his environment presents to him must be confirmed, corrected, or revoked at every instant of his life.

Thus M. de Petter [5] is right when he says that the essentially educative act is that of the subject himself, by which he himself is formed, in his vital and autonomous activity, by all which he has recognized and appreciated as having a value in itself. These considerations show us clearly that education differs, because of the necessity for the fulfillment of moral freedom, from any form of training. Neither the positive sciences nor metaphysical speculations have any decisive influence on our research. . . .

The human being of the child is fulfilled only through his existence, his being *in* the world and *for* the world, through his physical being. In this existence, the consciousness of the child becomes at the same time consciousness of the world and consciousness of self, that is to say, consciousness of his initiative, of his autonomy and of his independence.

Doubtless, the child lacks, at the beginning of his life, any clear image of self and consequently of his freedom, but he discovers himself to be free even in his random activities, although he has only a quite nebulous and diffuse sensation of this freedom. This consciousness is the first consciousness of experienced freedom. The soil in which this freedom can take root is offered to the child by the body and it is nourished by the animal life in which he participates.

That is why this first consciousness of freedom is so strong in the healthy child. In him, vivacity and a spontaneous bent toward movement are clearly manifested. To be more than a

<hr>

[5] De Petter, *Studia Catholica* (1948), p. 51.

feeling of force and health, to become an experienced freedom, this vital spontaneity, at this stage of the child's development, must be considered as a possible refusal. It must first of all mean a resistance to being governed, then later an upsetting of the order of things, and finally it must mean a revolt against the order. Let us try more precisely to define this first way in which experienced freedom is presented to us.

In the first place, we may state that this first phase of experienced freedom is not the consciousness of true freedom, that is to say of that freedom "indissolubly, essentially attached to the mind," and which "is real only when it defends itself and conquers itself." There can be no question of this in the first phase.

In the second place, we may state that primary experienced freedom depends on emotional dynamism. Le Senne has thrown light very well on the difference between freedom of initiative and freedom of power. This latter is realized only in proportion as reason and, generally, value, confer it. "In this sense, Erostratus, who set fire to the temple of Ephesus, was not free; he was the slave of his passions and of his errors.—He was free in the sense of freedom of initiative—he was free in the sense that he would have been able not to set fire to the temple." [10]

It nevertheless seems to me that Erostratus was not entirely determined by his passions, but that he chose rebellion and revolt against a reasonable moral order and that he wished to set them in the context of a world projected in its totality as refusal. This projecting of a world of refusal, in which the person becomes involved and to which he submits, means the choice of primitive experienced freedom. Thus we define it more precisely as the *freedom of caprice and of revolt.*

There is in every man, and certainly in every child, an almost unquenchable need for the experiencing of this irrational freedom—a freedom even senseless and absurd. We recall that Dostoyevsky, in his *Memoirs of the Underground,* showed us the tragedy of this apparent freedom. The consciousness of initiative may easily evolve into consciousness of caprice, as a

[10] René Le Senne, *Introduction à la philosophie* (Paris: P. U. F., 1939), p. 49.

means of attaining the experience of a feeling which is commonly called freedom.

There is no one who is not inclined, from time to time, to assume the role of a child in revolt, in order to do "what he wants to do." Thus we are not at all surprised that the child keeps this tendency so long, if an appropriate environment and a judicious education do not offer him the means of attaining a higher stage of freedom. However, it is common knowledge that *all* children do not use revolt as the means of acquiring the feeling of the experience of freedom.

There is general agreement in recognizing that it is especially small boys who revolt, that they are more apt to follow their caprices, and that they more often attack the order and value of things. It is evident that this difference between the sexes, which is manifested even at an early age, rests on a difference of innate disposition and of education during the first years of life.

Elsewhere I have tried to show that the innate difference is manifested in the fundamental form of the dynamism. Dynamism displays a predominant tendency either toward expansion or adaptation. For this reason, the very first contacts of each sex with the world differ.

The expansive movement causes us to encounter the world as an obstacle; the adaptive movement, on the contrary, causes us to discover a world of qualities, of form, of values. The meeting of obstacles arouses, by reaction, a reinforced expansive dynamism. Thus the child, physiologically stimulated, develops a greater muscular tension, and is thereby more predisposed toward a more aggressive behavior.

This aggressiveness is not itself an innate and physiologically determined quality. It is not an inevitable outcome. Does not the teacher himself impose on the "real" little boy, strong and energetic, different demands than on the little girl? Therefore he stimulates aggressive conduct, or at least he does not modify it as much as he could.

Whereas the little girl is especially praised when her movements and occupations help her conform to the traditional image, fitting for her age, we demand, on the other hand, that the "real" boy *do* something, no matter what, so long as he acts. We prefer to see the boy, in his approach to the world, as a

builder, as a conqueror, as a dominator, a little *homo faber*
(*homunculus faber*). In my opinion, this opposition of the
sexes, artificially cultivated from early childhood, is one of the
principal faults of education. . . . However, at the beginning of
life, all activity is determined negatively rather than positively.
This may be explained by the fact that the world is not offered
to the child primarily as a structure full of meaning, but as an
obstacle and an opposition with relation to his expansive spontaneity.

This expansivity is in itself blind to all value. This means that
it has, chiefly, a negative relation toward all reality and that this
relationship immediately becomes self-conscious in the form of
revolt, as soon as anything energetically resists this expansivity.
The *thing* may be an object which bars the way in the true sense
of the word, but it may also consist of an order, a command, an
imperious look, existing *as such* for the child. But there exists
nothing for man, and consequently for the child, which may not
be projected, in its structure of meanings, by an intentional act,
or by an instance of perception, of refusal, or of acceptance.

From the moment we understand clearly this fundamental
characteristic of human existence, the relation and the difference between experienced freedom, which is primarily nothing
other than freedom of caprice and of revolt, and moral freedom,
are already somewhat apparent to us. Thus we may note that
experienced freedom cannot be expanded except through opposition to a demand emanating from the world—that is to say,
from things and people—which is understood as such, but
which is refused. Caprice and revolt are possible only with
respect to a value which seems to announce itself to be irresisti-
ble. Thus we have arrived at a first conclusion.

The small child who breaks an object, tears it up, destroys it,
who resists, who does "what he wants," is not, animal-like,
following a non-ordered and non-directed impulsiveness. The
child gives to its impulsiveness, also aroused in him by physical
stimulation, the meaning of a revolt. Therefore his acts become
really a revolt with respect to the positive values of being,
discovered and denied as such in refusal. The child is, while still
very young, a true man, and for this reason he is not a represen-

tative of a nature obedient to blind laws, but always that of a normative and consequently moral consciousness.

The mother, in her intuitive wisdom, is thus to a certain extent right when she says that the baby is "naughty" when he *gleefully* throws his plate on the floor, watching it fall with evident pleasure. However, the child who takes the initiative which first wells up in him without interior order, from his impassioned vitality, is awakened to a first human reality, to which he has a right. In this awakening, he encounters things in their apparent autonomy, their mass, their weight, their inertia, their form, their possibility of movement.

The first happiness of the child is in becoming acquainted with this autonomous world of obstacles, but he can make this acquaintance only through free activity, through his caprices. The capricious thought is both an initiative and a happenstance, at the same time a negation and an affirmation of the real value of what is encountered. This encounter is transient, because blind expansiveness admits only of itself and excludes the possibility of choice. Through the obstacle offered by things, expansive impulsiveness, as we have said, is reinforced anew, and this time in a highly reactive manner, and it may even become true aggression.

Thus we see that the primary and primitive freedom of caprice is impregnated by another aspect of freedom. It is an acquired freedom, an experienced liberation, and this is identical to the consciousness of victory and the victor. At this moment, the child enters into the *second* phase of his human reality and of his experienced freedom.

He forms his being for himself in his self-consciousness as a being of power. It is the first step on the road where man finds himself as ipseity. But a resolute attitude and an intention of freeing one's self, of conquering, presuppose, to a still higher degree than caprice, that the thing conquered will be encountered as a value—a *value which is worth the effort*. We all still retain the memory of this experience, and can always experience it anew, through the youth which never completely leaves us. Who does not know the joy and the feeling of freedom of the swimmer or the mountain-climber? I refer to such experiences for the precise purpose of disclosing the phenomenal structure of experienced freedom in the consciousness of conquest. . . .

But let us return to the development of the child. The stage which we have described as the second phase of human reality in which the child performs his actions is certainly existence as power, but it is a relative power, rendered *relative* by the situation of our power.

"The idea of situation excludes absolute freedom at the beginning of our activities," says Merleau-Ponty. To this we add: to accept a *relative freedom* is identical with accepting the reality of the world in its own value for us. By this acceptance, the child has the experience of a new characteristic of his freedom. He feels himself free only in his *own* world, the world assumed and projected as his. Things, in this world, are no longer chance obstacles and autonomous objects with respect to a blind expansiveness; they are no longer entirely dependent on the taking of initiative. They appear and are formed in their autonomy, but yet as the property of the subject, as parts of his world.

The child gains, by means of the conqueror's freedom, a relative freedom, and thereby he conquers his own world, in which he confronts a hierarchy of values. Thus the *third* phase of his development marks the appearance of another experience of freedom. To understand this phase correctly, we must understand clearly the modification which relationships undergo. To this end, we must again start from the original dynamism of the child. We have already indicated two basic types of this dynamism, namely, expansive movements and adaptive movements. These latter are endowed with less muscular tension and consequently with less rigidity of articulation, a weaker impulsiveness, and are especially characterized by the enjoyment of tactile sensations. Through his adaptive movements, the child encounters from the very first qualities and forms, that is to say, sensed values.

This valueful world in turn arouses an adaptive motility, modifies the blind expansiveness, and consequently the aggressiveness. Every child is capable of this adaptation to values. But in our traditional culture we consider interest in tactile sensations to be characteristically feminine, and consequently so consider sensitiveness to quality, to form, to color, to sounds, to weight, etc.

Researches in child psychology prove, in fact, that girls are much more capable than boys of executing delicate and subtle movements of the hands, and that they possess a greater sensorial sensitivity.

However, each normal child will acquire, if he receives an appropriate education, the experience of sensed qualities. But he will be able to appreciate them only when he has attained, toward his environment, the attitude which we have indicated as the *third* phase of existence. Certainly this does not mean that the other phases will be liquidated. All the human possibilities are ever present, and it is by virtue of the environment offered to the child by education that one possibility or another will be more or less perfectly realized. Now the existence inaugurated by adaptive dynamism is characterized by the appearance of a double and ambiguous tendency to communicate and to grasp from a distance, tendencies which are equally original.

They are both expressed by an attitude of expectation and attention. This attitude of recoil is the disposition which gives rise to attitudes of surprise, of admiration, and of respect. They are the natural consequences of the adaptive dynamism and they are the condition which must be fulfilled in order to awaken the consciousness of relative freedom.

This latter is identical to *freedom of choice,* which is the prelude to true freedom—moral freedom or freedom of action (C. Marcel). Thus there is manifested in the child, through choice and recognition of values, through surprise and admiration, the true meaning of the "absorbent mind." With M. Madinier, one may call it "a true rational instinct which appears in the first years of life." [11]

How this desire to know and to understand still remains enveloped in random consciousness may be gained from a remark by the same author: "The emotion which corresponds to this 'rational instinct' is surprise, which is nothing other than the principle of sufficient reason or of universal intelligibility, not considered as logical rule but as *vital demand.*"

[11] Gabriel Madinier, *Conscience et amour; Essai sur le "nous"* (Paris: P. U. F., 1947), p. 75.

Surprise is in truth the first expression and intimation of the "absorbent mind" which, once formed, will determine the structure of the child's existence during all of childhood.

It is interesting to note, in our investigation concerning the development of experienced freedom and its relation to moral freedom, that surprise is the source of admiration and the latter the source of respect.

We must distinguish carefully these three intentional attitudes. Surprise signifies the arrest of the consciousness before the opaque and massive factuality of a perceived object. At the same time, this arrest, which we call attention, is impregnated with a presentiment of a possible translucidity. The novelty by which one is surprised must have somewhere an already known trait, should anticipate a certain familiarity.

So far as admiration is concerned, familiarity dominates the situation; it opens the vista to a value which is encountered with a beginning of enjoyment.

This enjoyment is of another character than the joy of the conqueror or the joy accompanying the freedom of caprice. In admiration, the subject rejoices in a disinterested manner; rather, he enjoys aesthetically. He participates in the disclosed value. The objects chosen and admired enlarge his vital space, because the subject assumes the values of his own world, the world in which he is situated.

Through admiration, man enriches himself. For the child, this circumstance is of high importance. Adaptive dynamism can realize only a very few values, but admiration becomes a participation in a universe without limits; it becomes the forgetting of self in the enjoyment of a world of implicit truth and beauty. In this act of fusion, the child exteriorizes himself, and he finds his own value in the admired objects.

He participates in their intelligibility. The consciousness of freedom at the same time undergoes an essential transformation. Experienced freedom becomes the life experience of a freedom, of which "the heart dwells"—according to a profound thought expressed by M. Lavelle, "in an act of acceptance, in a *yes* which we give to being and to life." [12]

[12] Louis Lavelle, *Les puissances du moi* (Paris: Flammarion, n.d.), p. 51.

Can we call this freedom moral freedom? That depends on the emphasis of the *yes*. If this *yes* means only an affirmation, of the nature of a declaration that a value exists, there is no moral element in admiration. But it is not possible to make precise distinctions in the realm of the relations between the human mind and the world.

Admiration, especially in the child, is often at the same time respect, that is, "the disposition by which the ego recognizes the right of obligation over itself." [13]

The child who admires a design, a flower, a bird, is not an aesthete as such, but his intention surpasses pure admiration and is recognized as an obligation to admire and respect beauty, the cleverness of the designer, the mystery of life, the wisdom of the creator.

The unfolding of moral freedom in the child is accomplished in situations which arouse surprise, admiration and respect. This truly human freedom surely draws its vital energy from the experienced freedom of initiative and power. But moral freedom does not reach its full unfolding and its full fecundity until it goes beyond freedom of choice and becomes a creative activity: which implies an act for which the child decides to bear the responsibility. This act is one in which the ego accomplishes and presents itself, in its human dignity, as a personality.

The way in which the three phases of child existence and the three modes of freedom are connected may be illustrated by means of an example.

For this purpose we choose the well known picture of a child who, in a Montessori school, carries a brim-full glass of water to the teacher. Freedom of caprice is suppressed, but the freedom of the conqueror still fills the child's consciousness. At the same time, consciousness is present as the relation of the ego to the person of the teacher, beloved and respected. But it is, in particular, the experience of *objective obligation* which gives to the child experienced evidence of the beginning of his moral freedom.

This objective obligation is identical to the act of comprehending objective demands and assuming them as a responsibil-

[13] René Le Senne, *Traité de morale générale* (Paris: P. U. F., 1942), p. 575.

ity with respect to the situation. It is only through this structure of significance that true moral consciousness is formed, for the obligation proclaims the ego to be double: "*below,* the empirical ego, limited in time and space by the body which incarnates it, a given ego, having a nature resulting from a history; *above,* the ego of value, whose goal is, through obligation, to raise up the first." [14]

The dividing of the ego means only consciousness of a moral conscience and of freedom considered as moral freedom. In our example, the request of the teacher had no other aim or result than that of constructing a situation which, through its objective structure, will be easily assumed by the child as a personal obligation.

In my opinion, one of the most important contributions of Mme. Montessori is the invention of situations of an imperatively obligatory character. Through this educational method, the development of moral freedom no longer depends on the individual orders of the institutor, but is related to a world presented to the child as concrete.

The disclosure of Mme. Montessori rests on an absolute dependence on the value and intelligibility of reality. This reality appeals to the spontaneous dynamism of the child. If this appeal is addressed exclusively to the expansive dynamism, the child will develop only the consciousness of a freedom of initiative and of conquest. If on the other hand the educational situation appeals to the adaptive dynamism . . . freedom is developed in another way. The first two phases, namely freedom of caprice and that of conquest, are thrown off at the beginning of their autonomy. They will be integrated into freedom of choice. That happens from the time of the systematic exercising of sensory experiences.

At the beginning the child certainly lets himself be captured by the joy of the sensations. At the same time, consciousness, in the encounter with things, is formed into a consciousness of the valueful existence of the world. At this moment—we may even say at this historic moment—a new chapter begins in the life of the child. It is the *fourth* stage in the relation of experienced freedom to moral freedom.

---

[14] Le Senne, *Traite de morale generale,* p. 571.

In this encounter, there is more than an agreeable perception, more than admiration of a value. The "valorized" being becomes a valid state in itself which, in the situation of the encounter, presents itself as a compelling reality.

The child is appealed to, and he must, and he can, respond. By this response, his admiration will be metamorphosed into respect, his aggressiveness transformed into prudence, the things desired transubstantiated into things loved with a disinterested love. This first love of the child for things, plants, animals, comrades, means the introduction into the moral relations of the true unity of society.

"Love appears"—in the child's existence—"as the highest category and the very expression of intelligibility: if we want the world to be intelligible, we must understand it as a work of love." [15]

What the child learns through personal experience in these encounters is that "love is the very end of all things; it depends on itself and justifies itself. It does not consist in wishing well, it is *the Good* itself. It is not good, in fact, because it gives to those which it unites the meaning of exchanging values. . . ." "Values are such because love has produced them in order to fulfill itself." [16] . . . This latter gives the child the possibility of transforming, through his own initiative, experienced freedom into moral freedom. This transformation is demanded by the experience of obligation toward all the reality of his environment.

This reality contains, in a form accessible to the child by means of example, all the fundamental categories of the human world: that is, perceptions, thought, nature, and culture. While self-consciousness realizes the ego as redoubled by the obligation which is the response given to reality, the child's existence, in its ipseity, is affirmed toward the intelligibility of his world. But there is more: the child . . . is not isolated. He is in a truly human small society. The ideal reality of this society is union and peace, respect and love. . . . Children, unregimented and unconfined, modify their freedom of caprice and of conquest

[15] Madinier, *loc. cit.,* p. 83.
[16] *Ibid.,* p. 102.

under the effect of the objective power of social relations. Through their more serious cooperative tasks, through mutual aid, and also through the enjoyment of their games, the children build up the "we" as the reality within which each is responsible for the other. Thus is formed, through the experience of social relations, a moral freedom, truly experienced.

It seems useful to summarize briefly this ensemble of ideas and to note the result of our phenomenological analysis. We have encountered freedom as the pure climate in which the mind is able to develop to its full perfection. This development receives its principal force from spontaneous life, and herefrom can be manifested, through expansive dynamism, the *first* phase of experienced freedom, as freedom of caprice, with respect to which the world is only an obstacle.

As soon as this freedom takes on the meaning of a subjective resistance, we note a relationship with respect to moral freedom. By the reactive reinforcement of resistance, the primary consciousness of freedom is linked to the secondary freedom of the conqueror. In this *second* stage, the child builds his existence as power and the world as a thing which is *worth the effort,* as a relatively positive value.

Consciousness of activity is relatively free choosing, and signifies the approach of a *third* phase of the development of existence. In this stage, freedom of choice, the prelude of freedom of undertaking, is built on the basis of adaptive dynamism. Little by little the ambiguous attitude of the encounter is generally differentiated into special attitudes of surprise, of admiration, and of respect, through which moral freedom is created in the form of an acceptance of obligation which the concrete world of the child himself demands. The *fourth* stage is attained in the unity of experienced freedom and of moral freedom, in child love, and in the encounter of the "we" as a reality of responsibility.

The development of freedom which I have tried to sketch is not the natural transformation of vital spontaneity into normative conduct. It is only compelling situations which can awaken morality. But a situation can have an obligatory character only for a being already having a normative consciousness to start with.

The most perfect education is that through which integration of nature and mind is best approached and in which, consequently, life is humanized and morality vitalized. The secret . . . is the perception of the reality of love which is identical with love of reality.

LEARNING AS UNIFYING

B. Othanel Smith

. . . What is needed is a method of instruction which will develop discipline in dealing with conflicting loyalties and perspectives comparable to that now developed around the search for
facts. The nature of such a method is here indicated. It centers
in what is referred to as a *normative unit* to distinguish it from
units in which the concern is primarily with informational problems.

The normative unit is a means of studying those unsettled
situations in which people are divided over loyalties and social
goals. It deals with situations in which the ends are uncertain,
confused, or in conflict, situations in which little consideration
can be given to the problem of means without giving primary
attention to the clarification of the goals to be attained. The
personal character of the individual, as we have pointed out, is a
central factor—one of the problematic elements of the situation.
In other words, the issues studied in a normative unit involve
relations among persons. . . .

In a social problems course [1] in which the teacher developed
a normative unit on the status of the Negro in American society,
the unit began with an effort to locate the points of difficulty
within the student group. The points were revealed in various
ways—by assertions of assumed facts, statements of policy, and
affirmations of normative principles. . . .

As the teacher finally noted, the major points of conflict in
the group took forms which could be stated as follows:

Reprinted from "The Normative Unit of Instruction," *Teachers College Record,* 45 (January, 1945), 219–220, 222–229. By permission of
the author and the editor of *Teachers College Record.*
[1] The writer is indebted to Mr. S. H. Engle, University High School,
University of Illinois, for this illustrative material. It is recognized that
many teachers have taught along normative lines, doubtless with many
of the ideas expressed in this paper more or less in mind. But we have
lacked an adequate rationale, and in some cases any sort of rationale, for
such work. We have therefore been unaware of the methodological
principles which alone would enable us to develop the discipline of
character which normative problems require for solution.

"Negroes are all right if they keep their place" *versus* "Negroes are Americans like the rest of us and should have equal political, economic, and social rights."

"If Negroes want a better status, let them attain it for themselves" *versus* "It should be the responsibility of white people to help the Negroes in their struggle for freedom and equality."

These points of general policy, however, are built up in a context of other general ideas, many of them also practical in nature. A good instructional procedure will open up this context. This is a sure route into the characters of the persons involved. The teacher sensed this. He directed the students in the search for generalizations which were related in one way or another to the issue and were not at first recognized as part of the significant thinking of the group.

Some of these general ideas were suggested in the exploratory discussion, others in later discussion. Before the different types among them are located, a general list should be noted:

1. Negroes should not hold public office.
2. Whites and Negroes should be separated in street cars and trains.
3. Negroes and whites should be permitted to attend the same schools.
4. The current fair employment regulation should be continued in peace-time.
5. All men should be treated as equals regardless of race, religion, or social position.
6. Each individual should be accepted as a person and given an equal opportunity to develop to his fullest capacity.
7. Negroes and whites should be separated in the community.
8. White people should be the judges of whether Negroes are behaving properly.
9. Labor unions should admit Negroes on the same basis as they admit whites.

These practical ideas may be divided into two interrelated types: those applicable to all men, and those applicable only to Negroes or to particular circumstances. . . . These two types may be recognized as . . . (1) broad *practical generalizations* (also called general normatives) and (2) *policies*.

While this case involved differing policies, it was at the same time wrestling with broad general normatives. The one stated is seen to be a basic democratic credo. The democratic creed in America comprises just such principles of general application. Practically everybody in America accepts these general principles verbally at least; few escape their molding influence. Nevertheless, in formulating and choosing public policies and measures, persons lacking ability to see and deal with the relations between these and the broad generalizations are more strongly motivated by special interests and prejudices than by the broader generalizations. The ability to deal with the relations between policies and generalizations can be developed by giving direct attention to them. One may, for instance, learn the fallacy of affirming loyalty to the idea that men should be free while yet holding that Negroes should not be admitted freely to theaters. When a person subscribes to freedom for all men and then sees this commitment come into conflict with special policies, as it will in decision making, he can at least learn to control the impulse to act only in accordance with the latter.

The students in this case were confronted with these interrelations of general normatives and proposed policies. They found that if unreasonable loyalties are to be rooted out, these must be brought under the influence of the normative generalizations which form the heart of the democratic creed. One of the prime conditions for examining prejudices from this standpoint is a clear comprehension of the broader ideals. The verbal symbols of equality, freedom, equal opportunity, and the like often become loaded with meanings imported from specialized perspectives and interests, and hence, while they are symbols of the common good, actually operate to the exclusive advantage of special groups and classes. In the normative unit, therefore, clarification of these value terms is one of the objects of study. This clarification must be sought partly in the literature of the democratic tradition, in the writings and public utterances of the great spokesmen of democracy, and not in the narrow experiences of the class group or in the rationalizations of the defenders of partisan views and special privilege. It must be sought also through the study of the value content of democracy again and again, in conflict after conflict, in unit after unit; for the meaning of these important social-moral norms cannot be gained in isolation from concrete issues where varied interpretations of the norms come to the surface and require attention.

The class group had already studied the democratic principles in previous units, but the students were again encouraged to search for the proper meanings in this new context of racial prejudices and tensions. They read and studied valuative stories and political literature bearing upon the ideals of freedom and equality applied to minority races as well as to people in general. This study, together with class discussions, served to clarify still further the general normative principles which effective, practical intelligence requires as a part of every democratic character. In accordance with the criterion of voluntary (uncoerced) common acceptance, one of the tests of policies is their consistency with these democratic principles, for they are the expression of a sort of standing consensus. They are the community in its ideological form. This test is often confusing because advocates of both good and bad policies often seek to justify them as deductions from democratic ideals. Everyone wishes the great symbols of the people to be on his side. But this is even further reason why attention must be directed to the clarification of basic, practical generalizations and to establishing consistency between these and policies.

The students were aware of conflict and confusion in their group regarding what a more desirable state of affairs in race relations would be. They were trying to find a conception which they could hold in common. This is the first phase of a complete judgment. . . . Then . . . they repeatedly stated the facts in the case. This is the second phase. . . . Throughout the discussion they were searching for a plan or plans of action. The policies they were after were these plans of action, the plans which would move race relations toward the better state of affairs. This is the third phase. . . .

The first part of the students' discussion turned around questions of fact. In support of discriminatory policies, assertions of fact were made which as such were seriously open to question: "Negro people are not as intelligent as white people," "They were happier when they were slaves," "Negroes cannot be trusted," "They are dirty and smelly." These assertions of fact, although usually not facts at all, serve to create the illusion of sound reason and reliable authority. One who entertains such "facts" very easily defends the policy that Negroes be not admitted to theaters, restaurants, and hotels on equal terms with whites. Indeed, persons often hold these false "facts" as a *result* of emotional commitment to the discriminatory policies. . . .

What is thus true of the relation of policy to facts is often equally true of the relation between broad general principles and facts. Sometimes there is no factual support for these broad ideas. . . . At other times the factual support is there but not seen, and the broad normatives are called visionary.

The students gave much attention to the claims of factual support for the differing ideas of good policy. They were invited to supply the source of factual statements offered as evidence of the rightness of their biases. This led the group into the literature bearing upon the comparative intelligence of the races, the criminal tendencies and public behavior of Negroes and whites, and other assumed facts about races and their relations. In this activity they were learning not only how to locate facts, but also how to examine facts for their accuracy and sufficiency as evidence in support of beliefs about social realities as well as about loyalties and policies.

It is, of course, patent that indefensible ideas of policy will not necessarily melt away under the heat of facts. Such popular beliefs are reinforced by institutional arrangements, customs, personalities, and a thousand hidden irrationalisms. But by subjecting them to the test of facts, their "good" explanations —rationalizations—are unmasked and the relentless processes of erosion begin to operate. The individual will not again be able to give "good" reasons for these prejudices and judgments. He may continue to hold them, but he knows they are factually indefensible, and that is an exceedingly uncomfortable state of mind, even for the untutored. Those ideas which do have an adequate factual foundation, however, will be strengthened by it.

The movement of thought toward a decisive conclusion and program of action is the lash which makes judgments responsible and rigorous. As a result of their study of the facts and normative ideas in this case, the students could turn with new equipment to the shaping of rules and policies in race relations.

They worked out a new "bill of rights" for Negroes, extending to them most, if not all, of those rights which they themselves enjoyed. They were able to choose more intelligently among the positions on the treatment of Negroes expressed at the outset of the unit and to come to a majority consensus about them. The right of the minority to formulate and to express its judgment was respected. But it was made clear wherein the majority considered the dissenting judgment factually in error and morally inadequate. The belief—so often expressed at the end of undisciplined discussion—that, after all, one opinion is as good as another was thus not left unchallenged. . . .

All that we have considered heretofore as belonging within the discipline of practical intelligence is indeed necessary, but unless conditioned to action it is of little worth. Ideals taught without regard to the conditions of their attainment may be little more than irresponsible moralizing. The study of facts divorced from personal and social values becomes meaningless and memoriter. The study and teaching of facts and ideals would become more responsible if commitment to a course of action were the final conclusion of the unit of instruction.

The students in this case have become conscious of the social-moral principles operating in themselves and in their community—principles of social equality, of economic opportunity, of political liberty, and the like. They have sought to clarify the meaning of these principles as these have bearing in race relations, and have learned to use them in formulating and judging racial policies and programs. These principles have taken on life and substance and are that much less shibboleths into which can be poured any sort of content to rationalize short-sighted and undemocratic policies and actions about race relations. In short, in this unit the students have been building into their personal characters the moral content of democratic culture. Their mastery of these great standards of judgment constitutes the heart of their discipline as democratic people.

The chief content of the normative unit is thus social-moral. It is the forms of knowledge and understanding which comprise the *common* sense of the people and arise out of the less specialized activities and experiences—religion, economics, government, etc. It consists of standards of conduct and beliefs created by generations of seers, sages, and common folk: norms and beliefs upon which the policies and choices of the people ultimately rest and by which they order their institutions and carry on their collective life. It is heavily weighted with judgments of value, with descriptive and explanatory judgments playing an auxiliary role. This social-moral knowledge is the prime content of the normative unit. It is subject matter not solely to be learned; it is to be critically examined and often shaped into better forms. But it is the central object of attention. All else is contributory. . . .

The normative unit also makes wide use of facts, descriptive generalizations, and skills. But it is different from other kinds of units in one important respect. It requires that facts and descriptive principles be geared to the task of clarifying and reconstructing normative principles, to the formulation of social directions and programs of action. They are studied and learned in their social-moral role and not as ends in themselves.

The normative unit emphasizes those habits of thinking which facilitate the attainment of dynamic consensus. In units whose content is chiefly facts and descriptive principles, discipline may be developed in habits of thought related to the determination of the accuracy and sufficiency of facts and to the logical validity of descriptive generalizations. The normative unit, on the other hand, includes not only these habits but extends intellectual activities into such spheres as the social-moral orientation of oneself and others, requiring that one become objective toward himself by conscious recognition and criticism of his own motives, aspirations, beliefs, and outlooks. Such a unit stresses the sympathetic recognition and valuation of opposing positions not only as proposed policies and courses of action but also as expressions of traditions and of the character of persons. The method of resolving moral conflicts within and among individuals and social groups is one of its central features.

In short, the normative unit gives discipline in the methods of practical thought and action. . . .

As a class works through unit after unit dealing with a variety of social-moral issues, the teacher helps them to abstract the method of practical intelligence and to become aware of its principles and techniques. This raises discipline to the level of conscious purpose and control and makes it a generalized tool for attaining uncoerced consensus where community life is divided over significant issues.

Moreover, the students have been *learning to use language as an instrument of social understanding, control, and action.* . . .

Finally, they are *learning to take social responsibility* not only through the clarification of social directions and standards of judgment but also because the unit requires a fusion of these directions and standards with the facts and descriptive principles into programs and plans of action. This discipline in constructive thinking about the future, this learning to make choices about the future in making plans and decisions now, this orientation to the future which normative units require is not the least of their contributions to the needed social discipline of these years.

LEARNING AS CRITICIZING

Robert E. Mason

The teacher who has accepted responsibility for moral leadership in his educative efforts hopes to stimulate students as well as impress them; he tries to encourage critical use of knowledge as well as mastery of knowledge; he wishes students to apply the products of learning, not to sit fondling them forever in an ivory tower. He has come to feel that the educational objective is the good of the individual and of society. But having adopted such a functional, dynamic, ethical conception of the educational endeavor, competence and proficiency have come to mean not mere mastery of knowledge but using knowledge toward good ends.

How, then, is one to mark the student who has mastered the facts in Social Studies IV, but who is president of the local Young Fascists League? Does he get an *A* in Social Studies IV? On the other hand, there may be in the group a student who is terribly and wonderfully confused about the facts in Social Studies IV, but who holds and practices devotion to democratic ways in dealing with his fellows. Does he get a *D* in the course? In the name of professional ethics, responsible teachers have sometimes entered the *A* for the fascist, and the *D* for the democrat, insisting that, after all, the person-in-Social-Studies-IV, not the whole person, is being evaluated. Thus, the progress report and the official school record preserved for posterity have said that the fascist is a good student, the democrat a bad one. Yet the objective of the course, as stated by the teacher, perhaps even as described in course announcements, faculty meetings, and in conferences with parents, was to make good citizens in a democracy, not fascists.

Such action seems morally questionable when judged against an ethical conception of professional responsibility. Not mastery of dead information but ability to use that information was said

Reprinted from "Student Evaluation and Academic Freedom," *Educational Theory,* 3 (April, 1953), 104–110. By permission of the author and the editor of *Educational Theory.*

to be of central importance. The young fascist mastered the information, but more, he used the facts in formulating and strengthening a personal philosophy. . . . The *A* had some justification if the teacher's job was no more than to introduce him to certain intellectual tools. Perhaps the question whether the student used what was given him for the good of mankind was not properly a concern of the teacher. To take such a position is to suggest, however, that the teacher is engaged in an amoral, neutral kind of activity, and is in flat contradiction, of course, with the broader conception of education as an ethical endeavor. . . .

When marking is thus seen as a moral-ethical judgment rather than a technique of mathematical measurement, it becomes tremendously important that the values guiding the teacher's judgments be clearly defined, recognized, and applied in the judgmental acts involved in evaluating student accomplishment. For a teacher who is genuinely devoted to the democratic way of life, the highest value is free exercise of critical intelligence. In the light of this supreme moral standard, the teacher must welcome positions honestly arrived at by thinking students, even when those positions seem to him to be evil and false. If the teacher's highest loyalty and deepest faith—a loyalty and a faith underlying all lesser faiths—is in free exercise of critical intelligence, then, paradoxically, there is a sense in which the highest morality involves a kind of moral irresponsibility. For, in this view, truth itself is seen as something wrought out of the clash of mind on mind, and subject to continuous re-shaping. The teacher's higher faith lies in the power of human intelligence, through deliberation and controversy, to re-shape conceptions of good and evil—even conceptions precious to him.

If so much be granted, the implication appears to be that the instructor should ignore the conclusions arrived at by students if students observe recognized canons of free inquiry. If this be done, the instructor is apparently justified in giving the "good student who is a fascist" the *A* and in giving the "bad student who is a democrat" the *D*. In other words, methods of arriving at conclusions but not the conclusions are evaluated. . . .

The issue . . . might be stated thus: *Has the student based his thinking on competent experimentation and research?* There is no pat formula for deciding which experimentation and research are admissible. But limits should be set; a major responsibility of the instructor is to set the limits; and the instructor's evaluation of student achievement should have as one of its fixed points of reference the extent to which a student has based his thinking upon evidence declared to be admissible. It might be added that an instructor has an obligation to defend before his students the limits which he sets. Upon occasion it is quite possible that an instructor may extend the limits of admissible evidence on the basis of student criticism. It is not, however, on the ground of some special authoritarian status that the instructor sets the limits; rather, it is his awesome and awful responsibility as a scholar and as a teacher to do so. He has the temptation and opportunity to set the limits in such a way as to support his special preferences, in the face of good evidence challenging such preferences. This, however, he will not, as an ethical professional person, do. On the other hand, the operation of his "point of view" in setting the limits must be and should be fully granted.

Again, the method of intelligence demands not only that thinking be based on competent experimentation and research, but it demands that this experimentation and research be understood in its own terms and under its own conditions. A student, then, should be held responsible not only for basing his thinking on admissible materials, but he should be held responsible for correct and sympathetic interpretation of those materials. There is an old principle of disputation which holds here; namely, you must understand your opponent's argument before you can attack him. The scholarly ordeal demanded as proof of such understanding is the ability to state the opponent's point of view to the opponent's satisfaction. The instructor, having taken the responsibility for defining the limits of admissible evidence, mediates that evidence in his work with his students. Thus, one of the criteria which he may use in evaluating the work of one of his students is *the degree to which the student can state satisfactorily the data, meanings, and knowledge* upon which their work together is based. Here again, the temptation to take special advantage of one's status as teacher to "cook the evidence" is great. Another danger is that the instructor may expect more of his students than he can expect from his professional colleagues. . . . Nonetheless, it may be suggested that only in such a persisting effort do we have the distinction between propaganda and honest reporting, and that only to the degree that reporting is honest can men build a democratic community on solid foundations.

Another condition which may legitimately constitute an evaluative criterion is the student's participation. The method of critical intelligence is one which opens continuously to public criticism. *Has the student shared his thinking with others in the class group? Has he opened his views to criticism and has he criticized the views of others?* If this principle of participation is to become a criterion, instructors must try always to understand and allow for differences in emotional make-up and sensitivity. For temperamental reasons, it is much more difficult for some persons to give and receive criticism than others. Some persons react defensively at first when their thinking is criticized, but modify their views to accommodate to the criticism after the heat of argument. Probably the instructor should not demand of every student the same degree of informal, spontaneous oral criticism in class discussions. But quiet, retiring students who do not like to talk should give clear indication in writing or in action that they are giving and are taking criticism, and modifying their ideas in the light of criticism.

This mutual give and take—this opening of one's thinking to the criticism of his fellows—this earnest, sincere effort to criticize the thinking of one's fellows—is as important an evaluative standard as any we have. A student may know the competent research, and he may be able to state clearly the basic data, meanings, and knowledge, while doing nothing in the way of creative thinking with these materials. He may have trained his memory to the point where he has great facility in parrot-like repeating of words. But he may not be *thinking.* . . . The letter grade issued a student becomes, thus, a judgment by the teacher of the student's competence in the field represented by the course. The "A student" is one who has done some careful, critical thinking in the field, has participated in a process of mutual criticism in which he has refined his opinions in response to criticism, and has criticized opinions of others. In his criticism, he has based his thinking on admissible evidence as defined by the instructor. He understands the research in the field as demonstrated by his ability to state alternative positions fairly and accurately, and to describe basic data, meanings, and knowledge in the field.

Thus, the "A student" has not only mastered a body of information, but he has demonstrated ability to appreciate and use that information. Both are important. Encyclopedic information alone certainly remains dead. Lively criticism not founded on precise command of admissible data, meanings, and knowledge is dangerous. . . . So much bad practice has gone on under the symbols "A,B,C,D,E,F" that probably we would do well to use an entirely different set of symbols. Perhaps personal notes or letters should be filed rather than any list of symbolic abbreviations. But the tradition that upon completion of a period of association, an instructor is obligated to evaluate the work of a student and report that evaluation to the student is, as much as faculty tenure provisions, a type of expression of that respect for truth—for freedom of inquiry and criticism—which is close to the heart of the educational enterprise in a free society.

In the last analysis, however, the instructor cannot mark a student on the end-point conclusions which the student reaches in a course. The standards of evaluation must have to do with the extent to which a student masters knowledge instrumental for thought, and the way the student uses this knowledge in thinking. Canons of inquiry having been met, inquiry and criticism must range at will, even when—as the instructor sees it —the most precious values are at stake. The school or college should be a haven, a protected place, where students and teachers may think freely, letting their minds go where evidence leads. . . .

LEARNING AS UNDERSTANDING

Reginald D. Archambault

What, then, should our aims be when we are engaged in moral instruction? The answer to this question would help us to delineate the responsibility of the school in this regard. . . .

The problem is complicated by the fact that we quite properly mean different things by "moral instruction" at different stages of the child's development. For example, if we are engaged in teaching a norm of honesty, we might construe it in these different ways,[3] depending on the maturity of the pupil:

(1) To teach Y to be honest through habit, using certain sanctions to insure honest behavior (Training).

(2) To teach Y that honesty is more desirable than dishonesty (Teaching the rule and reasons for it).

(3) To teach Y to believe in the rule that honesty is more desirable than dishonesty (Teaching the student to reflect on the rule and to provide his own reasons for accepting it).

(4) To teach Y to be honest out of conviction, and to ask him to offer objective and impartial reasons for this conviction (Teaching the student to be committed to certain rules and to act in accordance with his convictions).

The tests for success in each of these instances would be different. In (1) success would consist of Y's simply exhibiting a pattern of honest behavior; in (2) the test would determine whether Y could reproduce appropriate statements relative to the belief that honesty is a desirable norm; in (3) the acquisition of the belief itself would be tested by asking Y to give adequate reasons to support the belief; in (4) Y would be expected not only to give reasons for commitment to the belief, but evidence that he acts in accordance with the belief.

Each of these interpretations probably has a valid place in any program of moral instruction, for some might be considered

Reprinted from "Criteria for Success in Moral Instruction," *Harvard Educational Review*, 33, no. 4 (Fall, 1963), 474–481. Copyright, 1963. By permission of the President and Fellows of Harvard College.
[3] This schema is prompted by the Scheffler analysis; see Israel Scheffler, *The Language of Education* (Springfield, Ill.: Charles C. Thomas, 1960), pp. 94–95.

prerequisite to the later acquisition of knowledge or behavior deemed desirable and sufficient for success in moral instruction. The crucial question to be raised is: What are the minimal conditions sufficient to indicate success in moral instruction at the *end* of the teaching interval?

. . . And at first blush, the answer would seem to be an easy one. To teach someone *about* honesty, or even to expect him to give reasons for holding that honesty is the best policy, would, after all, seem quite vacuous, since we have not taught and tested for moral conduct. Similarly, if we are successful in merely inculcating moral habits, there is no indication that this was done by having our students act out of conviction. We are tempted to conclude that moral instruction consists in the attempt to get students to acquire a norm or pattern of action, and to reflectively support these norms in an "objective" or "impartial" manner.[4] A necessary condition for success would then be the demonstration by the student of the appropriate moral behavior (acting honestly, paying one's debts, etc.). But this suggests a much more extensive responsibility for the school in insuring moral conduct. It suggests a much more "practical" environment where teaching and test were not "merely intellectual" and where students could demonstrate "actively" the successful acquisition of norms of conduct.

The dilemma is more apparent than real. . . . The ambiguity involved in this discussion can be related to the classic problem of whether virtue can be taught. The crucial case is the one in which the student who demonstrates that he has been taught, in the non-active sense, that honesty is the best policy proceeds to act in ways incompatible with an adoption of the norm of honesty. . . . Two interpretations of this case are possible, depending on one's position regarding the relation between knowledge and virtue. One view would maintain that X had successfully taught Y, but that Y's failure to act on this knowledge can be attributed to a failure of the will. The other view would hold that the teaching has not been successful, since the appropriate moral conduct did not result.[5]

[4] *Ibid.,* p. 95.
[5] *Ibid.,* pp. 83–84. Traditionally, moral philosophers have held that moral training consists not only in leading the student to an intellectual

This points up the complexity of problems involved in deciding on the ends and means of moral instruction. . . . The problem of the relation between knowledge and virtue is . . . the most basic issue to be dealt with in defining the aims of moral instruction, for the basic question here is the criterion for ascertaining success or failure in teaching. The choice is not arbitrary. We certainly have ample evidence to suggest that intellectual apprehension, understanding, and avowal of norms do not guarantee an acquisition in conduct of the pattern of action prescribed by the norm. Since the transfer between belief and action is not automatic, the attainment of the aim of moral conduct must, then, involve not only intellectual apprehension and support of norms, but also a training of the will so that the student can bridge the gap between belief and action. This would make the task of moral instruction much more complex.

It is thus that we arrive at the crucial question as to whether the responsibility of the school is to strive for success in the attainment of moral conduct on the part of its students. The answer to this, is, I believe, a qualified "yes." . . . The more interesting question is the extent of this responsibility and precisely how this responsibility is to be fulfilled. Is it necessary to convert the school into a microcosm of society as the progressives would suggest, so that moral conduct in the school mirrors that in the "world outside"? Must we have direct moral training such as we find in religious schools?

In order to answer these questions we must be clear as to what we mean by "moral conduct," so that we can see what would be involved in achieving it. Moral conduct does not consist merely in acting in accordance with a norm. Such behavior may come about through compulsion or force, or may be performed automatically. To be properly considered moral,

---

apprehension of norms, but also in a training of the will. Aristotle, for example, emphasized the importance of habituation or practicing right acts, so that the student's will would be trained to do what his mind told him was right. William Frankena puts it this way: "We may perhaps take for granted, then, that the problem of producing virtue in the next generation is a twofold one: (1) that of handing on a 'knowledge of good and evil' or 'knowing how' to act, and (2) that of insuring that our children's conduct will conform to this 'knowledge'." "Toward a Philosophy of Moral Education," *Harvard Educational Review,* 28 (Fall, 1958), 302.

conduct must entail a "reflective and impartial support of norms." [7] This involves, then, four factors, jointly sufficient to entail moral conduct: (a) belief in a norm; (b) a tendency and capacity to offer a rationale supporting the norm; (c) a disinterested or impartial application of judgment concerning the norm; and (d) a tendency and capacity to act in accordance with the norm. As teachers engaged in moral instruction we may strive to achieve any of these objectives. The manner in which we attempt to achieve them would probably differ in each case because of what is entailed by the objective itself. Nevertheless, as I have already suggested, we would be properly considered to be engaged in moral instruction at any of the levels listed. The crucial point is that if we aim to achieve moral conduct (d) as a result of our instruction, *all* of the above objectives must be met. Can this be accomplished within the framework of the school? Should it be?

I have suggested that striving for moral conduct is a qualified aim of the school. The school's responsibility is not to insure moral conduct, for such insurance is impossible. The school hopes that the student will achieve various kinds and degrees of understanding, but it does not insure understanding. Rather, it makes available the means by which understanding can be acquired by presenting data, principles, and techniques to students, and testing for their success in learning these. It teaches for knowledge that promotes understanding. One of the conditions necessary for success in understanding rests with the pupil. We do not speak of failure in getting students to understand as a failure in teaching, unless our lesson has for some reason been incomplete. When we have offered a reasonable opportunity to the student to achieve understanding and he fails to do so, we attribute the failure to the pupil rather than to the instructor. Hence we say that we *promote* understanding rather than *teach* understanding. In this case we assume that understanding will be a by-product of our instruction. We try to make ourselves knowledgeable about those subsidiary learnings that are most conducive to the promotion of understanding and then proceed to teach and test for them. . . . The final success in achieving

[7] *Ibid.*, pp. 94–95.

understanding rests with the learner rather than the teacher.
. . . This, after all, is not surprising, for education, properly
conceived, is concerned with the development of the freedom of
the learner. It can be distinguished from training in that it
involves unpredictable responses at the end of the teaching
interval. In order to achieve this aim it is necessary to encourage
independence in the learner, and with this independence, responsibility for final learning outcomes. This is what makes the
process educative. We promote not only understanding, but
freedom as well.

The promotion of moral conduct is analogous in some respects to the promotion of understanding. We cannot teach
understanding. Nor can we "teach" moral conduct if we construe it in sense (d) above. What we can do is to promote moral
conduct by providing the means by which students can arrive at
beliefs, defend them, demonstrate a commitment to them, and
develop a method for criticizing them.

If we seriously set about to promote understanding in the
pupil, we are reasonably specific about the types of understanding we wish to promote. We then choose a set of rules, techniques, and principles which will be most conducive to the
promotion of that understanding, and teach directly for them.
For the teacher this necessitates a ruthless process of choosing
and specifying objectives of instruction, and then formulating
means by which these objectives can be most efficiently attained. When testing for the attainment of them, our tests must
be specific and must deal with the subject matter chosen for
instruction. If our teaching has been successful, learning will
have taken place. The knowledge derived will pertain not only
to the specific subject matter used as a means of attaining
knowledge, but to analogous situations as well. We assume that
there will be a transfer of learning to other situations. If such
transfer were not possible we would need to start afresh every
time we taught anything.[9]

In promoting moral conduct our task is similar. We aim at
the acquisition of certain principles, skills and dispositions, but
we are definitely limited, for example, in the number of rules

[9] In this regard see Israel Scheffler, "Justifying Curriculum Decisions,"
School Review, 66 (Winter, 1958), 470–472.

and principles that can be taught, and in the scope of skills we can teach for specifically and directly. Here again we must assume a transfer in knowledge of principles, and skills, to wider areas of experience analogous to those taught for specifically in the teaching interval.

In promoting moral conduct, then, we are concerned with achieving objectives conducive to its attainment. Chiefly, these objectives are a knowledge of moral principles, a commitment to certain of them, and the ability and tendency reflectively to support moral convictions objectively arrived at. We have suggested that the true indicator of the objectives of moral instruction is the test that is given to determine its success or failure. How then would we test for the achievement of these objectives? We could do so by getting our students to present defensible moral positions and to indicate their convictions on ethical issues. We could teach for these objectives by presenting problems for apprehension and solution.[10] Are we then not open to the charge that the attainment of these objectives, as measured by the tests we have designed, yields evidence only of intellectual apprehension of norms, and that we have not really striven for the attainment of those objectives that will promote moral conduct? We are presenting problems for intellectual apprehension and solution, but the *manner* in which these problems are studied and solved, and the manner in which norms are criticized, represent moral activity of a significant kind. If the student is involved in an active formulation, critique, and defense of norms, he is engaged in moral activity. Moral instruction thus construed aims at (a) intellectual commitment to norms; (b) reflection and criticism of norms held; (c) inculcation and promotion of a method of objective criticism and evaluation which in itself represents an important form of moral activity. Developing skill in scientific method involves the use of rules of evidence and procedure. Historical analysis involves considerable honesty in scholarship. The teacher of literature deals constantly with the understanding and resolution of moral problems.

[10] These problems, of course, need not be those of "pure" ethical character generally associated with courses in moral philosophy. They might well be issues that arise in the normal course of study that have ethical implications.

These points suggest two implications. The first is that the process of reflecting on and criticizing norms is in itself moral activity, even though it takes place intellectually. The second is that in moral instruction, as in all other instruction, we assume that there will be a great deal of transfer (intellectual, to be sure) from the limited area of instruction to a wider range of situations in present and later life. In these important aspects moral instruction is analogous to instruction in other areas.

At this point we can postulate a notion of responsibility for the school in moral instruction. It should not aim directly for the attainment of moral conduct except insofar as the conduct can be taught for in the intellectual curriculum. (It is also necessary, of course, to *train* the child in practical moral matters.) But that curriculum is pregnant with possibilities for moral instruction. Indeed, it might be argued that the successful teaching of history, literature, and science necessitates the reflection on, discussion of, and criticism of moral issues in an objective and impartial fashion.[11]

Thus we see that successful intellectual instruction often involves moral instruction, and that the successful attainment of the objectives of intellectual instruction entails the attainment of skills, attitudes, and commitments that are essential to the acquisition of moral conduct. Specifically, this entails getting the student to arrive at a position on issues that are moral, justifying that position, and demonstrating consistency in its application to other moral issues.

This indicates the manner in which moral instruction can take place, as well as the limits of the school's responsibility for it. The school should not directly strive to achieve aims that promote moral conduct except insofar as this is possible and feasible within the bounds of normal intellectual curriculum study. But as we have seen this gives a considerable responsibility to the school for developing habits, skills, and sensitivities that are

[11] Of course, this is not meant to suggest that the direct inculcation of norms should not take place at appropriate points. It is an essential function of schooling. Yet it in itself, as Scheffler so clearly demonstrates, is not moral conduct. However, we should also note that in using examples of practical maxims such as "honesty is the best policy" and "pay your debts," Scheffler unwittingly focuses too often on the area of practical maxims that are conducive to inculcation by training.

conducive to moral conduct.[12] If the student later fails to exercise these capacities in which success has been demonstrated, we must then attribute this to a failure of the will rather than a failure of instruction.

Perhaps the principal point to be made here is that the dichotomy suggested by the distinction between "intellectual" and "moral" instruction is not necessarily valid. As several recent writers have pointed out, the *manner* in which the process of instruction is carried out is a crucial factor in developing moral sensitivity, even in the supposedly "morally neutral" field of science. Demonstrated success in the techniques and procedures of valid investigation and conclusion in these disciplines does represent a form of *moral* activity, behavior which will hopefully transfer to wider areas of moral experience. It is, in an important sense, a training of the *will*.

---

[12] Bertrand Russell shares this point of view. Taking his cue from Aristotle's analysis of the relation between intellectual and moral virtues, he says: "Although improvement of character should not be the aim of instruction, there are certain qualities which are very desirable, and which are essential to the successful pursuit of knowledge; they may be called the intellectual virtues. These should result from intellectual education; but they should result as needed in learning, not as virtues pursued for their own sakes. Among such qualities the chief seem to me: curiosity, open-mindedness, belief that knowledge is possible though difficult, patience, industry, concentration and exactness." *Education and the Good Life* (New York: Liveright Publishing Corp., 1926), p. 149.

LEARNING AS HEARING

Giovanni Gentile

A more precise determination must now be given to . . . the *fundamental antinomy of education,* understanding by "antinomy" the conflict of two contradictory affirmations, either one of which appears to be true and irrefutable.

The two contradictory affirmations are (1) that man as the object of education is and must be free, and (2) that education denies man's freedom. They might perhaps be better re-stated in this way: (1) Education presupposes freedom in man and strives to increase it. (2) Education treats man by ignoring the freedom he may originally be endowed with, and acts in such a way as to strip him entirely of it.

Each of the two propositions must be taken, not as an approximate affirmation, but as an exact enunciation of an irrefutable truth. Therefore freedom here means full and absolute liberty; and when we speak of the negation of freedom, we mean that education as such, and as far as it is carried, destroys the freedom of the pupil. . . .

Education then posits this liberty in the pupil, for it presupposes in him a susceptibility of development—educability, as we may call it. The learner could not possibly be educable, that is, susceptible of receiving instruction, unless he were able to think. But thinking, we have already seen, signifies freedom. And not only is freedom presupposed by the educator, but it is the very thing he is aiming at in his work. As a result of his teaching, liberty must be developed in the same manner that the capacity for thinking and all modes of spiritual activity are developed. For the development of thought is a development of reflection, a constant increase of control over our own ideas, over the content of our consciousness, over our character, over our whole being in relation to every other being. And this growth of power is what we mean when we speak of the development of our

Abridged from *The Reform of Education,* trans. D. Bigongiari (New York: Harcourt, Brace, and World, 1922), pp. 40, 57–62. By permission of the publisher.

freedom. It has been said, in fact, that education consists in liberating the individual from his instincts. Surely, education is the formation of man, and when we say man we mean liberty.

Here we stumble upon our antinomy. How are we to reconcile this presupposition and this aim of the educator with his interference in the personality of the pupil? This interposition surely signifies that the disciple must not be left to himself and to his own resources, that he has to clash with something or somebody that is not his own personality. Education implies a dualism of terms, the teacher and the learner; and it is this dualism which destroys the freedom, which sets a limit, and therefore annihilates infinity in which freedom consists. The disciple who encounters a stronger mastering will, an intellect equipped with a multitude of ideas, with an experience which forestalls his own powers of observation and his innate zeal for investigation, sees in this more potent personality either a barrier obstructing his progress towards a goal which he spontaneously would attain, or else a goad which hurries him along the way which he would have indeed chosen of his own accord, but along which he would have liked to advance freely, calmly, joyously, as our Vittorino da Feltre would have it, and without any unwelcome compulsion. This pupil then would want to be left alone in order that he might be free, as free as God when as yet the world was not and he created it out of nothing by his joyous *fiat,* symbol of the loftiest spiritual liberty.

For these reasons we have come to believe that the most serious problem of education is the agreement between the liberty of the pupil and the authority of the teacher. Therefore great masters who meditated on the subject of education, from Rousseau to Tolstoi, have exalted the rights of liberty, but have fallen into the opposite extreme of denying the duty to authority, and have pursued in their abstractions a vague and unrealisable ideal of negative education.

But we must not cling to negatives. It should be our purpose to construct, not to destroy. The school, this glorious inheritance of human experiences, this ever-glowing hearth where the human spirit kindles and sublimates life as an object of constant criticism and of undying love, may be transformed, but cannot be destroyed. Let the school live, and let us cling to the teacher and maintain his authority, which limits the spontaneity and the liberty of the pupil. For this limitation is only apparent.

Apparent, however, when we deal with true education. For the school has for centuries been the victim of a grave injustice. People have been led to consider the classroom as a place of confinement and of punishment, and teachers have been cruelly lashed by the scourge of ridicule cracked in the face of pedantry. Through this injustice, the school has been burdened with faults that are not its own, and teachers, genuine educators, have been confused with the pedantic drill-masters that are the negation of intelligent education and of inspired ethical discipline. In order to see whether education really limits the free activity of the pupil, we must not consider abstractly any school, which may not be after all a school. We must examine an institution at the moment and in the act which realises its significance—when the instructor teaches and the pupils are learning. Such a moment should at least hypothetically be granted to exist.

Let us take a concrete example and consider a teacher in the act of giving lessons in Italian. Where is this something which I have called the Italian language? In the grammar, perchance? Or in the dictionary? Yes, partly. Provided grammar can invest its rules with the life of the individual examples that together constitute the expressive power of the living language; and provided the dictionary does not wither up all words in the arid abstraction of alphabetical classification, does not hang each of them by itself as limbs torn from the living body of the speech in which they had so often resounded and to which they will be joined again in the fullness of life and expressiveness, but does instead incorporate, as every good dictionary should, complete phrases, living utterances of great authors or perhaps of that nameless many-souled writer that somewhat confusedly is called the people.

But more than in the grammar and more than in the dictionary, the word is and exists in the writers themselves. The teacher should there point it out, as he guides his pupils through the authors who were able to express most powerfully our common thoughts. To his students who are striving to learn the language —that is the writers—he reads for example the poems of Leopardi. The poet's word, his soul hovers over the classroom, as the master reads. It penetrates into the minds of the pupils, hushes every other sentiment, removes every other thought, and throbs within them, stirs them, arouses them. It becomes one with the soul of each pupil, which speaks to itself a language of its own, using, truly enough, the words of Leopardi, but of a Leopardi who is peculiar to each of the listeners. Under this spell, the pupil who hears the poet's word echoing in the depths of his being, will he stop to reflect that this word is the echo of an echo? That he is under the influence of something repeated after a first utterance? Our own experience answers: No! But if any of the audience become absent-minded, if they should lose the rapt delight of poetical exaltation communicated to their soul by the teacher's voice, and should say that the word they hear is not their own but the master's, or rather, the poet's, then they would commit a serious blunder. For the word they intently listen to in their soul is their own, exclusively their own. Leopardi does not impart any poesy to him who, through his love, his study, and the intensity of his feelings, is unable to live his own poetry. And Leopardi (or the teacher who reads him) is not materially external to the enraptured listener; he is his own Leopardi, such as he has been able to create for himself. The master, as St. Augustine long ago warned us, is within us.

He is within us even if we see him in front of us, away from us seated in his chair. For in so far as he is a real teacher, he is ever the object of our consciousness, surrounded and uplifted in our spirit by the reverence of our feelings and by our trustful affection. He is *our* teacher, he is our very soul.

The dualism then is non-existent when we are educating. We do notice it before, and we are thus brought to examine the antinomy; but the difficulty is removed by the very act of education itself, by the first word that comes to the pupils' ears from the lips of the teacher. The dualism however cannot be resolved if the master's word fails to reach the pupils' soul, but then under those circumstances there is no education. But even in such cases, if the teacher is not sluggish, if he displays a real spiritual power, the abiding existence of the barrier between the two minds proves helpful to the spiritual growth of the learner, who, because of his incoercible freedom, is impelled by the insufficiency of the master to affirm his personality with increased vigour. So that the school is a hearth of liberty, even in spite of the intentions of the teacher. A school without freedom is a lifeless institution.

Further reading

Aschner, M. J., "Teaching the Anatomy of Criticism," *School Review*, 64 (October, 1956), 317–322.

Broudy, H. S., B. O. Smith, and J. R. Burnett, "Development of Norms through Exemplars," in *Democracy and Excellence in American Secondary Education* (Chicago: Rand McNally, 1964), pp. 214–230.

Curran, C. E., "Intelligence, Morality, and Democracy," *Educational Theory*, 5 (April, 1955), 65–78.

Donovan, C. F., "On the Possibility of Moral Education," *Educational Theory*, 12 (July, 1962), 184–186.

Kilpatrick, W. H., "In Retrospect at Ninety," *Studies in Philosophy and Education*, 1 (November, 1961), 146–152.

McClellan, J. E., "Two Questions About the Teaching of Moral Values," *Educational Theory*, 11 (January, 1961), 1–14 f.

Smith, B. O., "The Logic of Teaching in the Arts," *Teachers College Record*, 63 (December, 1961), 176–183.

CONCOMITANT LEARNING

If in the following selection Gusdorf is right about the nature and significance of speaking, then the teacher's speaking the truth, being true, and speaking truthfully are one and the same thing. Then the epistemological (speaking the truth), the metaphysical (being true), and the axiological (speaking truthfully) dimensions of teaching are united in the person of the teacher when the teacher is being true. Conversely, when the teacher enables the pupil to speak in his own voice, then the three dimensions of learning are united in the pupil's being true. Then the difficulty of determining which of the three dimensions should be considered primary and worthy of paramount concern is more theoretical than real. Perhaps Gusdorf is right when he says that all philosophical problems boil down to the one problem of men speaking. If so, the three dimensions of teaching and learning are united in the educative process constituted when the teacher and the pupil are speaking authentically, or they do not exist at all.

Independently of this issue, the following selection presents the recurring idea that the teacher is supposed to be some sort of example or value model so that the pupil can learn the values of the teacher by "osmosis," i.e., concomitantly with instruction in everything else. Its difference from other expressions of this conception of the teacher's "role" is its place in current thought, for it is squarely in the mainstream of contemporary European existential phenomenology. The particular values it depicts, embodied in the teacher's way of existing, might be highly appropriate for the times.

Other treatments of the concomitant learnings allegedly accruing when the pedagogic relation is dialogic are Winetrout's "Buber: Philosopher of the I-Thou Dialogue," *Educational Theory*, 13 (January, 1963), 53–57; Herbert Read's chapter, "The Teacher," in his *Education Through Art* (London: Faber and Faber, 1943), pp. 279–289; and in Buber's own *Between Man and Man* (Boston: Beacon Press, 1955). Other aspects of values learned concomitantly are shown in Dewey's "Appreciation and Cultivation," *Harvard Educational Record,* 1 (April, 1931), 73–76; in Reynold's "Children's Privacy and Compulsory Schooling," *Teachers College Record,* 68 (October, 1966), 33–41; and in Ulich's "Leadership and Education," *Educational Forum,* 19 (March, 1955), 261–269.

TEACHING AS SPEAKING

Georges Gusdorf

A more precise analysis of the conditions of dialogue ought to permit us, in effect, to go beyond this moment of despair. The most pressing need is to grasp speech in the context of the particular situation in which it emerges. A sentence is not uttered in a vacuum: it presupposes a certain state of relations between the speakers, and the horizon of a language corresponding to shared values. In ordinary usage, the context is taken for granted, so that the literal text seems to be self-sufficient. Familiar conversation or the newspaper article is based on an existing language, determined once and for all as a function of tacitly accepted average values. Talking at cross-purposes and misunderstanding only show up when one of the persons present repudiates that implicit mutual consent and denounces the social pact of everyday language. An automatic and approximative speech gives way, then, to authentic speech, which runs into all sorts of obstacles.

The examination of this authentic speech will nevertheless allow us to isolate the implications of valid language. The meaning of speaking depends, indeed, upon three distinct elements, the totality of which alone justifies it. First of all, one must consider *who* is speaking. In this respect, by virtue of what is the speaker speaking? Is he a man who lives hand-to-mouth, the man of the passing moment, scattering his words like seeds to the wind? Or rather is he committed to what he says, and to what degree? There is thus a personal characteristic that measures the intensity of speech. It can reveal being: promises and oaths directly affirm an inner value attitude in which a man comes to be one with what he says. But most of our sentences do not present that intimate tension; they are more or less disengaged from personal being. A proper appreciation must try to estimate the amount of authenticity which speaking man confers on his speech.

Reprinted from *Speaking,* trans. Paul T. Brockelman (Evanston, Ill.: Northwestern University Press, 1965), pp. 83–86, 101–104, 121–126. By permission of the translator.

But the reference alone to him who speaks remains one-sided: one must also take into account the other, him *to whom* the phrase is directed. That object is essential, because the spoken word is truly efficacious only if there is a reciprocity between the speakers. If they do not find themselves in agreement, but out of step with each other, misunderstanding will necessarily arise. The literal meaning of the words perhaps will be understood, but their value-meaning will escape. If someone thinks I am serious when I joke, or humorous when I am most sincere, my words lose their meaning en route. A deep and intense declaration, a confession, or a cry from the heart are as difficult to listen to as they are to say. For real communication to be achieved, there must be the same enthusiasm on both sides, a kind of preliminary communion. Each time that I speak, what I say depends upon the other whom my language intends: an indifferent person, an adversary, or a friend and ally. Meaning is always the trait of a collaboration.

Thirdly, that collaboration itself doesn't take place in a vacuum. The *moment* is the third dimension of any verbal expression. Each act of speaking is in its own way situational, each word is an historic word. The situation suffices to give value to any remark, which then becomes decisive because it is pronounced in a decisive moment. For example, some dying words might never have been remembered by humanity if they had not been the last words of some historically illustrious person.

Thus a sound exegesis must not be content to consider a man's every word, to somehow reduce his words to a single plane. One must carry out a kind of study in relief. It must be a study in which the statement each time takes on form and life according to the degree of personal commitment of the man who is speaking, according to the reciprocity of the encounter and according to the meaning of the moment. The apparent meaning of the speech gives way to its personal value. Besides, such an evaluation can only be carried out by those in whom the very sense of the situation is in some way restored. The extreme speech of a crisis only takes on its full meaning in a complementary critical situation. All true understanding is itself an accomplishment. The hero speaks to heroes, the poet to poets, and the appeal of the saint is only effective if it releases in us a dormant possibility of saintliness. Non-comprehension is a bar opposed to the demands of others, and at the same time a specification of one of our limits. So too we can become strangers to ourselves. Because one's life, at any given moment carried to the heights of awareness of value, can fall back into its customary mediocrity, we can cease to understand this or that attitude which once was ours, this or that promise we have made. Then it is that we renounce *keeping our word*. Like the voice that breaks because it is incapable of holding to a high note, we find ourselves incapable of holding to the locus of values that, at one time, enlightened us. . . .

The point of departure for the use of speech, then, is not monologue, but *dialogue*. Man shouldn't be alone when speaking. Monologue is the beginning of madness, the confrontation of others the beginning of wisdom. As the Spanish critic, Eugenio d'Ors, wrote: "All monologue is by nature unkempt. Thanks to dialogue, the soul of others penetrates into our own, as a comb digs its teeth into the tangles of disordered hair. It penetrates it, straightens it out, and tidies it up." [1] The image is ingenious. It calls to mind the effectiveness of *dia*logue to render meditation *intel*-ligible, that is to say to permit the solitary individual to read between the lines of his own naturally confused thought. Indolent fantasy gives way to obedience, for the other exercises a veritable shaping of my consciousness that, beyond the exchange of words, establishes a real collaboration. The other voice is not limited to the role of accompaniment or mere echo. It becomes the educator of the first voice in this learning of coexistence.

Dialogue, therefore, is the first and most crucial test of universality. If I desire to reach understanding with others and to have them share my certainty, I must proceed to portion out the difficulty step by step so as to keep both minds in unbroken contact. When the listener doesn't follow a train of thought, one must go back and lead him along, over and over again, until he understands. Thus Socrates, that midwife to minds, proceeds from question to answer, following the roundabout ways of the ironic method. But that illustrious example himself teaches us

[1] Eugenio d'Ors, *Au Grand Saint Christophe,* from the French translation by Mallerais, Corrêa, p. 117.

that the power of dialogue has limits. Socrates speaks. The listener, each time more edified, only intervenes from time to time to punctuate with respectful approval the dazzling developments of the master. This second voice only takes the part of pauses when the virtuoso must catch his breath. If authentic dialogue means to work together on an equal footing, Socrates, who takes over the dialogue, seems more like a person in monologue. . . .

However, there is no reason here to be surprised or upset. In fact, philosophic dialogue brings into confrontation matured personalities for whom the game is already up. They limit themselves to expressing a consolidated thought which they can't deny without denying themselves. Now, conversions are rare. True dialogue presupposes an open and receptive attitude, as opposed to sterile discussions in which each participant limits himself to restating his convictions, without ever giving an inch, and in which, as a last resort, he ends up by playing hide-and-seek or by hurling insults in a desperate effort to have the last word. The value of dialogue is thus not inherent in the genre itself, as rationalists sometimes seem to think. A new dimension is opened up to the life of the mind—but in this instance it is like a loveless marriage that has lost most of its meaning. The conjugal dialogue can be reduced to a long chain of domestic scenes. It may wrap itself around the couple absorbed in each other in an exclusivism that divorces them from the rest of the world and becomes a kind of monologue of two, a monologue in which the individual egos add themselves together instead of interacting. Dialogue offers the possibility of salvation. But the passage here from the possible to the real presupposes a receptive attitude, an openness to the world and the other. The interchange of words doesn't mean very much if it is not founded on the recognition of other people. The distinctive sign of man in dialogue is that he listens as well as he speaks, if not better. That is the effect of an attentive presence, a spiritual hospitality, as it were, that excludes the desire to dazzle or to conquer as well as the claim to sovereignty. Authentic dialogue characterizes the encounter of men of good will, each of whom testifies for the other, not to himself alone, but to their common values. That is why in the recent period of bondage [i.e., the occupation] the gift of dialogue already bore within itself an anticipated liberation. But these moments are rare, and are given only to those who are worthy of them. Most men exchange words without ever entering into dialogue. Commonplaces are the substance of their ideas, and the opinions prevalent in their little social circle take the place of values. . . .

In the final reckoning, then, the problem of speech seems to take all of its meaning from the moral order. Each man is responsible for constituting a universe for himself. That is to say, he is responsible for passing from the mental, moral, and even material confusion of infancy to the adult's presence to the world, a presence within the present moment articulated as a function of values which define his relations with the world and others. This is *the* adult task, a task which must be continually repeated because man is a historical being. The movement of time and the change of situation once again cast in doubt every balance once it is achieved. The very concern for continuity in truth obliges us to repeatedly create at each new moment. Thus speech defines any supreme moment of the person, the first or last word of his existence in its spontaneity, bearing witness to this unique being affirming and reaffirming himself over against the world. . . .

A kind of unconditional moral imperative arises here, clothed in that sublimity which Kant saw in duty. To give one's word shows the human capacity of self-affirmation despite all material restrictions. It is the disclosure of a human being as he really is, the projection of value into existence. In a particularly tense situation in which my fate was at stake, I gave my word as the word appropriate to the situation, the word that resolved the situation and made me a new being in a world transformed. Others had confidence in me and I united myself to them by a commitment of mutual faith. To respect one's word is thus to respect others as well as oneself, for it indicates what one thinks of oneself. He who breaks his word is dishonored not only in the eyes of others, but in his own eyes as well.

The religion of speech is thus a criterion for personal authenticity. Giving one's word shows that human speech, not content merely to indicate value, can itself become a value. One's word of honor is a fixed point amidst all our vicissitudes: it is through the promise that we pass from personal time to personal eternity. It raises up life, a domain of habit and desire, to the rule of the norm, the consciousness of value by means of which the person makes up his mind to become what he is. Every word in this sense, even if it has not been pronounced as an oath, is a promise, and we ourselves must be careful not to desecrate a language which others read as the symbolic representation of our personal life.

Man, capable of speaking, thus finds himself clothed in a prophetic dignity. In the face of an uncertain future, speech formulates an anticipation. It traces within the chaos of circumstances the first hints of the future. In his own personal world, man acts with a power of creative initiative. The man who gives his word enunciates himself and announces himself according to the direction he has taken, mobilizing all his resources to give birth to a reality fitting his demand. By the power of a word once pronounced, something begins to be which was not before. Speaking alters the form of the situation. It is a pledge and commitment, the signature of a contract which may appear to be a loss of freedom, but which in fact guarantees man's attainment of a new freedom through the power of obedience.

Thus speech at its most effective takes on the meaning of a *vow* or even a *sacrament*. It is speaking in action, a word that is a holy action, a moment of personal eschatology in which destiny is shaped. It is highly indicative of this sacramental value of speech that the Christian doctrine of marriage, all too often misunderstood, situates the sacrament in the mutual commitment of husband and wife. The priest is merely the first witness to a mutual assent whereby two lives are henceforth joined together. But it is also clear that if speech is promise, it is only valuable insofar as it is kept and in proportion to the capacity to keep it of whoever utters it. He has given a pledge. He remains master of the value that he himself attributes to this pledge. To keep one's word is to make an effort to maintain a certain sense of oneself that one once recognized as constituting his personal existence. Faithfulness, in marriage as in any other commitment, is not a routine, but corresponds to an inner repetition of the promise, a continual reactualization that makes of the word given an eternal present. It is not easy to keep speech as the only fixed point at the heart of a ceaselessly variable human reality, and perhaps any oath promises more than it is possible to hold to. But then the other danger arises of becoming slave to an out-of-date promise which time has made meaningless and which henceforth necessarily becomes a vain superstition. Man remains the master of his word, but he can only give up a dead fidelity in order to affirm a more living authenticity. In any case, the respect for commitments is self-respect, and everyone is judged in himself by his capacity for this essential loyalty.

Thus, it seems impossible in the abstract to fix rules for the correct use of speech. The task of the honest man cannot be assumed by anyone but himself. In any case, the cardinal virtues of fidelity, loyalty, and honor, and the vices of lying, hypocrisy, and perjury are bound up with the practice of language in good or bad faith. The man of his word is the one who, in a troubled world, strives to contribute to the realization of truth. Not that language by itself possesses a magical power. There are literally no more right words in this world than there are clean hands. Speech is worth no more than the man who uses it. The word appears in the flow of existence like a landmark or a guide —always both the beginning and the end. The spotless perfection of a definitive language, on the contrary, would bring language to a full stop and would ruin existence by stabilizing it.

The ethic of speech indicates a need for veracity as a daily experience. It's a question of telling the truth, but there is no telling the truth without being true. And so the necessity of clearing up the relations of self to others and self to self becomes definite. Here, the commandments are clear. First of all will be the refusal to pay lip-service, to pay oneself and others with words that are not, as they should be, so many pledges of the inner self. Let speaking be whole and always indicative of a real presence. Verbal facility all too often hides character flaw. The man of his word doesn't just give lip-service, but gives himself. And that purification of speech is double-edged; it implies a reciprocal clause. One must let others speak, being on guard against behaving like those who take over the whole conversation for themselves and never listen to what one says to them. To be open to the speech of others is to grasp it in its best sense, continually striving not to reduce it to the common denominator of banality, but to find in it something original. By doing this, moreover, by helping the other to use his own voice, one will stimulate him to discover his innermost need. Such is the task of the teacher, if, going beyond the monologue of instruction, he knows how to carry the pedagogical task into authentic dialogue where personality is developed. The great educator is he who spreads around himself the meaning of the honor of language as a concern for integrity in the relations with others and oneself.

The man of his word affirms himself at the heart of an ambiguous human reality as a guide and landmark, as an element of calm certainty. Doubtlessly, he runs the risk of loneliness and failure. One cannot be true all alone, nor play the game alone if all the others cheat. Such at least is the easy excuse of those who try to justify breaking their word by pointing to the laxity of others. Certainly if everyone spoke the truth, it would be easy to do likewise. But the moral task consists in taking the initiative in the direction of obedience to value rather than custom. One must be true without waiting for others to be so, and precisely so that others might come to be so. The strong personality engenders an environment of truth around itself. Its strictness is contagious and it carries others along with its momentum. The man of truth radiates a kind of light that forces each witness to see and judge himself. A Socrates, a Jesus, or a Gandhi imposes on his listeners that authority which he is the first to obey. His speaking exercises an intrinsic efficacy that makes others consent.

The man of his word, pursuing for his own good the goal of being true, thereby contributes to putting human reality in order. He knows perfectly well that he will never finish his work, but he has a faith in the possibility of a better understanding between men, of a more authentic communication. Our duty is for each of us to take on the creative initiative which is the function of the Word. A man's life must achieve on its own the elevation of nature to culture, animality to humanity. Of course, this emergence is facilitated by society itself, which takes charge of the child and fashions him according to the norms of his environment. But this environmental education is never completely sufficient. The passage from chaos to cosmos must be ceaselessly repeated. The upward struggle must constantly win out over the threats of coasting downhill. Speech fixes the determination of man, who, by means of the promise and the vow, proves to himself and others that he is the master of his temporal existence. But, while and by forming himself, the man of his word also works toward human unity.

CREATIVITY

Because schools are partly established to inculcate a society's values in the younger generation, and because teachers are partly surrogates for the community as well as standing *in loco parentis,* it might seem at first glance that there could be little scope for the pupil's creativeness in moral education. Two questions, however, suggest quite the opposite.

Can any values be justified? If values and evaluations are completely subjective and cannot be known in any way (i.e., the relation between axiology and epistemology), then is not any attempt to instruct in values tantamount to indoctrination and thereby reprehensible on moral grounds? Would not such attempts be morally wrong and logically self-contradictory? The selection by Atkinson argues this case from within the mainstream of contemporary Anglo-American analytical philosophy. If his argument is valid, that is, if there are irreducibly open options in values, then besides the creativity of the pupil in learning values so that they are evaluations, what else is there? Nothing? Do any of the readings in Section Two above indicate ways in which the ultimately unjustifiable nature of values can be evaded in education?

How does the learning of values transfer? Although transfer of learning is a general problem, it is complicated in the moral realm by the distinction between operative and professed values, that is, by the possibilities of hypocrisy and self-deception. If the pupil sees or thinks he sees that the values he learns are honored more in the speech than in the practice, then besides his creativity in the development of his own authentic values, what else is there? Morris does not argue this case (as Wirth does) but rather gives a method whereby values can be learned intellectually and yet related to the pupil's conduct of his own life such that the problem might be evaded. To find this combination he relies almost completely upon the pupil's creativeness. Would his suggestion be enough to go by?

Would Morris's suggestion suffice for the reader of this volume in respect to his future existence as a teacher? Which of the previous readings would be of help? Or is the whole matter not quite so simple?

ON CRITERIA OF VALUES

R. F. Atkinson

. . . Instruction, then, is essentially a rational process, both at
the giving and, in so far as it is successful, at the receiving end.
It involves, for instance, providing adequate support, by way of
proofs, reasons, evidence, whatever may be appropriate to the
field in question, for the conclusions it is sought to impart. No
higher degree of conviction is sought than is warranted by the
nature of the support available. Not conviction by itself, but
justified conviction, rational assent is the aim. The imparting
and acquiring of an understanding of what is taught is consequently involved in its realisation. Because of this, and in so far
as it succeeds, instruction puts its subject in the way of making
progress in the field by his own efforts. Indoctrination, on the
other hand, need not. It is subject to no such restrictions.
Conviction or assent is all that is sought, and any teaching
procedure is acceptable provided only that it is or is thought to
be effective in achieving this end. Understanding, awareness of
the grounds upon which opinions ought to rest, is not required.
If knowledge consists in justified (full) conviction, then the
object and result of instruction may be knowledge; whereas of
the man who is indoctrinated merely, although what he believes
may be true and capable of justification, it will not be possible
to say that he knows it.

With regard to teaching and learning how, the instruction/
indoctrination distinction manifests itself as that between, say,
training and drilling. The trained man knows how to achieve a
certain sort of result. The well-drilled man only knows how to
carry out certain routines which will, no doubt, in appropriate
circumstances, be effective in producing the results. The former
operates intelligently, whereas the latter does not. The trained
man knows what he is about, knows not only the rules of
procedure but also the reasons for them, and hence knows how

Reprinted from *Philosophical Analysis and Education,* ed. Reginald Archambault (New York: Humanities Press, 1965; London: Routledge and
Kegan Paul, 1965), pp. 172–176, 181–182. By permission of both
publishers.

to adapt the rules to non-standard conditions. The man who is merely well drilled has to make do with rules of thumb which he mechanically applies.

This does not pretend to be an account of teaching methods. I am not maintaining that teaching should or can consist entirely in instruction and training as I have described them. Even where the ultimate aims are knowledge and intelligent practice, it seems inevitable that some recourse will have to be had to non-rational teaching methods, that it will sometimes be necessary to try to impart information and techniques beyond the recipients' understanding, that there will be some learning by rote or drill. Nor, moreover, can anybody have a full grasp of all the information, techniques, etc., that he puts to use. We have all taken a vast amount on trust, and must continue to do so.

Instruction and indoctrination, training and drilling—this sort of distinction, whatever words may be used to express it, is, I believe, commonly taken for granted in discussions of the aims and practice of education. On what basis does it rest? Once the question is raised it becomes apparent that the distinction presupposes that there are clear criteria of truth, cogency, correctness in any field to which it applies. It is not required that there should be a body of established truths, facts, laws, practices in the field, only that there should be criteria for determining what is and what is not acceptable. Instruction, training, is then a matter of teaching with due regard to the criteria appropriate to the field in question: indoctrination, drilling, the reverse. Accordingly, the more fugitive the criteria may be in a particular field, the harder will it be to distinguish instruction and indoctrination.

It is, moreover, on this basis easy to understand why we are inclined to discriminate morally between instruction and indoctrination. Since the process of instruction is governed by criteria which are in principle accessible to any rational person, it is, to use the traditional, imprecise, but perhaps sufficiently well understood language, a matter of treating a person as an end in himself: it is not putting him to use, exploiting him, treating him as a mere means, as indoctrination so clearly is. And further, so long as the instruction/indoctrination distinction can be drawn within a field, we have, as it were, ready-made, a basis for evaluating and regulating the non-rational teaching procedures that we may be obliged to use, whether for lack of time or competent teachers or because of the immaturity and/or incapacity of the taught. We can restrict ourselves to the inculcation of information and practices which could be the content of rational teaching and, with regard to the young especially, employ only those non-rational methods which do not or as little as possible impair the recipients' capacity for subsequent instruction and training.

Before turning to the main enquiry of how moral education stands with regard to the instruction/indoctrination distinction, it might be worth while to take a look at two cases in which the need for such an enquiry has been overlooked—once very obviously, in the other case less so. No one can fail to see that in the following passage, which one must hope to be fairly untypical of ecclesiastical pronouncements on education, a relevant question has been begged: "Every education system makes use of indoctrination. Children are indoctrinated with the multiplication table; they are indoctrinated with love of country; they are indoctrinated with the principles of chemistry and physics and mathematics and biology, and nobody finds fault with indoctrination in these fields. Yet these are of small concern in the great business of life by contrast with ideas concerning God and man's relation to God, his neighbour and himself, man's nature and his supernatural destiny." [2] But John Stuart Mill's much weightier and in so many ways justly celebrated defence of the liberty of thought and expression suffers, it seems to me, from a similar defect. The chief ground on which Mill supports this liberty is that it is the necessary condition of people's acquisition and full understanding, which alone secures stable possession, of 'the truth.' [3] This is no doubt the case where truths of fact (scientific truths) are concerned, but the argument is meant to apply to thought and expression in morals, religion, and politics too. It has to be asked, therefore, whether there are truths of anything like the same sort to be discovered in these fields. Mill in his essay betrays an altogether inadequate aware-

[2] Quoted by J. S. Brubacher in *Eclectic Philosophy of Education* (Englewood Cliffs, N.J.: Prentice-Hall, 1951), p. 326.
[3] J. S. Mill, *On Liberty* (1859), ch. 2.

ness of the possibility of radical differences among the various fields of enquiry, speculation, and practical judgment. He appears to think that they can readily be placed on a simple scale of increasing complexity, running from mathematics, where 'all the argument is on one side,' through natural philosophy (science), to morals, religion, and politics. So very far is Mill from according any special status to moral 'truths,' which presumably must by their nature have some specially close relation to conduct, that he allows that they, along with all other opinions, lose their immunity when so expressed as to be direct instigations to action,[4] as if people were to be allowed any moral opinions they liked so long as there was no danger of them or anybody else acting upon them. It may be that sense can be found for the idea of truths in morals, politics, and religion, but unless and until it has, nobody is entitled to advocate liberty of thought and expression in these fields on the ground that it is a necessary means to securing the truth. . . . Is there then a firm enough basis for drawing the instruction/indoctrination distinction with respect to moral education? In many treatments of the topic attention is directed on to the contrast between direct moral teaching by explicit precept on the one hand, and reliance on example, on the candid discussion of moral issues as and when they arise in the teaching of other subjects, on the other. On the face of it at least, this contrast relates primarily to the method of moral teaching, whereas the present concern is with its content, or rather with the question whether there is a possible content for moral instruction. It is true that indirect methods of moral teaching, in so far as they engage the attention and judgment of the taught, to that extent differ from indoctrination as described above. All the same our question about the content of moral education remains to be answered.

What then is there to teach in morals? Not, it is clear, information in any ordinary sense, nor practical skills. As to the latter, moral progress is frequently understood in contradistinction from the acquiring of such skills as are necessary or helpful for achieving economic or social success, and, even if one takes more presentable candidates like promoting other

[4] *Ibid.,* ch. 3.

people's welfare, there is no getting round the fact that immorality is never viewed as a matter of lacking or losing a capacity. Incapacity is indeed a defence against charges of immorality. And as to moral information—what could this be? Take any moral position and its opposite can be maintained without logical error or factual mistake. It can, of course, be taught and learnt (is a possible object of knowledge) that a certain moral position is held by certain people, but, whatever adequate grounds for holding a moral position might be, it is clear that this is not among them. There can be moral teaching, instruction in, as opposed to instruction about, morality, only if there are criteria of truth, cogency, correctness, in the field. Are there such criteria?

Manifestly it is impossible even to list all the more important sorts of answer that have been given to this question. All I shall attempt is to illustrate a type of view which seems to be dominant among contemporary philosophers of a, very broadly, empiricist or, less happily, linguistic persuasion. There is no one who seriously entertains the hope of being able to establish a substantial moral criterion, a touchstone of moral truth. The possibility of formulating a criterion for applying the term 'moral' is, of course, another and less momentous affair. Morality, it is asserted or conceded, cheerfully or sadly, is a field in which there are irreducibly open options. . . . It might well be thought that the impossibility of establishing an ultimate moral criterion has received at least as much emphasis as it deserves in recent moral philosophy. I have, however, been struck by the absence of much reflection of it in most of the discussions of moral education I have seen. There is undeniably a widespread belief in the importance of moral education, and some attention is given to questions of method and approach, but it seems to be assumed that there is no room for serious dispute about what is to be taught. This assumption—but perhaps it is really a conspiracy of silence—needs very little consideration to be seen to be quite extraordinary.

PERSONAL CHOICE

Van Cleve Morris

We are told on good authority that the school is above all a *social* institution, that its principal function in modern life is to recreate in each individual the beliefs, outlooks, behaviors, and preferences of the society which it serves. To do this effectively and efficiently we in America have insisted via compulsory attendance laws that all of our youngsters participate in this activity. To assert that we have socialized the educational process in this country is to utter the most fatuous of understatements; we have taken John Dewey at his word and turned education into the crowning paradigm of corporate group life.

Now this is all very good and there is nothing particularly pernicious or monstrous about it. But it does tend to blur the image we have of the developing individual. The school is not just a social institution; it is also an "individual" institution, i.e., an institution for individuals. Indeed it is somewhat of an irony, pointed out some years ago by Prof. Boyd Bode, that while so-called progressive education pretended to give so much new prominence to the individual in its educational doctrine, it wound up burying him in group dynamics in the socialized learning process. We are now called upon to extricate the poor fellow from the crushing overload of social controls that he takes on in school and to find again that the school is a school for individual selves quite as much as it is a school for social integration.

What this means is simply that the school must direct its attention to the release of the human self, to the involvement of the child in personal decision and moral judgment to a far greater degree than he knows at present. He is too tangled up in group controls . . . to learn much about what and who he is. He is too enmeshed in peer-group response to discover that he is there himself as one of the peers.

Reprinted from "Existentialism and the Education of Twentieth Century Man," *Educational Theory*, 11 (January, 1961), 57–59. By permission of the author and the editor of *Educational Theory*.

We thought when we secularized the school that we had driven orthodoxy and narrowness out of the educational process. The great historical joke, however, is that while we have successfully driven sectarian, religious orthodoxies out of the school we have simultaneously driven the school into the waiting arms of another kind of orthodoxy, i.e., the tyranny of middle class society. The task now is to perform another bit of social surgery to separate at least a part of the youngster's school life from the moral tyranny of the community.

To take a concrete example, consider the matter of privacy and quiet reflection. How much opportunity is there in a typical school in America for a youngster to sit still and quiet and go over the personal choices he must make that day? I venture to say that it would be difficult to locate a minute and a half in a typical schoolboy's day for this kind of activity. We have elevated gregariousness to the status of a moral commitment for today's youth. It is now suspicious behavior to declare that one wants to be alone. Privacy has declined both as a behavior trait and as a worthwhile thing in our lives; it is a new and embarrassed form of immorality to separate one's self from other people, to reflect quietly on what one is doing, to locate where one is in the rolling ocean of social experience. The great doctrine of "shared experience," so novel and exciting when John Dewey first announced it, has flooded down over the social landscape as if it were a moral law, and it has flushed us all out into the public open where we can no longer call our private selves our own.

This . . . is the tragedy of modern Western life, and the super-tragedy is that American public education is presently designed to aggravate instead of rectify this sorry predicament. The first task, then, of any . . . program would be to provide for more private experience for the child while he learns in school. It is noteworthy, it seems to me, that there are tell-tale signs of this in the field of art.[5] In this portion of the school program, at both the elementary and secondary levels, there is a real and genuine interest in allowing the individual youngster to look at his world and to say with his hands what he sees,

[5] See V. C. Morris and I. L. de Francesco, "Modern Art and the Modern School," *The Clearing House* (October, 1957), 67–71.

without prior compliance with so-called artistic laws of form, balance, and line. . . .

But the provision of private experience in the program of the school is not all, simply because it is not enough. What one does with his privacy, what content he puts into his reflection is the vital statistic of learning. And the . . . educator is necessarily interested in having the youngster fill his quiet moments with the personal judgments he must make concerning his own life. That is to say, his reflections should contain the subject matter of moral choice. If the Humanists wish to fill the mind with the content of our intellectual past and if the Experimentalists wish to develop trained intelligence through the solving of problems, certainly there should be a little time in the school day for awakening the moral powers of young people to get them to ask who they are and what they are doing around here.

This might be done, I think, in a number of ways. Reference was made above to the so-called Existential Moment in each of our lives. . . . After we have been going to school for six or eight years . . . we do not, I say, know who we are; we do not even know *that* we are. We are not yet existentially awake. But once we come awake . . . the elementary school should seize upon every opportunity to present moral problems to the youngster—at the level of his understanding—to provide small beginnings for the long, slow climb to moral maturity. Preferably these problems should be the kind that have no answer, such as "What would you do if you knew everything?" or "Is it ever right to kill a man?" At the very least they should open up the moral sphere to youngsters to introduce them to the most difficult sector of the world they inhabit. . . .

Somewhat later in his schooling, a youngster should be given a more systematic exposure to the ethical questions of life. Perhaps he might be asked to imagine himself in complete charge of another individual, capable of making him do anything, experience anything, desire anything, know anything. What, for the assignment, would be his plan of life for this individual? Then when this assignment was complete, the teacher could ask the student to compare this program with what plans he has for himself.

From this point forward, into college and beyond, the individual should be constantly provoked to expand upon this plan for his developing self, checking here, amending there, but always mindful of the control he has over his own single life, the precious offering he is to contribute to the developing Idea of Man. We should all, I suppose, wish that we had more than one life to work on; there are so many mistakes. But one is all we are allotted.

INDEX

Abstraction: level of, 54, 61, 66, 79–80, 142, 144–145, 163–164

Action: as function of consciousness, 105, 131, 132, 133. *See also* Behavior

Actual entity, 137–144 *passim*, 184–188 *passim*

Actual occasion, 138–139, 141

Aesthetic experience: analogous to *satori*, 97; primacy of, 141–142; origin of the cognitive and practical, 143–144

Aggressiveness: neither innate nor physiological, 232; transformed, 240

Alienation: from self, 82, 146, 177–178; from classroom, 148; from world, 149; of teacher from herself, 149; from pupil, 150; from pedagogic relation, 156

Anomie, 82

Answers: consequences of teacher's zeal for, 176

Antinomy of education, 264

Aristotle, 132, 138, 142

Authenticity, 87, 155–157, 173, 269, 271, 275, 277

Authority: presupposed by programmed instruction, 76; educative questioning of, 78; nonviolent, 146; ascribed by pupil, 154; identical with education, 158, 160; falsely decried by progressivism, 165; direct use of, 220–221; not conflicting with freedom, 267; related to truth, 278

Bacon, Francis, 199

Behavior: as caused, 104, 109–110; as free, 105, 110, 112, 149, 168, 170–171, 188, 224, 225, 264, 276. *See also* Freedom

Behavioral change: as insufficient evidence of learning, 10

Bergson, Henri, 142, 227

Bode, Boyd, 287

Brameld, Theodore, 146–147, 157

Broudy, Harry S., 17, 19

Buddha, 92

Bureaucratic indifference, 83

Causality in teaching, 62–64, 71, 106, 168–169, 259–260

Communication, educative: rational, 7–8; experimental, 29–30, 80, 222–223, 254; inquiry, 32–33, 34–36; presentative, 43, 55; dialectical, 49–50; scholastic, 67; Zen, 95; existential, 153–154, 277–278; idealistic, 160–161, 266–268

Communication, presuppositions of: common sense, 106–108; existential, 271–273

Concrescence, 137–138, 140, 144, 184, 188

Conditioning: as kind of teaching, 6; compared to indoctrination, 8; as basis of teaching machines, 17; defined, 104–105; compared to teaching, 106–108

Consciousness: of world and self, 124–125, 230; phenomenological description of,

ILLINI BOOKS

Also available in clothbound editions.

IB-19	Black Hawk: An Autobiography	Donald Jackson, ed.	$1.75
IB-20	Mexican Government in Transition	Robert E. Scott	$2.25
IB-21	John Locke and the Doctrine of Majority-Rule	Willmoore Kendall	$1.25
IB-22	The Framing of the Fourteenth Amendment	Joseph B. James	$1.45
IB-23	The Mind and Spirit of John Peter Altgeld: Selected Writings and Addresses	Henry M. Christman, ed.	$1.25
IB-24	A History of the United States Weather Bureau	Donald R. Whitnah	$1.75
IB-25	Freedom of the Press in England, 1476-1776: The Rise and Decline of Government Controls	Fredrick Seaton Siebert	$2.25
IB-26	Freedom and Communications	Dan Lacy	$1.50
IB-27	The Early Development of Henry James	Cornelia Pulsifer Kelley, with an introduction by Lyon N. Richardson	$1.95
IB-28	*Law in the Soviet Society	Wayne R. LaFave, ed.	$1.95
IB-29	Beyond the Mountains of the Moon: The Lives of Four Africans	Edward H. Winter	$1.75
IB-30	The History of Doctor Johann Faustus	H. G. Haile	$1.45
IB-31	One World	Wendell L. Willkie, with an introduction by Donald Bruce Johnson	$1.75
IB-32	William Makepeace Thackeray: Contributions to the Morning Chronicle	Gordon N. Ray, ed.	$1.45
IB-33	Italian Comedy in the Renaissance	Marvin T. Herrick	$1.75
IB-34	Death in the Literature of Unamuno	Mario J. Valdés	$1.25
IB-35	*Port of New York: Essays on Fourteen American Moderns	Paul Rosenfeld, with an introductory essay by Sherman Paul	$2.25
IB-36	*How to Do Library Research	Robert B. Downs	$1.45
IB-37	Henry James: Representative Selections, with Introduction, Bibliography, and Notes	Lyon N. Richardson	$3.50

* Also available in clothbound editions.

IB-38	Symbolic Crusade: Status Politics and the American Temperance Movement	Joseph R. Gusfield	$1.75
IB-39	*Genesis and Structure of Society	Giovanni Gentile, translated by H. S. Harris	$1.95
IB-40	The Social Philosophy of Giovanni Gentile	H. S. Harris	$2.45
IB-41	*As We Saw the Thirties: Essays on Social and Political Movements of a Decade	Rita James Simon, ed.	$2.45
IB-42	The Symbolic Uses of Politics	Murray Edelman	$2.45
IB-43	White-Collar Trade Unions: Contemporary Developments in Industrialized Societies	Adolf Sturmthal, ed.	$3.50
IB-44	*The Labor Arbitration Process	R. W. Fleming	$2.45
IB-45	*Edmund Wilson: A Study of Literary Vocation in Our Time	Sherman Paul	$2.45
IB-46	*George Santayana's America: Essays on Literature and Culture	James Ballowe, ed.	$2.25
IB-47	The Measurement of Meaning	Charles E. Osgood, George J. Suci, and Percy H. Tannenbaum	$3.45
IB-48	*The Miracle of Growth	Foreword by Arnold Gesell	$1.75
IB-49	*Information Theory and Esthetic Perception	Abraham Moles	$2.45
IB-50	Outlawing the Spoils: A History of the Civil Service Reform Movement, 1865-1883	Ari Hoogenboom	$2.95
IB-51	*Community Colleges: A President's View	Thomas E. O'Connell	$1.95
IB-52	*The Joys and Sorrows of Recent American Art	Allen S. Weller	$3.95
IB-53	*Dimensions of Academic Freedom	Walter P. Metzger, Sanford H. Kadish, Arthur DeBardeleben, and Edward J. Bloustein	$ .95
IB-54	*Essays on Frege	E. D. Klemke, ed.	$3.95
IB-55	The Fine Hammered Steel of Herman Melville	Milton R. Stern	$2.95

* Also available in clothbound editions.

IB-56	*The Challenge of Incompetence and Poverty: Papers on the Role of Early Education	J. McVicker Hunt	$3.45
IB-57	*Mission Overseas: A Handbook for U.S. Families in Developing Countries	Harold D. Guither and W. N. Thompson	$2.95
IB-58	*Teaching and Learning	Donald Vandenberg, ed.	$3.45
IB-59	*Theory of Knowledge and Problems of Education	Donald Vandenberg, ed.	$3.45
IB-60	*The Art of William Carlos Williams: A Discovery and Possession of America	James Guimond	$2.45
IB-61	*Psychological Tests and Personnel Decisions (Second Edition)	Lee J. Cronbach and Goldine C. Gleser	$2.95
IB-62	*Mass Communications (Second Edition)	Wilbur Schramm, ed.	$4.50

*· Also available in clothbound editions.

University of Illinois Press   Urbana, Chicago, and London